Better Homes and Gardens®

STEP-BY-STEP

Kids' Rooms Projects

Better Homes and Gardens® Books
Des Moines, Iowa

Better Homes and Gardens® Books
An imprint of Meredith® Books

Step-by-Step Kids' Rooms Projects
Editor: Paula Marshall
Copy Chief: Terri Fredrickson
Managers, Book Production: Pam Kvitne, Marjorie J. Schenkelberg
Contributing Copy Editor: Carol Boker
Contributing Proofreaders: Sue Fetters, Ann Marie Sapienza, Donna Segal
Electronic Production Coordinator: Paula Forest
Editorial and Design Assistants: Kaye Chabot, Mary Lee Gavin, Karen Schirm

Produced by Greenleaf Publishing, Inc.
Publishing Director: Dave Toht
Project Designers: Dave Toht, Rebecca JonMichaels, Betony Toht, Jean DeVaty, Steve Cory
Contributing Writers: Steve Cory, Dawn Kotapish
Graphic Design: Jean DeVaty, Melanie Lawson Design
Ilustrations: Tony Davis
Photography: Dan Stultz Photography

Cover Photograph: Dan Stultz Photography
Cover Production: David Jordan

Meredith® Books
Editor in Chief: James D. Blume
Design Director: Matt Strelecki
Managing Editor: Gregory H. Kayko
Executive Shelter Editor: Denise L. Caringer

Director, Retail Sales and Marketing: Terry Unsworth
Director, Sales, Special Markets: Rita McMullen
Director, Sales, Premiums: Michael A. Peterson
Director, Sales, Retail: Tom Wierzbicki
Director, Book Marketing: Brad Elmitt
Director, Operations: George A. Susral
Director, Production: Douglas M. Johnston

Vice President, General Manager: Jamie L. Martin

***Better Homes and Gardens®* Magazine**
Editor in Chief: Jean LemMon
Executive Building Editor: Joan McCloskey

Meredith Publishing Group
President, Publishing Group: Stephen M. Lacy
Vice President, Finance and Administration: Max Runciman

Meredith Corporation
Chairman and Chief Executive Officer: William T. Kerr

Chairman of the Executive Committee: E. T. Meredith III

Library of Congress Catalog Control Number: 2001130199
ISBN: 0-696-21195-5

All of us at Better Homes and Gardens® Books are dedicated to providing you with information and ideas to enhance your home. We welcome your comments and suggestions. Write to us at: Better Homes and Gardens Books, Shelter Editorial Department, 1716 Locust St., Des Moines, IA 50309-3023.

If you would like to purchase any of our books, check wherever quality books are sold. Visit us online at bhgbooks.com

Note to the Reader: Due to differing conditions, tools, and individual skills, Meredith Corporation assumes no responsibility for any damages, injuries suffered, or losses incurred as a result of following the information published in this book. Before beginning any project, review the instructions carefully, and if any doubts or questions remain, consult local experts or authorities. Because local codes and regulations vary greatly, you always should check with local authorities to ensure that your project complies with all applicable local codes and regulations. Always read and observe all of the safety precautions provided by any tool or equipment manufacturer, and follow all accepted safety procedures.

TABLE OF CONTENTS

Introduction 4

Babies through Preschoolers

Changeable Changing Table 6
Soft Cells 10
Pickup Pocket Quilt 14
A Bedspread That Grows Up 18
Big Top Tent 22
Laundry Monster 26
My Mannequin 30
Make the Art Gallery Scene 32

Elementary-School Ages

Van Gogh to Go 36
Fantasy Canopy 42
Handy Headboard 48
Storage by the Cord 54
It's a Jungle in the Closet 58
Dreamy Double-Decker 62

Middle Schoolers

Sitting Witty 70
Delightful Dividers 76
Gum Ball Footstool 78
Made in the Shade 80
Work Space Station 82
Cityscape Screen 88
Homegrown Loft 90

Patterns and Basic Skills

Project Patterns 96
Cutting and Shaping 104
Routing and Drilling 107
Fastening 108
Sewing 109
Working with Kids 110
Resources 112
Metric Conversion Chart 112

INTRODUCTION

When equipping a kid's room, parents often seek more originality than kids do; many children would be happy to fill their room with posters, window treatments, rugs, and bedclothes based on the newest cartoon series or movie. Introducing kids to the pleasures of making something themselves, of using materials and colors they choose, regardless of what fad is being currently merchandised, is an important first step in helping children develop confidence in their own taste and judgment.

And buying kids' furnishings off the shelf can be expensive. Too often, a major investment becomes obsolete as children grow and their interests change. The projects in this book don't cost a fortune. Most depend more on "sweat equity" than on a pricey materials list. Many are just as stylish, often more so, than something that could be purchased. However, some items—bookcases are a good example—can be purchased easily and inexpensively and are do-it-yourself projects worth avoiding.

Age-Graded Projects

We've collected 21 projects geared to children. The projects are assigned to three age categories: babies through preschoolers, elementary-school ages, and middle schoolers. Of course, these categories are a guide only. A preschooler may love to have the double-decker bus shown on page 62, a project intended for elementary ages. The "Pickup Pocket Quilt" shown in the baby through preschooler chapter may well be something a middle schooler would love to have to display treasured stuffed animals. However, the chapter related to your child's age group is a good place to start as you browse through the book with your son or daughter.

Basic Materials

It's very frustrating to get excited about a project only to find that a key ingredient is almost impossible to find. The projects in this book require only readily available materials. All of the materials are available from your local home center, fabric store, or art supply store.

Basic Tools

In like fashion, these projects can be made with readily available tools. In some instances, we suggest renting a specialized tool that will help the job go faster, but no project depends on such tools. You'll always find an alternative method listed that involves a more basic tool.

Basic Skills

Basic tools imply a knowledge of some basic skills. These projects are designed to go together as easily as possible. Most can be made by do-it-yourselfers with average carpentry or sewing skills. Some are so simple that you can plunge in with little prior do-it-yourself experience. None requires fine woodworking or expert sewing skills. Where a project or step is challenging, fair warning is given.

With all of the projects, kids can participate to a significant degree. For a refresher course in cutting, shaping, drilling, fastening, and sewing, see pages 104–109. Often, the steps for the project you choose to make will cover these or will present a needed variation on a basic skill.

Customized Projects

Many of the projects can expand or contract to suit your specific needs. For example, the art table shown on page 36 has optional legs that can be lengthened as your child grows. With few exceptions, these projects can be readily adapted to suit the dimensions of the space you are dealing with. The closet treatment that's shown on page 58 can adjust to suit a closet door anywhere from 30 inches wide to 8 feet wide.

In addition, these projects are simple enough that you can freely add individual touches. Pay close attention to structural details (the type of lumber and fasteners that bear the load in a project, or the requirement that a project be fastened to a wall), but chart your own course with decorative details and nonstructural functional elements.

Step-by-Step

As you make these projects, work sequentially, following the steps provided. Never cut more material than is asked for in the step you are working on. Always double-check measurements against your project—often an earlier change or mismeasurement will have a bearing on the exact size of the piece you are about to cut. Rest assured that your version of the project can vary somewhat from that presented in the book and still be every bit as successful.

Clear Patterns

For those projects that would be difficult to sketch freehand, or where cutting fabric is involved, patterns are provided beginning on page 96. A scale is provided for each so that you can readily transfer the pattern to your material. In many cases, a slight variance from the pattern will make no difference at all—most of these projects have a forgiving design.

Feature Boxes

In addition to clear steps, easy-to-follow diagrams, and clear patterns, you'll find plenty of tips throughout this book. For every project, a "You'll Need" box tells you how long the project will take, what skills are necessary, and what tools you must have. A "Materials" list specifies the lumber, fabric, fasteners, and adhesives you'll need to complete the project. The other tip boxes shown on this page are scattered throughout the book, providing practical help to ensure that the work you do will be as pleasurable as possible and that it will result in safe, long-lasting projects.

TOOLS TO USE

If you'll need special tools not commonly found in a homeowner's toolbox, we'll tell you about them in Tools to Use.

Money $ Saver

Throwing money at a job does not necessarily make it a better one. Money Saver helps cut your costs with tips on how to estimate your material needs accurately, make wise tool purchases, and organize the job to minimize wasted labor.

MEASUREMENTS

Keep an eye out for this box when standard measurements, critical tolerances, or special measuring techniques are called for.

CAUTION!

When a how-to step requires special care, Caution! warns you what to watch out for. It will help keep you from doing damage to yourself or the job at hand.

EXPERTS' INSIGHT

Tricks of the trade can make all the difference in helping you do a job quickly and well. Experts' Insight gives you insiders' tips on how to make the job easier.

CHANGEABLE CHANGING TABLE

The diaper-changing stage may seem to last forever, but after a couple of years, the changing table becomes obsolete. This project lets it grow with the child.

Begin by finding an unfinished or used chest that is 38 to 46 inches tall. If it has a finish, begin by lightly sanding or preparing the surface with deglosser. Add the guard rail and paint the chest, and then make the changing pad. The cover can be removed easily from the pad for washing. Consider making an extra cover as a spare.

Home centers and hardware stores provide hundreds of options for stylish pulls. For paint, consider latex spray paint for ease of use and a kid-safe finish.

As with all changing tables, the guard rail keeps only the pad in place: Never leave a child unattended on the table.

YOU'LL NEED

TIME: 4 to 6 hours to add a protective guard, sand, paint, and attach drawer pulls. 2 to 3 hours to sew the changing pad.
SKILLS: Beginner carpentry and intermediate sewing experience.
TOOLS: *Chest:* Measuring tape, straightedge, speed square, pencil, geometry compass, saber saw, drill, miter box, fine-toothed handsaw or backsaw, nail set, sanding block, screwdriver, drop cloth, paintbrush. *Pad:* Sewing machine, rotary cutting tools or scissors, straight pins.
MATERIALS: *Chest:* Clear pine 1×4, 4d finishing nails, white glue, masking tape. *Pad:* 1¼ yards of muslin, 1½ yards of fabric, matching thread, 6 yards of piping, ½ yard of hook-and-loop tape, 6 square feet of 2-inch foam, primer, paint.

ABOVE: *Take an unfinished or used chest of drawers and make this colorful changing table. It only takes paint, new pulls, the addition of a simple rail, and a sew-it-yourself changing pad.*
LEFT: *With a change of paint and pulls, the same project can grow with your child to become a handsome, customized chest of drawers.*

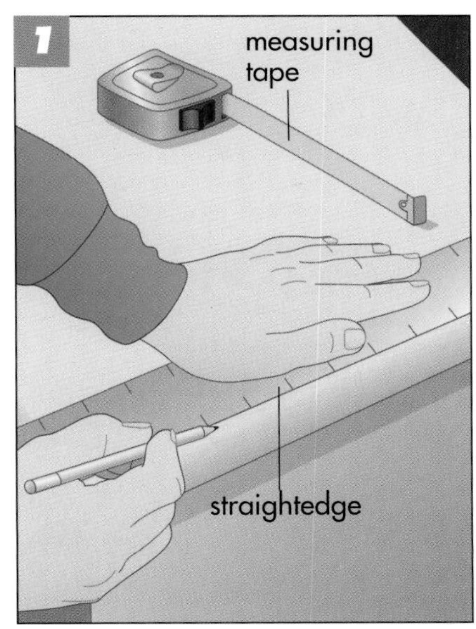

1. Measure and mark top.
Use a straightedge to mark a light guideline for positioning the sides of the changing area. Measure in about ¾ inch from the edge of each side. The back of the changing area should be flush with the back of the chest of drawers.

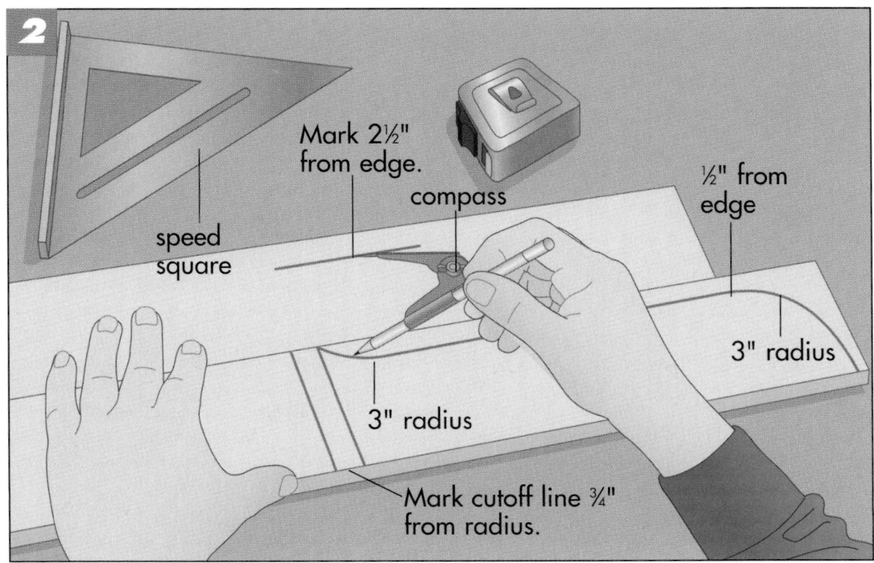

2. Mark 1×4 with design.
Select a piece of 1×4 as straight and knot-free as you can find, or pay extra for "clear" (knot-free) lumber. Before trimming it to the needed size, lay it on a work surface and strike a line ½ inch down from the top edge. Set a standard schoolroom geometry compass so it is open 3 inches. Use it to mark the cutoff for the rounded front end of the side piece. Place a scrap of 1×4 above the piece and use the compass to mark the cutout where the piece will abut the back of the changing area.

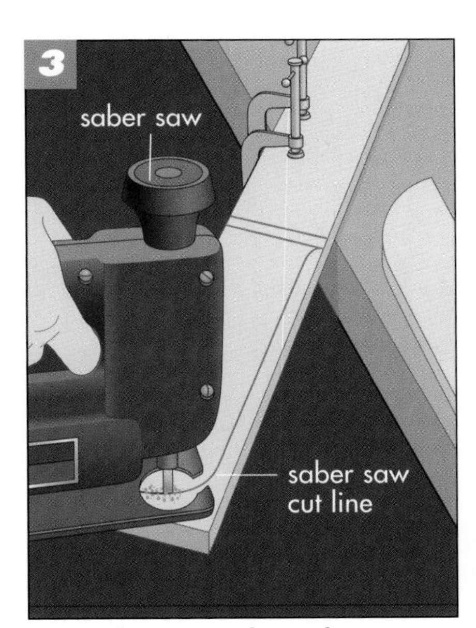

3. Cut the 1×4 with a saber saw.
Clamp the piece to a solid work surface. Start the saw before pushing the blade into the wood. (See page 106 for more on how to use a saber saw.) Smooth edges with rough (60-grit) sandpaper. Use the first piece you cut as a template for the second.

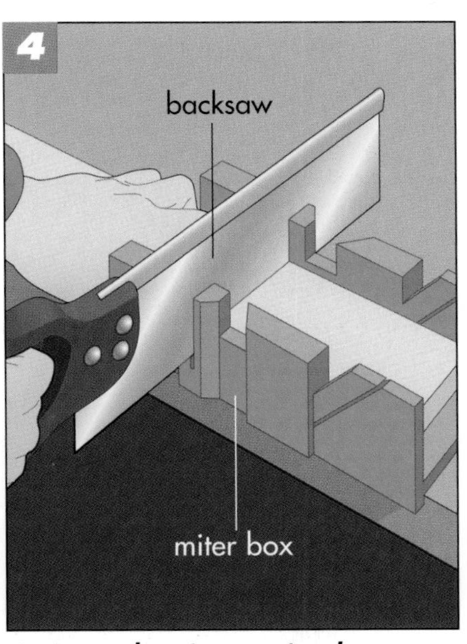

4. Cut ends using a miter box.
Using a miter box and a backsaw or fine-toothed handsaw, make the final cut on each of the side pieces. Position the side pieces on the chest, mark the backer piece, and cut it to length.

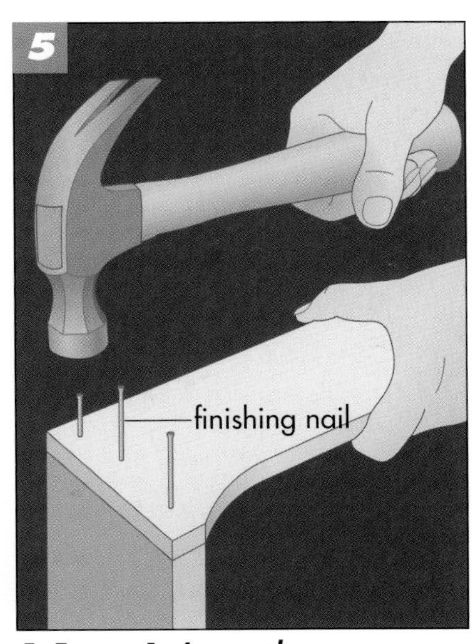

5. Fasten 1×4s together.
Drill pilot holes with a 1/16-inch bit to avoid splitting the wood. Pound 4d (2-inch) finishing nails into the holes until the points carefully protrude. Apply white glue to the backer and complete the nailing. Re-sand, first with 60-grit, then with 100-grit sandpaper.

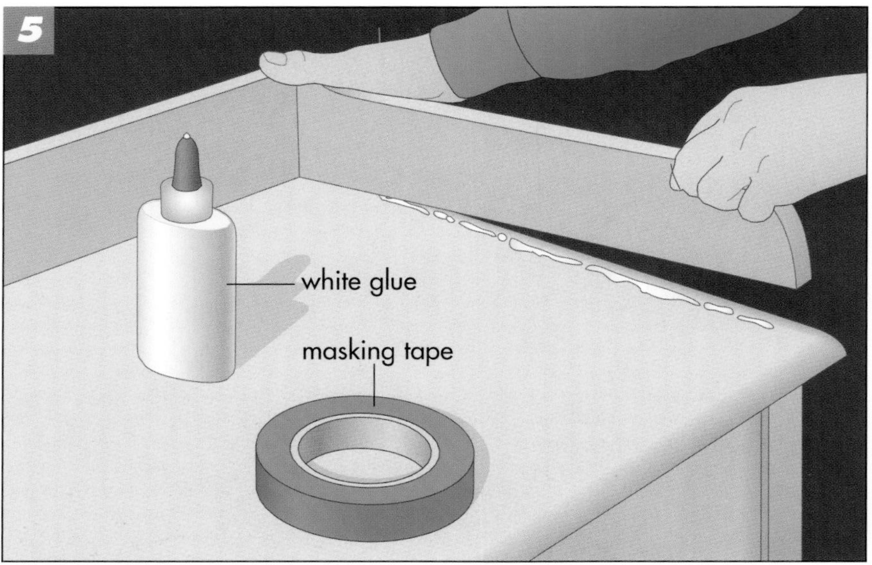

6. Glue 1x4s to top of drawer.
Run a smooth bead of white glue where the side rail will be attached to the chest. With the rail nailed together, set it on the chest with the back of the rail flush with the back of the chest. Fix it in place with masking tape. Gently lay a couple of boards across the rails and set four to six books on top until the glue dries.

7. Secure the rail.
Beneath the side rails, drill $\frac{1}{16}$- or $\frac{3}{32}$-inch pilot holes every 3 to 4 inches. Pound in a 4d or 6d finishing nail (select whichever is about twice the thickness of the top). Fine-sand the entire unit with 150-grit sandpaper, prime, and paint.

CHANGING-TABLE PAD

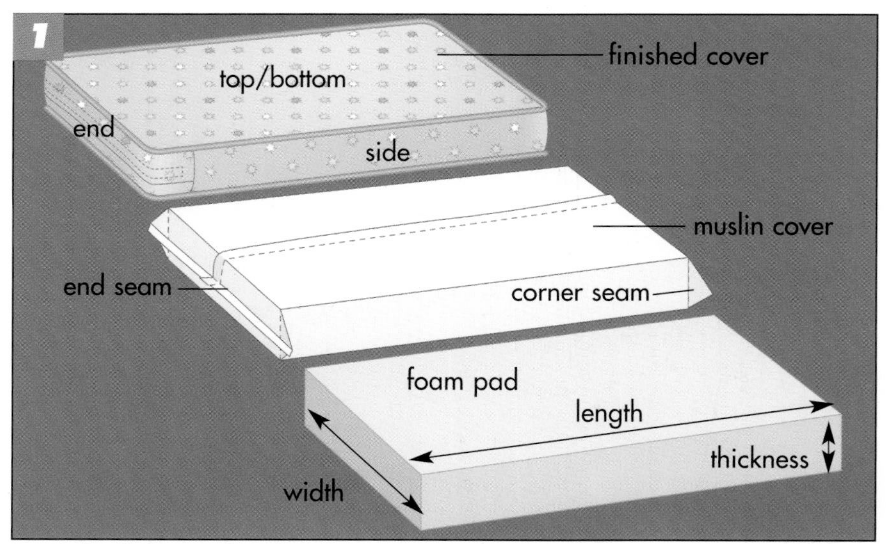

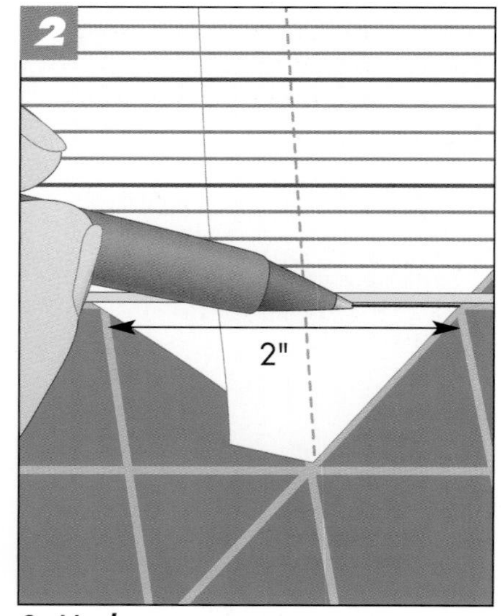

1. Make foam pad and cover.
Measure the length and width of the chest top; then cut 2-inch medium-density foam ½ inch shorter in both dimensions. Next make a muslin cover. To determine the cover's width, wrap a measuring tape around the foam pad width and add 1 inch for seam allowances. For the length, add the length measurement to the thickness and add 1 inch for seams. Cut muslin to these dimensions. Sew the lengthwise edges together, using a ½-inch seam allowance. Press the seam to the center of one side.

2. Mark cover corners.
Join the ends, leaving an opening at one end to insert the foam. For crisp corners, fold each corner as shown above and mark across the point. Stitch on marking. Turn to the right side and insert the pad. Turn the raw edges to the inside and stitch the opening closed.

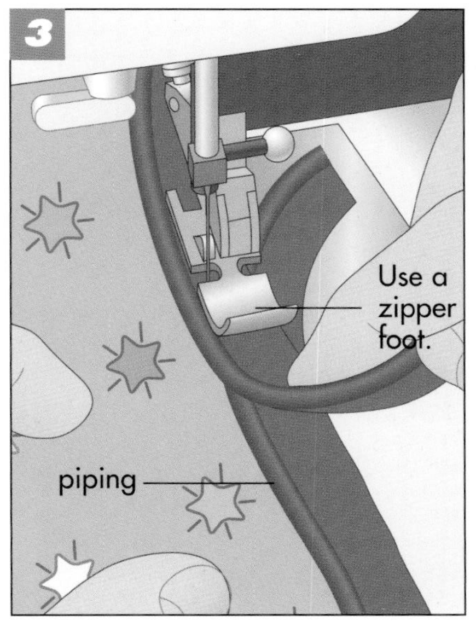

3. Cut side strips and sew piping.
The width of the side strip is the pad thickness plus 1 inch. The length of the strip is two pad lengths plus one pad width minus 3 inches. The opening end is made of two strips, each 4½ inches wide by 1 pad width plus 5 inches. Cut two pieces for the top/bottom, adding 1 inch to each dimension of the pad. Baste piping to the outer edges of the right side of the top/bottom. Curve the piping off the edge of the fabric at the beginning and end, overlapping to form a smooth transition.

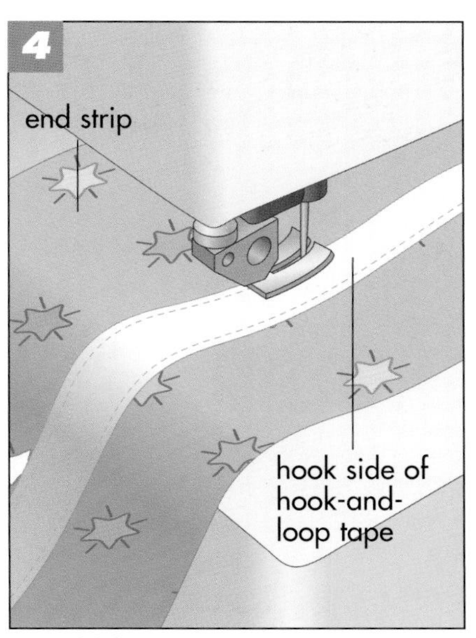

4. Add fastening tape to opening.
Press each end strip in half widthwise with wrong sides facing. Open up one strip and stitch the hook side of a strip of hook-and-loop tape ½ inch from the center fold. Refold the strip and topstitch along the fold. Overlap the end strips to form a 2½-inch-wide strip. Determine the placement of the loop side of the tape; stitch. Overlap and stitch across the ends.

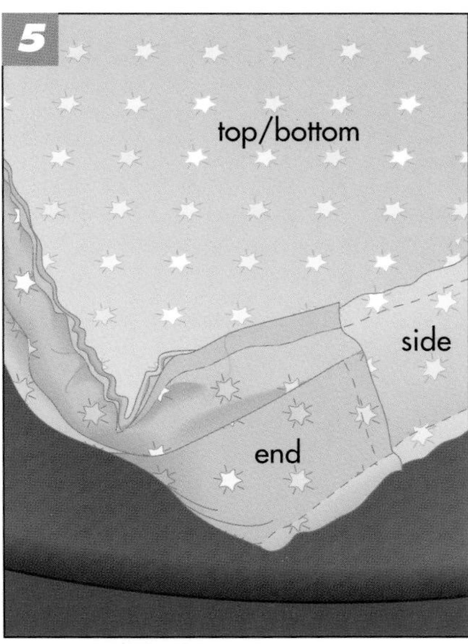

5. Assemble the outer cover.
Join the ends to the short edges of the side strip, forming a loop. Pin the side loop to the outer edge of a top/bottom, with right sides facing, clipping the strip to the seam line at each corner. Then place the opening at one end. Use the zipper foot and sew along the piping seam line. Pin, then stitch the other top/bottom in place.

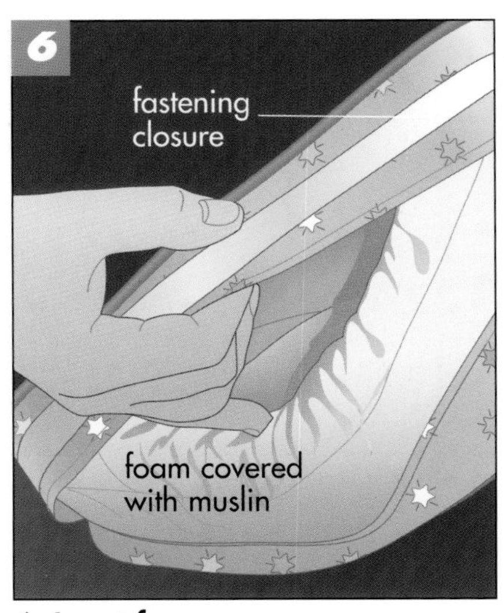

6. Insert foam.
Turn cover to the right side. Insert the cushion and press the fastening tape strips together to secure. Remove the fabric cover to launder before use.

PULLS THAT GROW UP

If you choose drawer pulls fastened with one screw, you can change them as your child grows up. When you're buying pulls for younger ages (*above left*) or pulls suitable for older kids (*above right*), be prepared to pay $3 to $7 each.

SOFT CELLS

Every generation of kids loves the limitless playability of blocks. Here's a project that builds on that theme. Imagine these colorful blocks, made of foam and covered with thermal fleece, used for building forts, playhouses, furniture—even a mattress for sleepovers. With practice, you can make one every 30 minutes and have a roomful in a weekend.

The sizes of the blocks shown are based on increments of 5 inches. That way, the blocks are stackable in any direction. If you choose foam of another thickness, plan the dimensions that are multiples of the thickness. Fabric options include canvas, duck, denim, and pant-weight cottons. Brushed denim and some twills have a nap that helps the blocks cling to each other when stacked.

BELOW: *Use them for lounging or stack 'em high. However your kids use them, these soft, colorful blocks make for a gentle landing.*

YOU'LL NEED

TIME: About 30 minutes per block.
SKILLS: Intermediate sewing skills.
TOOLS: Sewing machine, rotary cutting tools and mat (optional), scissors, straight pins, bread knife, ruler/straightedge, fine-tip permanaent marker, string.
MATERIALS: For each block, about ⅝ yard of batting, ⅝ yard of thermal fleece, matching thread, and 2 square feet of 5-inch-thick foam.

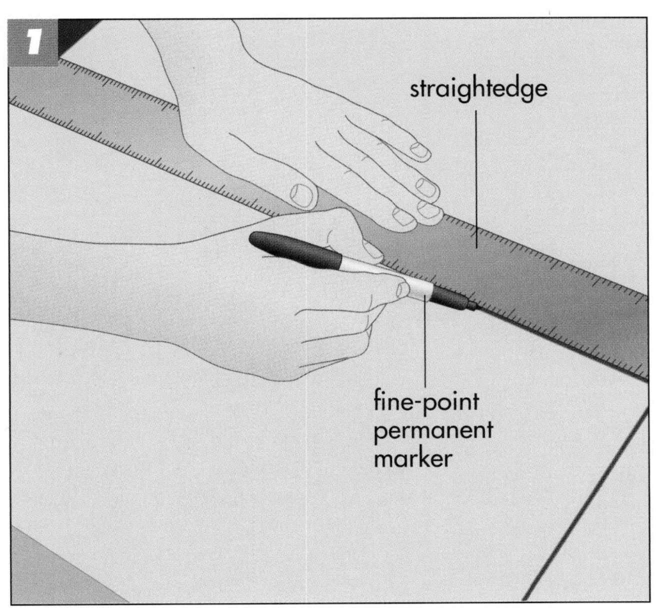

1. Mark foam.
Determine the sizes of blocks desired. With the 5-inch-thick foam shown, the dimensions are multiples of 5 so that the blocks will stack evenly: 5×10×20-inch rectangles and 5×10×10-inch squares. Plan the most efficient layout of your sheet of foam, and mark cutting lines with a ruler and a marker.

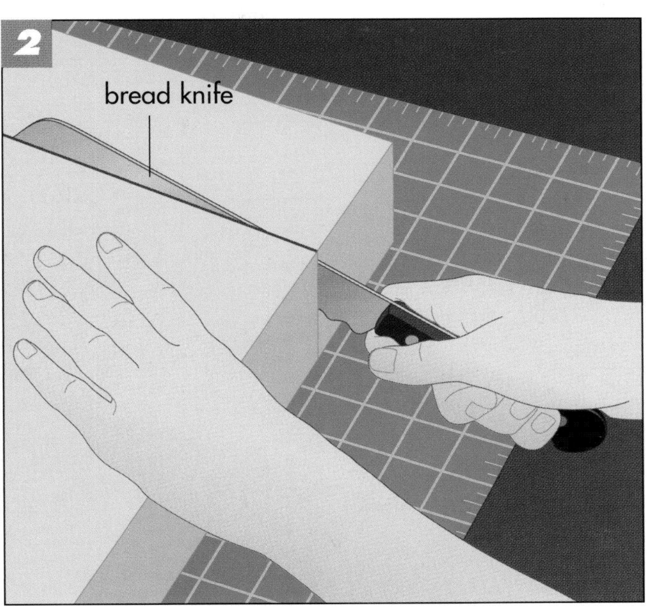

2. Cut foam with a bread knife.
Cut the foam to block sizes desired using a bread knife or, for an even smoother cut, an electric carving knife. You may wish to mark the foam on both sides to help you cut the edges evenly.

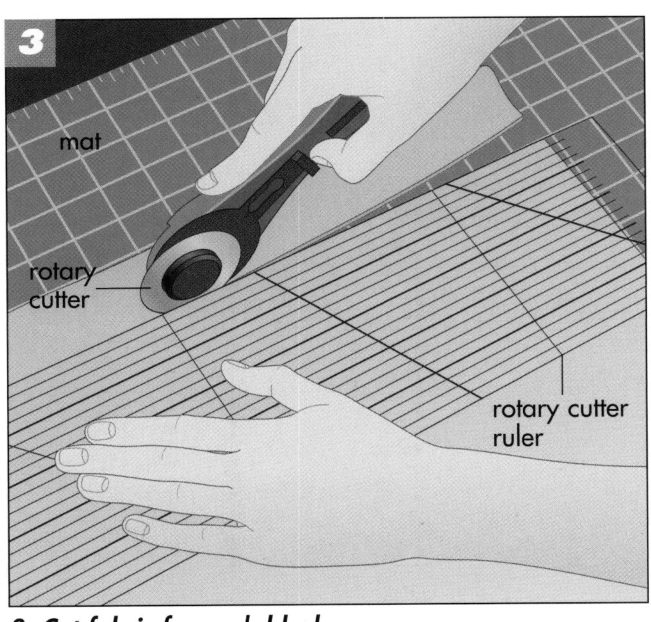

3. Cut fabric for each block.
For each block, cut two 6×21-inch rectangles for the sides and two 6×11-inch rectangles for the ends. Cut two 11×21-inch rectangles for the top/bottom. If you choose to cover in three colors of fleece, as shown, use one color for the side pairs, another color for the ends, and the third color for the top/bottom pieces.

Where to Buy Foam

If you have an upholstery shop in town, stop by for a quote on the foam. Ask for a price on 25- to 35-density foam—anything heavier might be too hefty if your kids happen to throw blocks at each other. The upholstery shop will have samples for you to inspect. Most commonly, the foam is sold in 24×82-inch pieces. An upholstery shop can order thicknesses ranging from ½ inch to 6 inches. Check, too, for scrap pieces—double-sided tape allows you to join scraps into usable blocks.

Upholsterers have a machine that cuts with an almost "factory" edge and they may be willing to cut pieces to size for you.

Fabric stores also carry foam. They usually won't cut it for you, and the selection might not be as broad, but the price may be slightly lower.

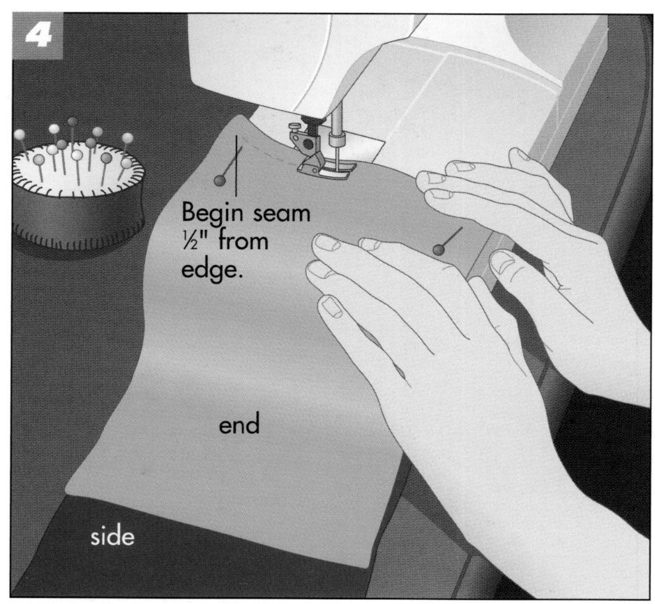

4. Join the side seams.
Pin the fabric together with right sides facing. Join a side to an end along the short ends, beginning and ending ½ inch from the edges of the strip. When sewing thermal fleece by machine, use a stretch stitch to prevent the seams from breaking. Sew a side to an end to a side to an end, forming a loop.

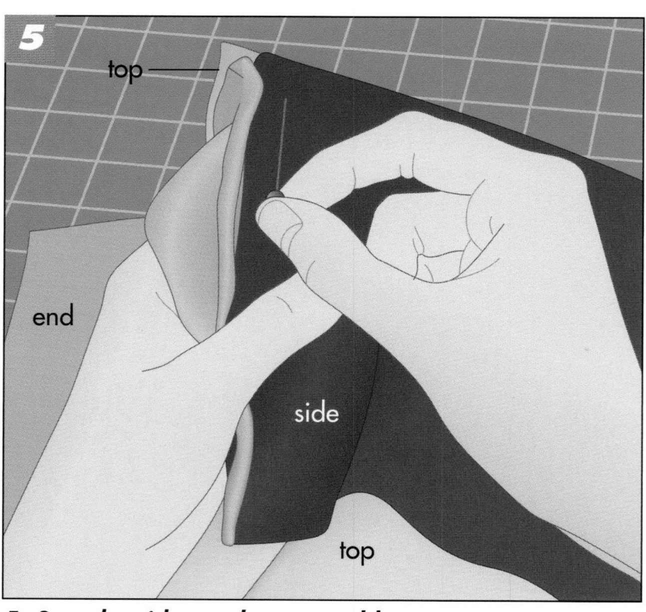

5. Sew the sides to the top and bottom.
Pin one side to a long edge of a top/bottom rectangle with right sides facing. Join the seam, beginning and ending ½ inch from the edges. Then pin and sew the other side, then both ends, to the top/bottom. Repeat with the other top/bottom, leaving one end open to insert the foam.

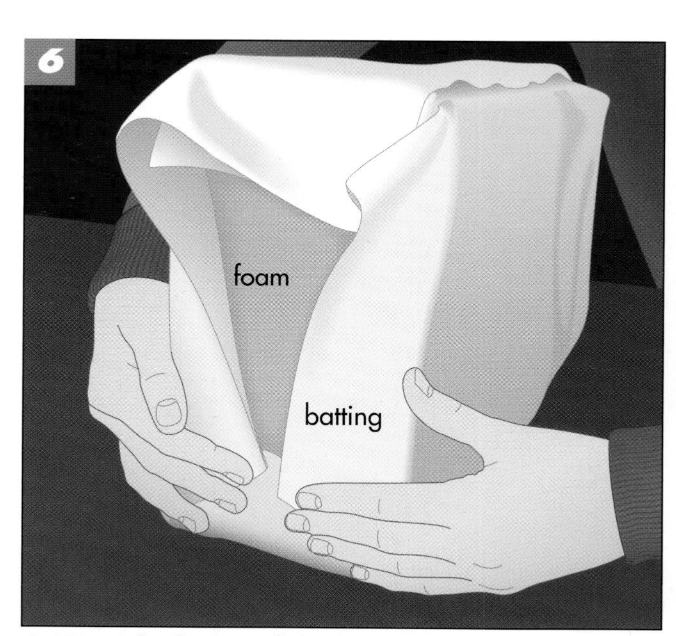

6. Wrap the foam with batting.
The cover slides over the block more easily when the block is wrapped with batting. Cut 35×25-inch rectangles of batting and wrap each block. The batting will cling to itself; if desired, you can tack the batting where it overlaps.

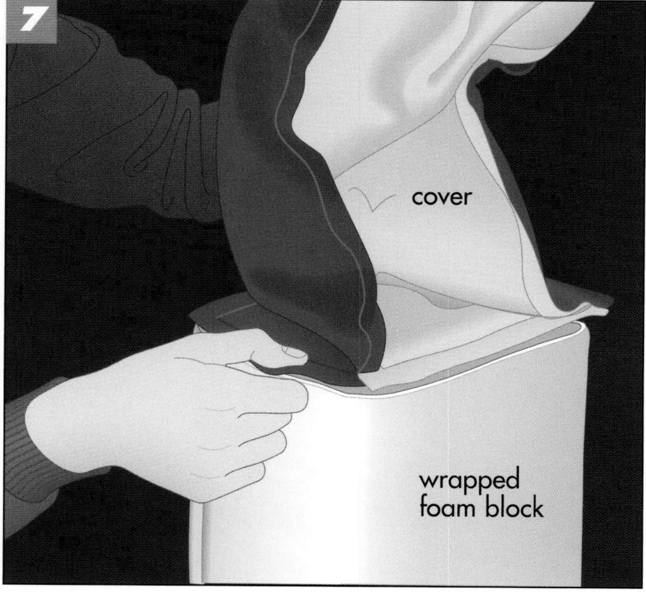

7. Set the cover on the block.
Here's a trick for easily getting the cover on. First, set the completed cover, wrong side out, on the top edge of a block. Line up one end on the end of the foam block.

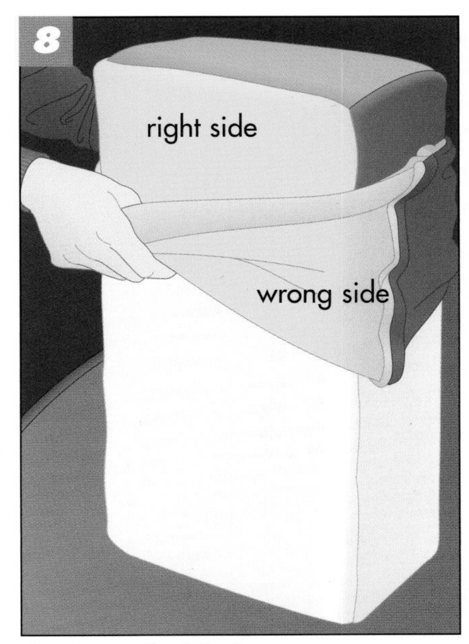

8. Cover the block.
Next, slide the cover over the block, turning it to the right side as you go. Keep the layer of batting smooth.

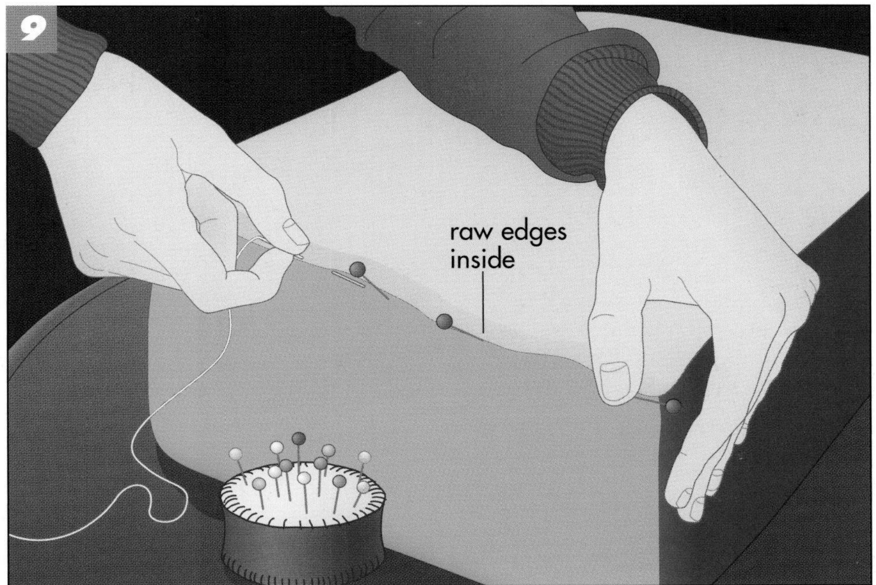

9. Hand-stitch the last seam.
Overlap the open edge, turning the raw edges to the inside. Pin one edge to the other, keeping the seam as straight as possible. Hand-stitch the opening closed, using doubled thread.

HOW TO MAKE BLOCKS OF OTHER SHAPES

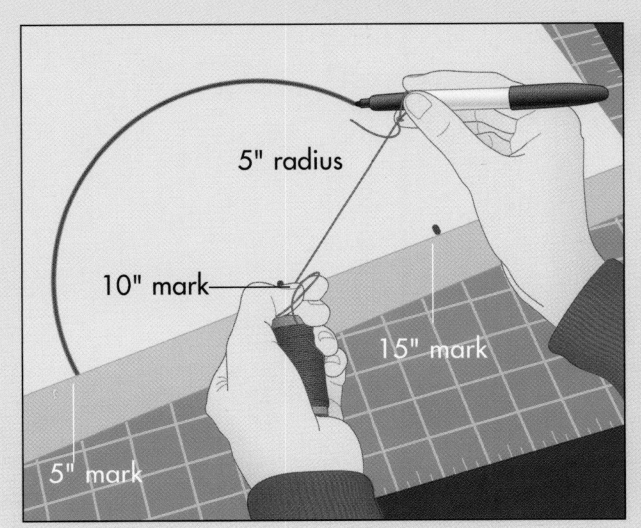

1. Mark an arc.
Along a 20-inch side of a 10×20-inch rectangle, mark 5-inch increments. Using a string as a compass at the center mark, mark a semicircle from the 5-inch mark to the 15-inch mark. Cut out the half circle. Make covers for both the semicircle and the remaining shape.

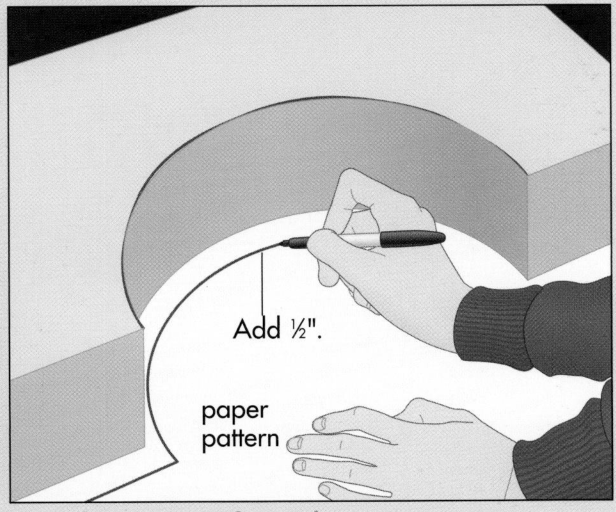

2. Make a pattern for each cover.
Draw around each shape to make a pattern. Add ½ inch for seam allowances around all sides. To determine the length of the curved part, lay a measuring tape along the edge and add 1 inch to the measurement for seam allowances. Make covers as for the larger, rectangular block, leaving one straight side edge open to insert the foam.

PICKUP POCKET QUILT

All quilts are comforting and decorative—this one is useful as well. The alternate blocks of the quilt provide pockets for storing a child's treasures. This project offers an ideal home for stuffed animals and beanbag toys.

Use 100-percent cotton fabric for quiltmaking; it's a pleasure to work with and comes in a wide array of colors. For a child's quilt, find a pet, doll, space, or sport-themed pattern to mix with solid color fabrics to create a truly individual quilt.

Quilts are made in stages. First, cut the fabrics and piece together blocks to create a pattern or design. Join the blocks, sashing, and posts to create the quilt top. Layer the top, batting, and backing, and pin or baste the layers together. Hand or machine quilt the layers.

The pieces for this project include: squares, triangles, sashing strips (the pieces between the blocks), and hanging loops. After you've assembled the pieced blocks, make the storage pockets. Once you've laid out all the pieces of the quilt together, sew the blocks into rows, then join the rows. As a finishing touch, quilt the sashes.

BELOW: Pocket blocks have two layers of fabric, and they expand for storage. Small tucks at the bottom edge tidily control the extra fabric.

YOU'LL NEED

TIME: About 12 hours for a 26×58-inch quilt.

SKILLS: Moderate sewing skills.

TOOLS: Sewing machine, scissors, straight pins, iron, and drill. Optional: rotary cutting tool, ruler, and mat.

SUPPLIES: 3 yards of a dark-print fabric for sashing, backing, and hanging loops, 1¼ yards of light-colored print for triangles and pockets, ⅓ yard total of assorted prints for center squares, ¼ yard of print fabric for sashing posts, 30×62-inch piece of batting, matching thread, 60-inch cafe-curtain rod with hooks or brackets.

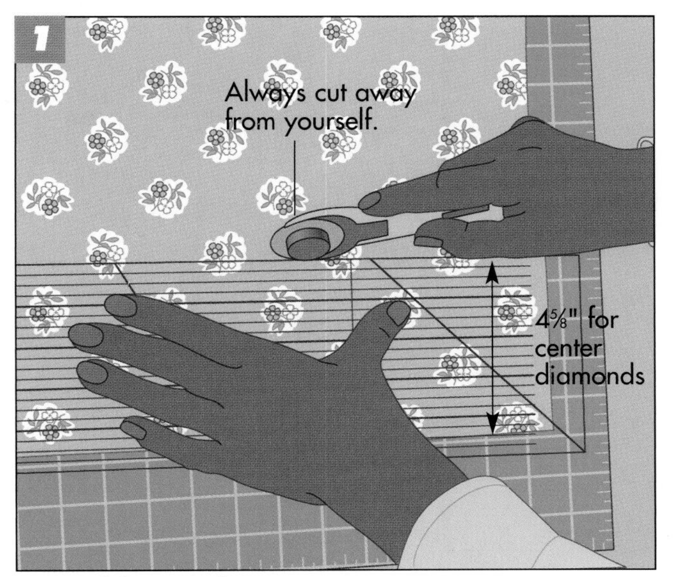

1. Cut fabrics with scissors or rotary cutter.
From an assortment of print fabrics, cut eleven 4⅝-inch squares for center diamonds. From the light-colored print, cut ten 8½×6½-inch pockets and ten 6½×6½-inch pocket backing squares and twenty-two 4-inch squares. Cut each 4-inch square in half to make forty-two triangles. For sashing posts, cut thirty-two 2½-inch squares from the print fabric. From dark-print fabric cut fifty-two 2½×6½-inch strips for sashing strips, eight 4½×9-inch strips for hanging loops, and a 30×62-inch rectangle for the backing.

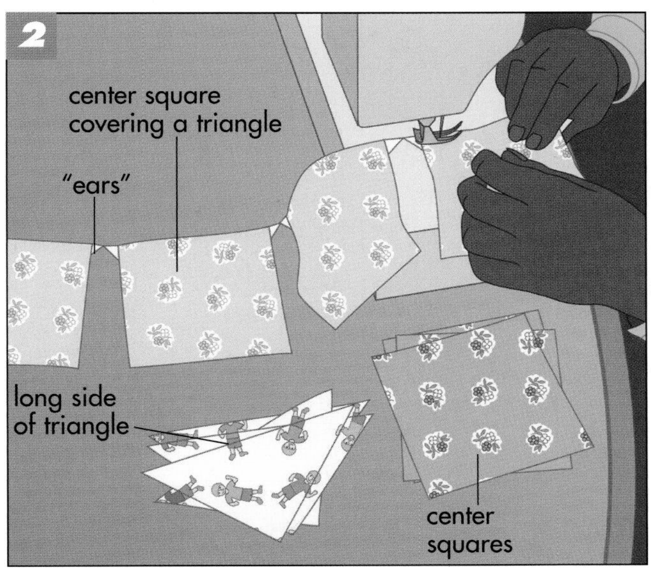

2. Chain the blocks.
Center a square on the long side of a triangle, with right sides facing and an "ear" extending beyond each edge. Using a ¼-inch seam allowance (the distance of the stitching from the cut edge), join the pieces. Without cutting the thread, put the next unit in place and continue sewing. When all are joined, clip apart the units. Stitch another triangle to the opposite side. Press the seams flat toward the triangle.

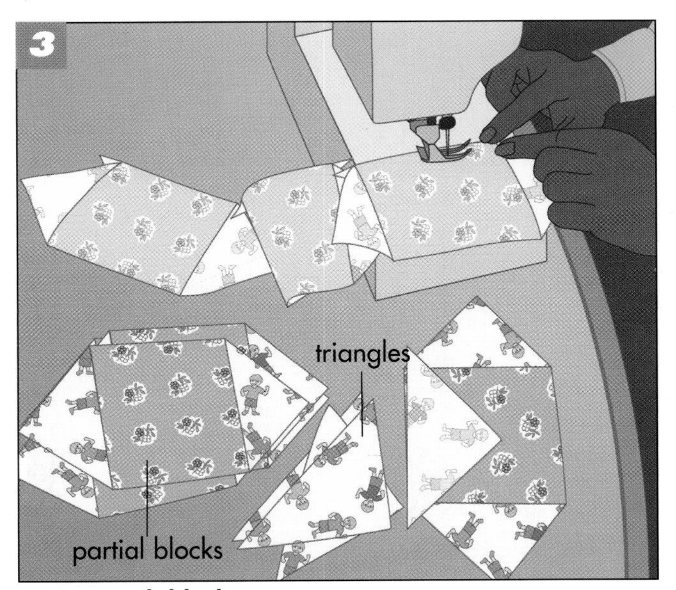

3. Sew quilt block.
Trim off the ears that extend beyond the center diamond. Sew a triangle to each remaining edge of the center square, chaining the blocks as in Step 2. Press the seams away from the center square and trim off the ears.

EXPERTS' INSIGHT

KEYS TO SUCCESSFUL QUILTMAKING

■ Cut precisely. Invest in a rotary cutter, a mat, and a ruler. These tools are fast and accurate; take time to learn to use them. Be safe: Always retract the blade every time you set down the rotary cutter.

■ Sew accurate seams. Having a true ¼-inch seam allowance makes a big difference in making sure the quilt top fits together smoothly. To check your machine, sew together two 2¼-inch strips, press the seam flat, lay the strip open. The width should measure exactly 4 inches. Begin each project with a new needle in your sewing machine.

■ Press the seams flat before joining one block to another. Be careful when pressing bias edges to avoid stretching the fabric out of shape.

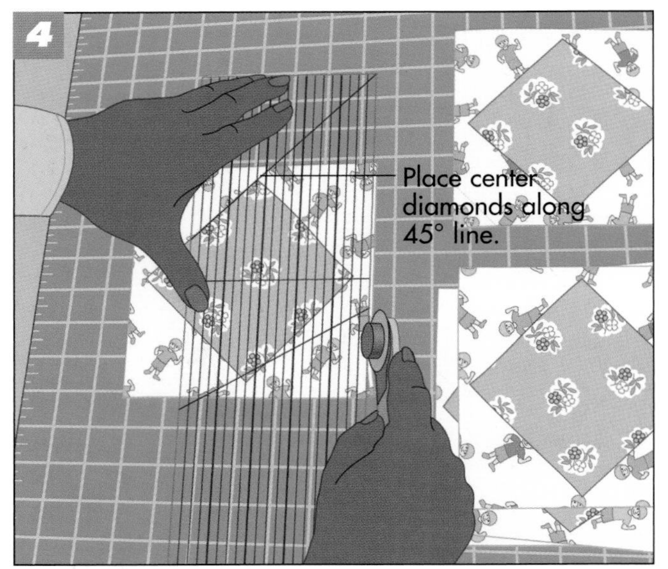

4. Trim the pieced blocks.
Using a 6½-inch square cut from a piece of lightweight cardboard, trim each block to the exact size. If you're using a rotary cutter and quilt ruler, align the center square with the 45-degree line on the ruler, and trim the blocks to 6½-inch squares using the rotary cutter.

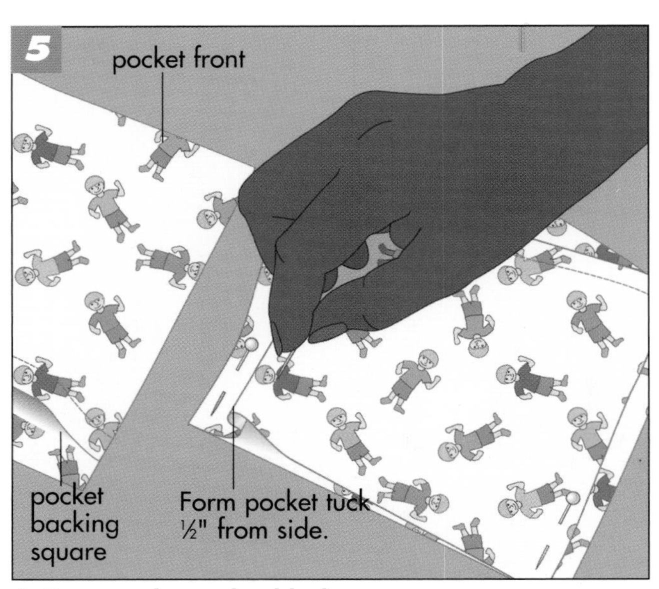

5. Prepare the pocket blocks.
Press each 8½-inch pocket edge under ½ inch; fold over ½ inch again and press; topstitch. Pin the side and bottom edges of the pocket to the edges of a backing square. Fold the excess width of the pocket into a tuck at each edge of the backing square, and pin. Machine-baste the raw edges, using a ¼-inch seam allowance. Be careful not to catch the top edge of the pocket in the seam allowance.

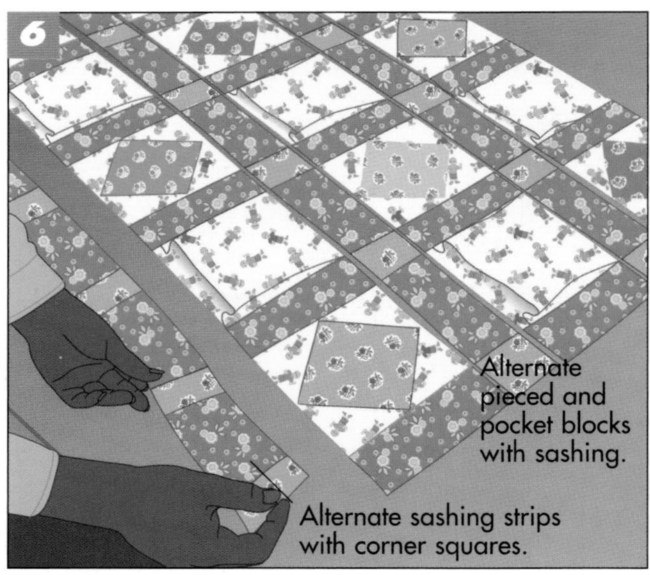

6. Lay out rows.
Lay out the pieced blocks, pocket blocks, sashing strips, and corner posts in a pleasing arrangement. You may wish to pin a paper label to each block to keep them in order. Sew the blocks of each horizontal row together. Iron the seams of the blocks toward the sashing strips and the seams of the corner posts toward the sashing strips.

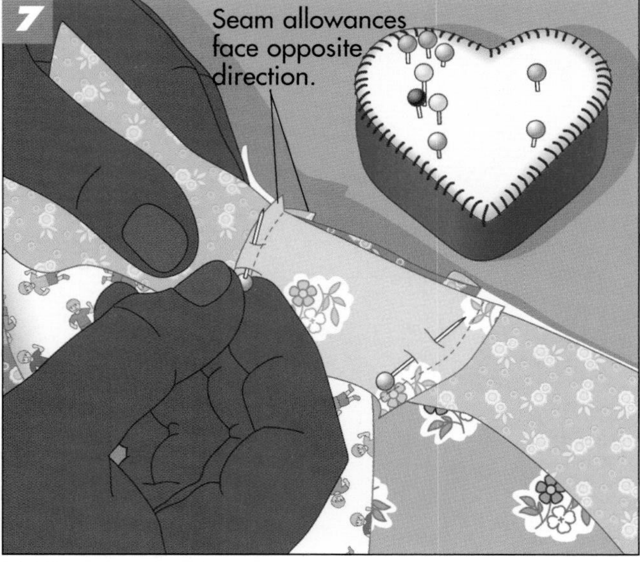

7. Pin rows together.
As you pin the rows together, butt the seams, matching the seam and alternating the seam allowances. This reduces the bulk at the seams. Join the horizontal rows to assemble the quilt top.

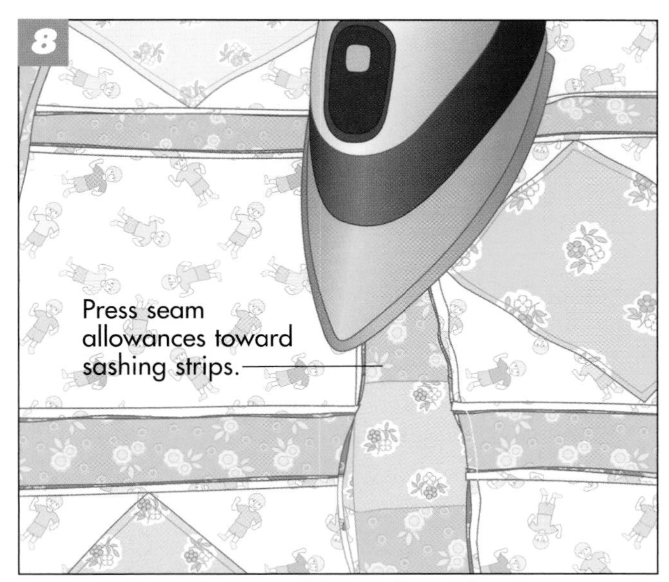

8. Press the quilt top and layer the quilt.
Press the seams toward the sashing strips. Trim loose threads. Pin the batting to the wrong side of the quilt top. Baste around the perimeter of the quilt, using a ½-inch seam allowance.

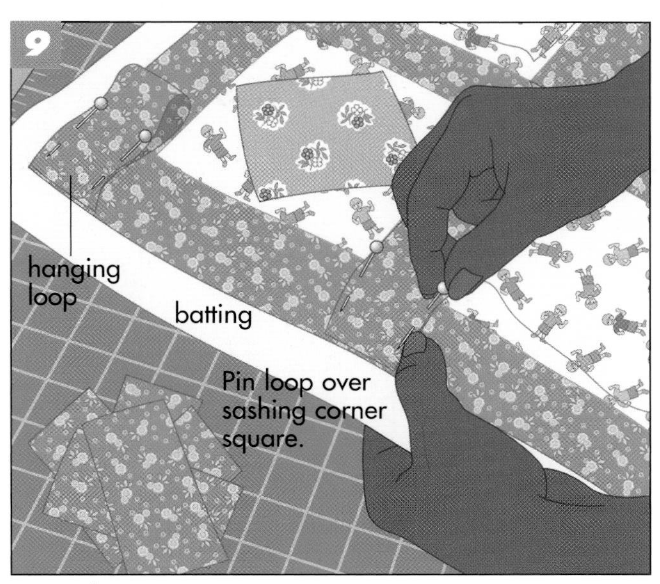

9. Pin loops.
Fold the 4½×9-inch hanging loops in half lengthwise with right sides facing. Using a ¼-inch seam allowance, sew the long edge of each strip to make a tube. Turn to the right side and press, centering the seam allowance on one side. Fold each tube in half, with the seam to the inside and matching raw edges. Pin a loop to the top edge of the quilt over each sashing post.

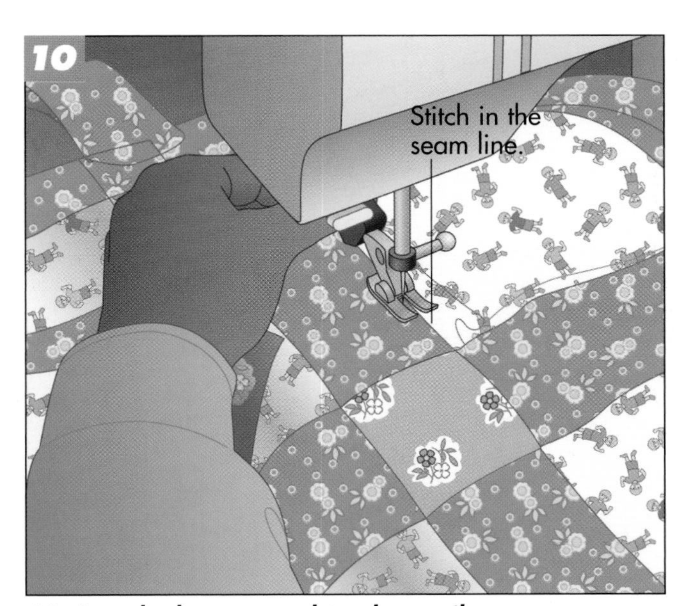

10. Sew the layers together, then quilt.
Pin the backing to the quilt top with right sides facing. Sew around the perimeter, using a ¼-inch seam allowance and leaving a 6-inch opening for turning. Trim the excess fabric at each corner and turn to the right side. Press, turning the raw edges at the opening to the inside. Hand-stitch the opening closed. Stitch in the ditch (along the seam lines) to quilt. Quilt within the pieced blocks as desired.

11. Hang quilt.
Screw brackets or hooks into wall studs. Place a curtain rod through the hanging loops and hang the quilt. To hold the quilt close to the wall, use cup hooks instead of curtain-rod brackets. Install one hook, set the rod in place, and level it (see page 33) to determine the location of the second hook.

A BEDSPREAD THAT GROWS UP

Children's interests change so quickly, why not make a bedspread that can change with them? Using simple ribbon ties to hold decorated napkins, this bedspread allows children to design their decor—and alter it as the years go by. The napkins are big enough to make a design impact, while small enough to be convenient for child-size projects.

The simplest method uses fusible webbing to adhere fabric pieces to the napkin base. Young children can draw out patterns and trace them onto fusible webbing, while older children can cut out ironed pieces. An adult should do the pressing step, which requires a hot iron and a wet pressing cloth.

Explore other themes such as neighborhood houses, farm animals, fancy dresses, or tropical fish. The simplicity of the process allows for complex designs and a variety of colors.

BELOW: *This colorful bedspread grows with the child. When it's time for a change, make new blocks and tie them into place.*

YOU'LL NEED

TIME: Allow 1½ hours to prepare the bedspread; ½ hour to decorate each square.
SKILLS: Basic sewing skills.
TOOLS: Measuring tape, iron, pressing cloth, scissors, straight pins, eyelet pliers or tool, and sewing machine (optional).
SUPPLIES: Twin bedspread or duvet cover, 12-pack of restaurant-quality napkins, 48 16-inch lengths of ⅜-inch-wide grosgrain ribbon, and 48 large eyelets.

BEDSPREAD PREPARATION

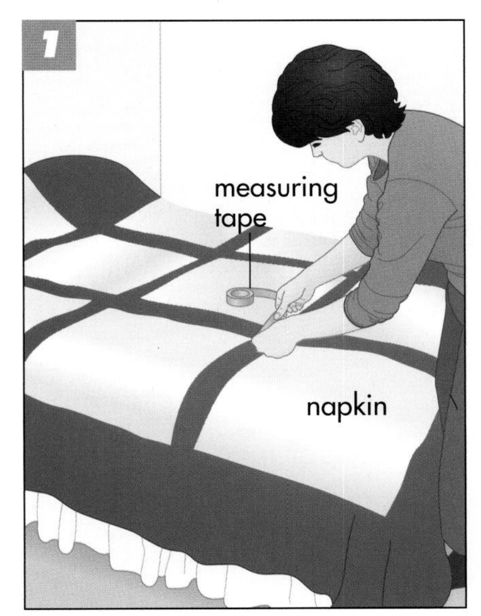

1. Plan layout.
With the bedspread on the bed, plan the layout of the napkins. Position them in equidistant rows. Using straight pins, mark ½ inch in from each napkin corner to indicate the placement of the ribbon ties.

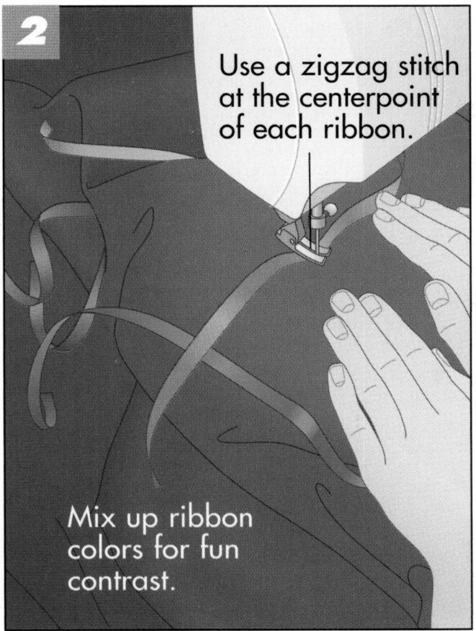

2. Stitch grosgrain ribbon ties.
Pin the centerpoint of each 16-inch length of ribbon into the places marked in the previous step. Stitch ribbon ties to the spread with a sewing machine using a zigzag stitch, or hand-stitch with doubled thread.

3. Attach eyelets.
Trace the eyelet hole ½ inch in from each napkin corner. Cut a hole with scissors or with the eyelet pliers. Insert an eyelet from the right side of the fabric. Grab fabric and eyelet between pliers and squeeze firmly.

OPTIONS FOR DECORATING

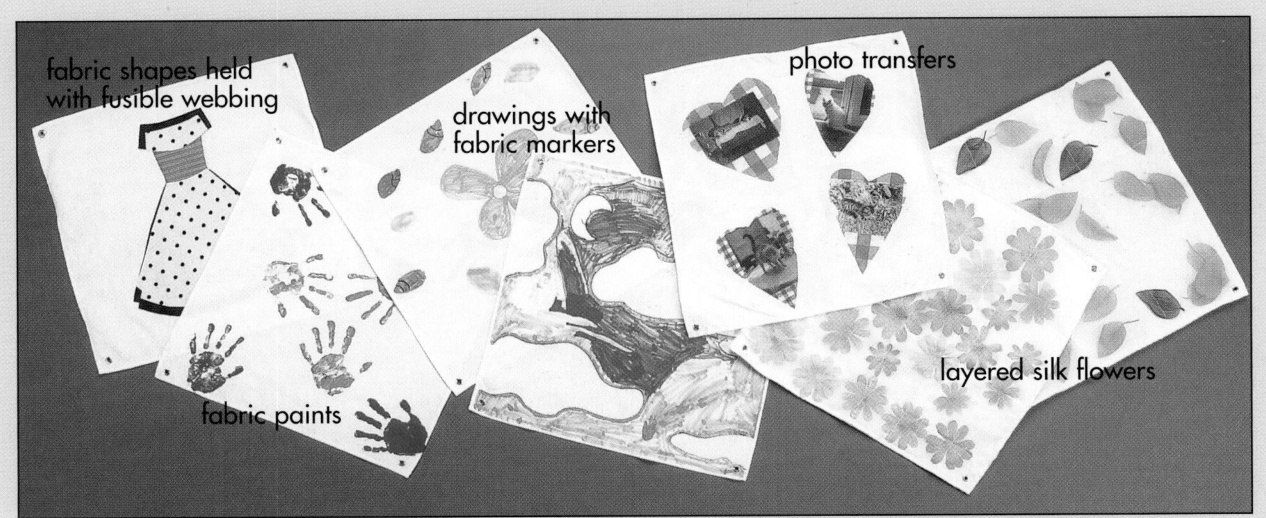

Fusible webbing makes complex designs simple to execute. Have a younger child make handprints or draw on napkins with fabric markers using fabric paint. Older children can apply pictures of friends, rock bands, or family pets to fabric using a photo transfer solution. They also can sew silk flowers or leaves between layers of netting for an ethereal effect.

FUSIBLE DECORATING

1. Transfer patterns to webbing.
Create a pattern and draw each design element on the paper side of webbing. Cut out around each piece. Using a hot, dry iron on the paper side, iron the webbing side to the wrong side of the fabric.

2. Peel paper from fabric.
When the fabric has cooled, cut out each piece along the pattern line. Remove paper slowly and carefully, leaving the webbing on the back of the fabric.

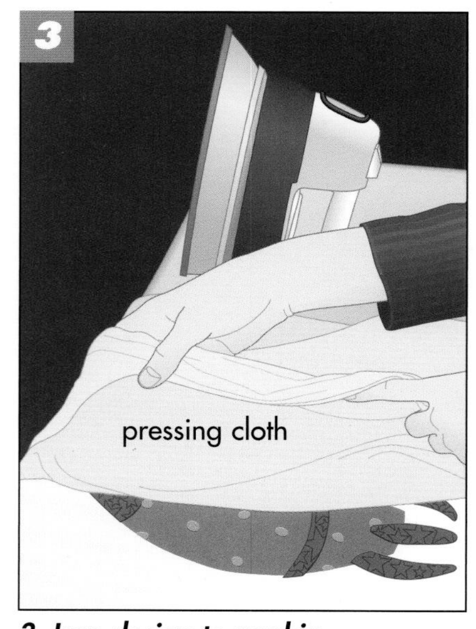

3. Iron design to napkin.
Place each piece, web side down, on a napkin. Cover it with a damp pressing cloth. With the iron at its hottest setting, press down for 15 seconds. Repeat until fabric is dry. Iron each layer of design in turn.

DECORATING WITH HANDPRINTS

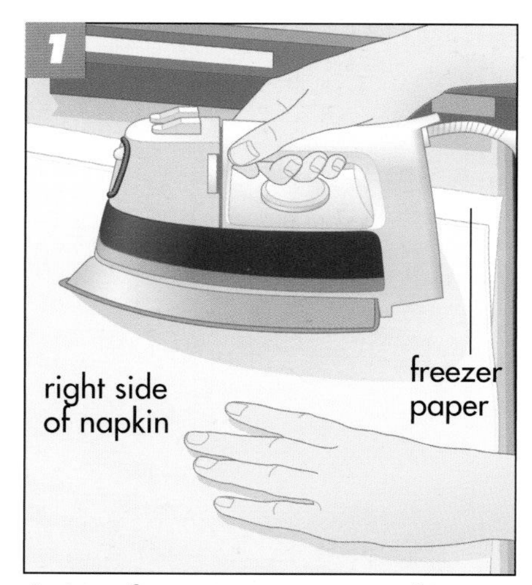

1. Iron freezer paper to napkin.
To stabilize the fabric of the napkin, place the shiny side of freezer paper on the underside of the fabric. Iron from the top of the napkin.

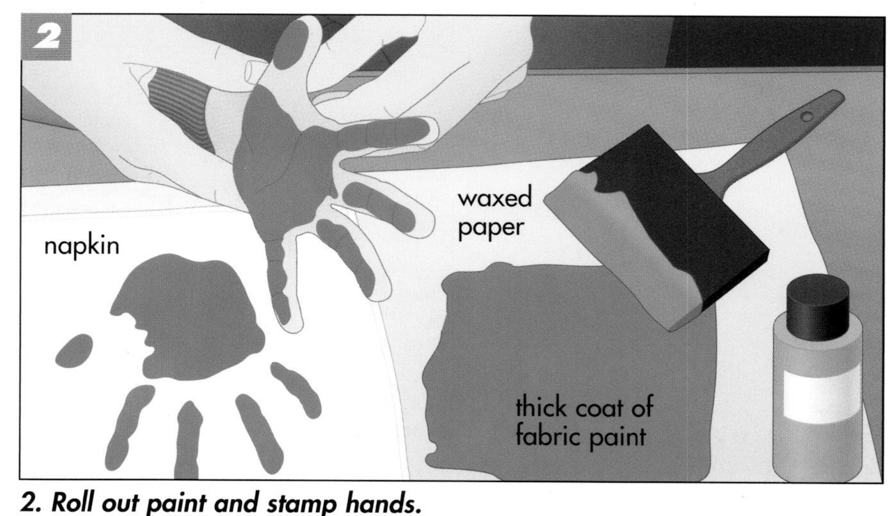

2. Roll out paint and stamp hands.
Pour fabric paint onto a piece of waxed paper or a disposable plastic-coated plate. Using a foam brush or roller, smooth a thick, even coat of paint over the surface. Older children can place a hand into the spread-out paint and press it firmly down on the napkin, leaving a print. An adult can guide smaller hands to ensure a clean imprint. After the paint has dried, pull off the freezer paper.

PHOTO TRANSFER

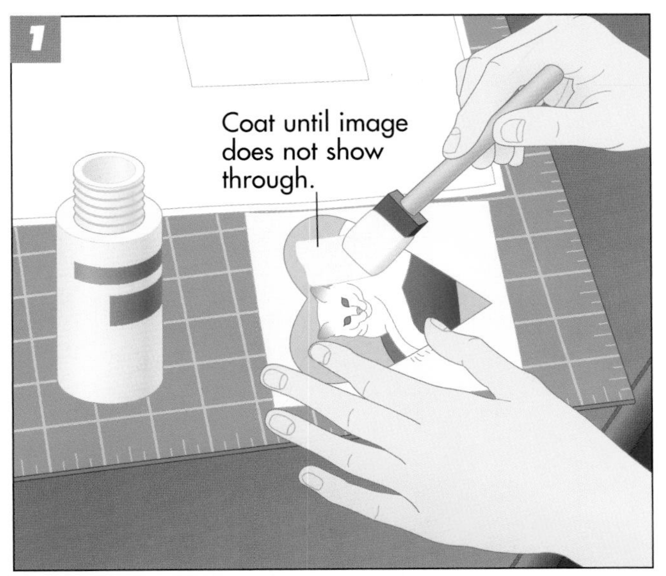

1. Paint transfer solution onto photocopy.
Make photocopies of images, then cut into the shape desired. Using a foam brush, paint transfer solution thickly over the top of the image. Press face down on a napkin, placing a paper towel over the top. Roll the bottle of transfer solution over the top to remove excess liquid. Remove paper towels and allow to dry for 24 hours. (Check manufacturer's directions.)

2. Soak and rub off paper with a sponge and water.
Dip a small sponge in water, and saturate shape. Let it stand for 2 minutes. Rub off paper using a circular motion, starting in the center of the image. Repeat every 30 minutes until all paper is removed. If after you've repeated the process the image appears cloudy, rub in a small amount of baby oil.

LEAFY LAYERS

Enclose treasures between netting and napkin.
Cut netting or a sheer fabric 1 inch larger than each napkin. Iron the napkin in thirds horizontally and vertically to mark stitching lines. Place silk leaves or flowers between the netting and napkin layers. Pin items in place. Add a few items to the top surface. Fold the raw edge of the fabric over the napkin on all four sides and pin. Topstitch around the napkin. Sew seams across the napkin on the fold lines.

REPLACING PANELS

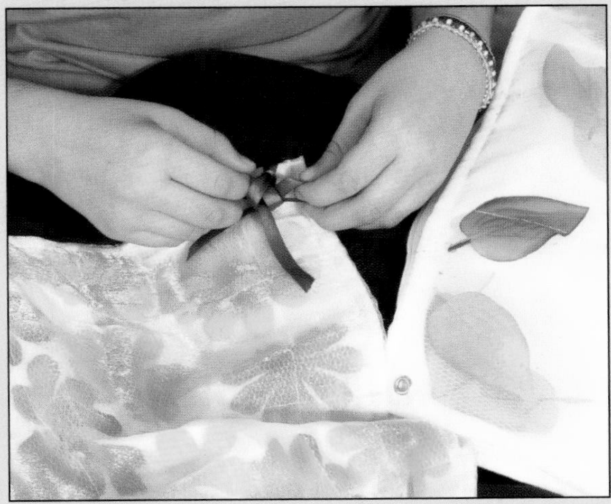

When it's time for a change, make new panels and add eyelets. Untie the bow on each corner and remove the old panels. Thread one end of a ribbon through each eyelet on the new panel and tie a bow to secure it in place.

BIG TOP TENT

This colorful variation on the tried-and-true card table and blanket tent is simple to make and will brighten many a rainy day. Designed as a combination of a circus tent and a puppet theater, an imaginative child will transform it into a playhouse, castle, or shop.

To make this project, begin by constructing the PVC pipe frame. Follow the dimensions provided for a tent that's roomy enough for younger children without being too large for indoor play. Or adjust the size to suit your space. If you enlarge the project, remember that most fabric is a maximum of 45 inches wide. If you make your tent any wider, you'll have to seam pieces of fabric together first.

Once the plastic pipe pieces are cut to length, the frame assembles quickly with a handful of standard pipe joints. Sewing the tent is simple—even simpler if you omit the ornamental points (see page 98). The fabric tent drapes over the frame without fasteners. Use light-colored fabric for the tent roof to keep the interior bright.

YOU'LL NEED

TIME: About 2 hours to cut and assemble the plastic pipe frame and 6 hours to sew the tent.
SKILLS: Moderate sewing experience; simple measuring and sawing.
TOOLS: Fine-toothed handsaw, miter box, measuring tape, iron, permanent marker, string, pencil, ruler, sewing machine, scissors, pins.
MATERIALS: Fabric: 3½ yards of yellow, 4 yards of blue, 4 yards of red, matching thread; four 10-foot pieces of 1-inch PVC, six tees, six 90-degree elbows, four 45-degree elbows, slow-dry adhesive.

ABOVE: *Indoors or out, this simple tent/theater provides a colorful place for play that also enhances a child's imagination. With some basic sewing skills and the willingness to saw a few pieces of plastic pipe, you can make this versatile project.*
LEFT: *A puppet theater at the back of the tent provides space for improvised performances. A simple puppet storage bag hangs from the support member inside the tent.*

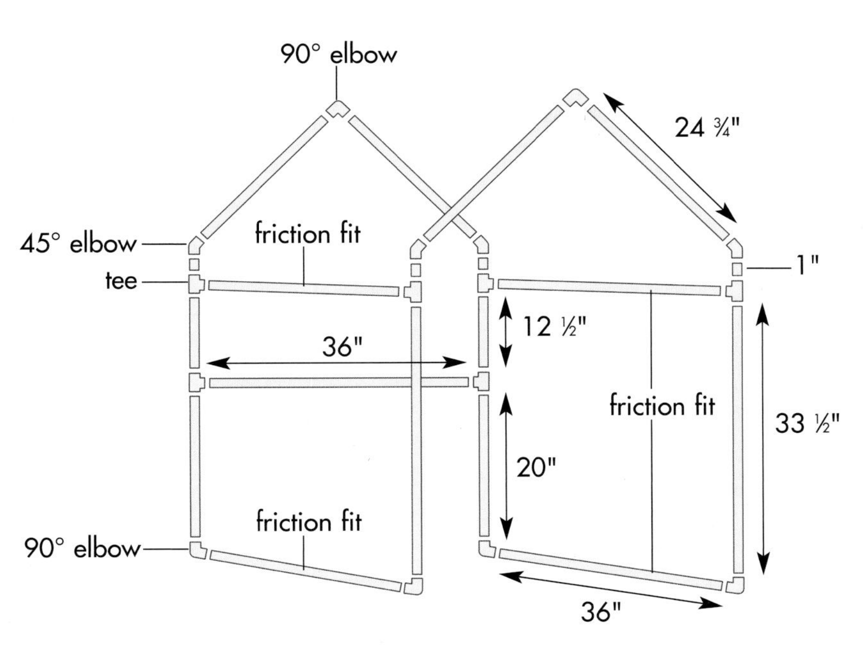

Frame overview.
The frame for the tent is made from 1-inch PVC pipe, available from home centers and hardware stores. When you buy the tees and elbows, double-check their type and diameter; you will find many options. You can remove the blue labeling on the pipe with a small amount of acetone. Or spray-paint the frame with a nontoxic paint. For easy storage, leave the side pieces unglued.

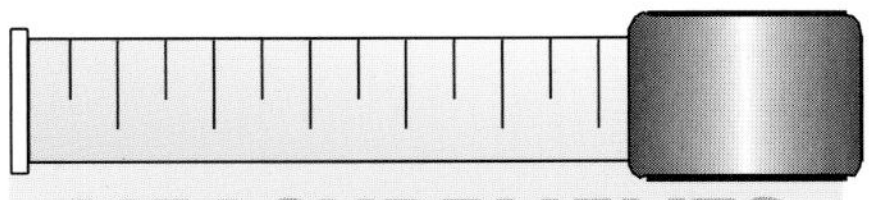

MEASUREMENTS

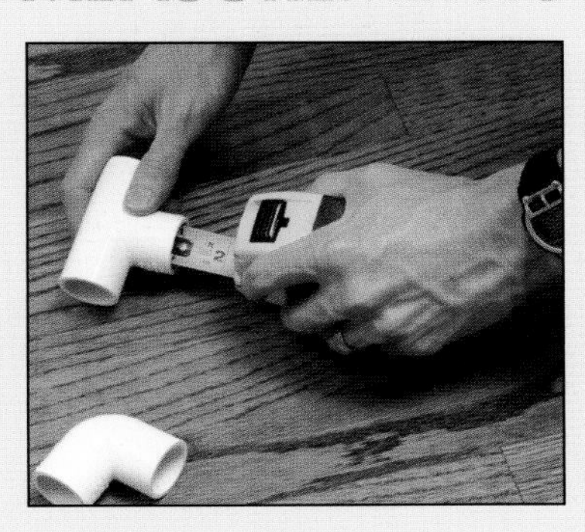

Enlarging the Frame

If you alter the frame dimensions, remember that the end of each pipe inserts 1 inch into a joint. Rough together one gable until you get the size that you want; use it as a guide for making the other gable. Then, measure between the joints and add 2 inches to get the cutting length of the side piece.

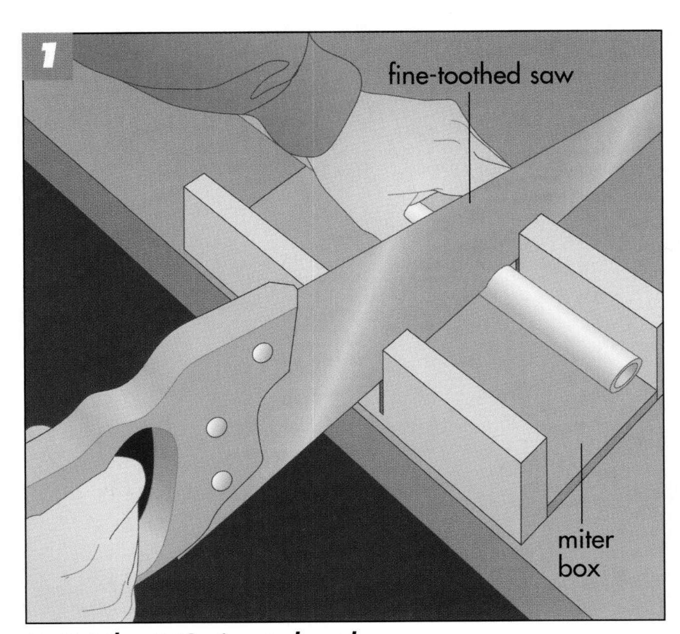

1. Cut the PVC pipe to length.
Mark the pipe with a fine-point permanent marker. Hold or clamp the pipe firmly in a miter box, and cut at the mark with a fine-toothed handsaw. Make long, smooth strokes, letting the saw blade do the work. Sand away any burrs on the inside and outside of each piece of pipe.

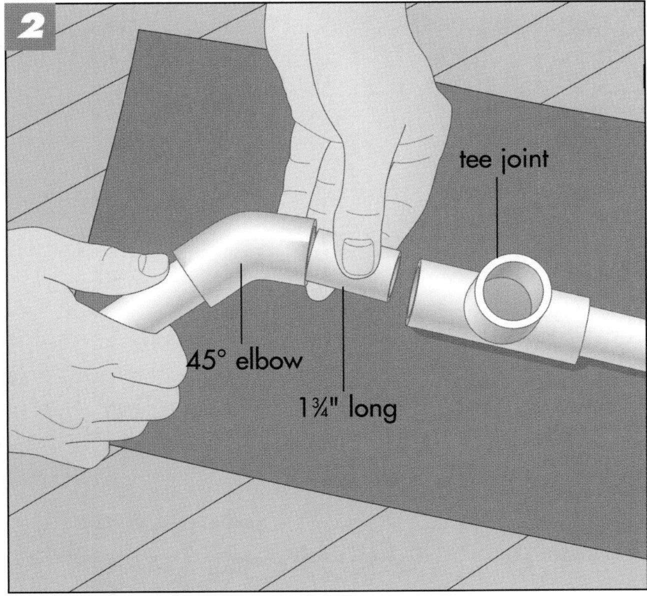

2. Piece together the gable.
Do a dry fit of the entire frame, being sure to push each pipe section fully into each joint. If you have to take apart the frame, use a scrap of wood to tap the joint away from the pipe. At the base of the roof gable, cut 1¾-inch pieces to join the 45° elbow and the tee joint (shown above).

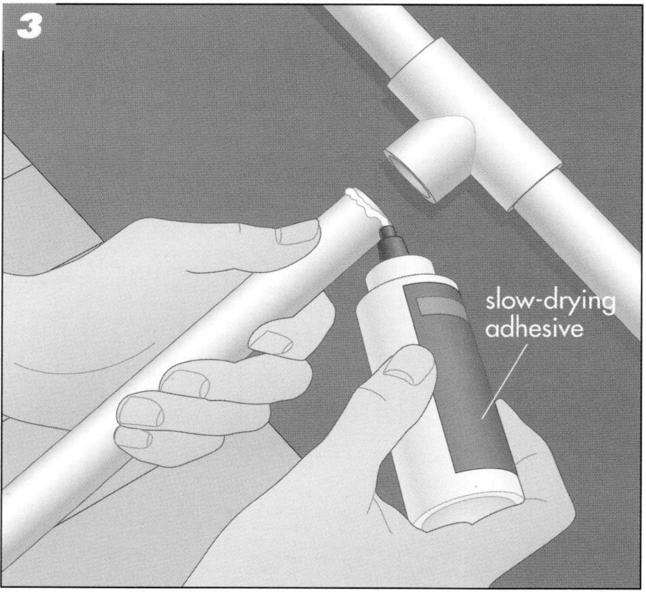

3. Glue gable joints.
Do not use plumber's PVC solvent and glue—it is designed to dry very quickly to make a watertight joint. Instead, use a vinyl glue with enough drying time to adjust joints (20 minutes is ideal). Glue the gable ends only; leave the ends of the side pieces unglued so the frame can be taken apart for storage.

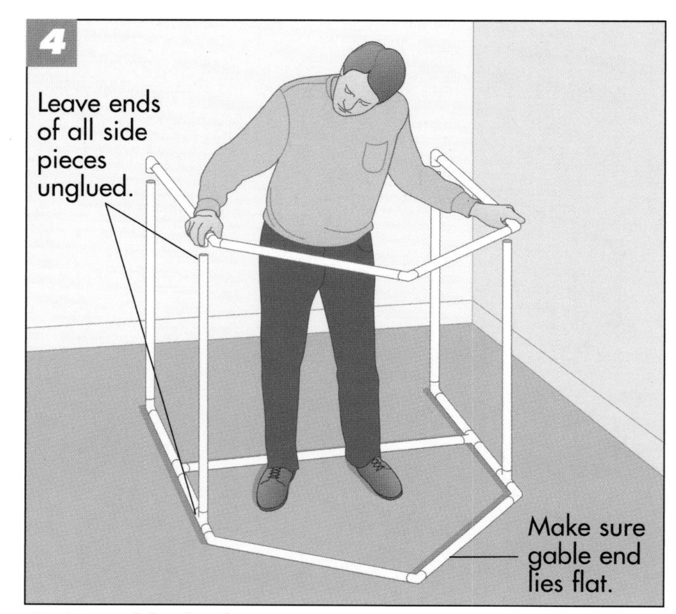

4. Assemble the frame.
Before the glue dries, lay each gable on the floor and gently step on the sections until the whole gable lies flat. Next assemble the entire frame and recheck the alignment of the tees and elbows. Then add the side pieces (without glue) to one gable, as shown, and attach the other gable.

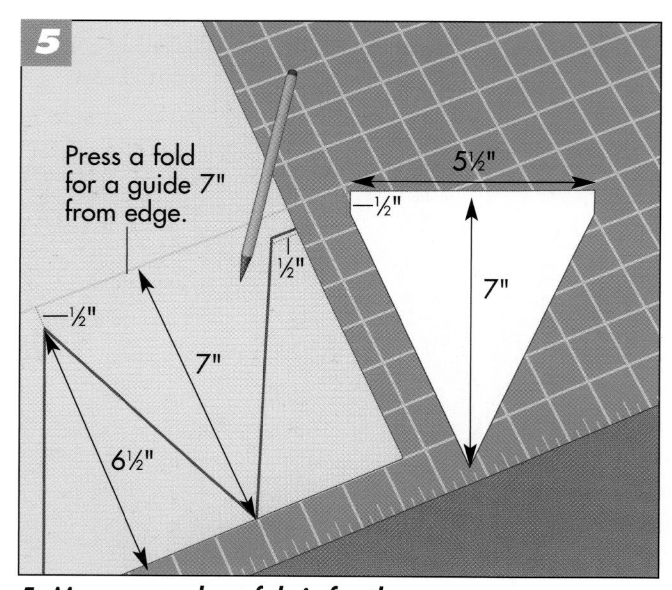

5. Measure and cut fabric for the tent.
Cut out all tent pieces, referring to the pattern on page 98 for fabric layout and measurements. The tent roof and sides meet in a decorative border. Make a paper pattern with the dimensions as shown above and trace around the point along the roof edge, beginning ½ inch from the edge. Use the cut edge as a pattern to cut the top edge of each side.

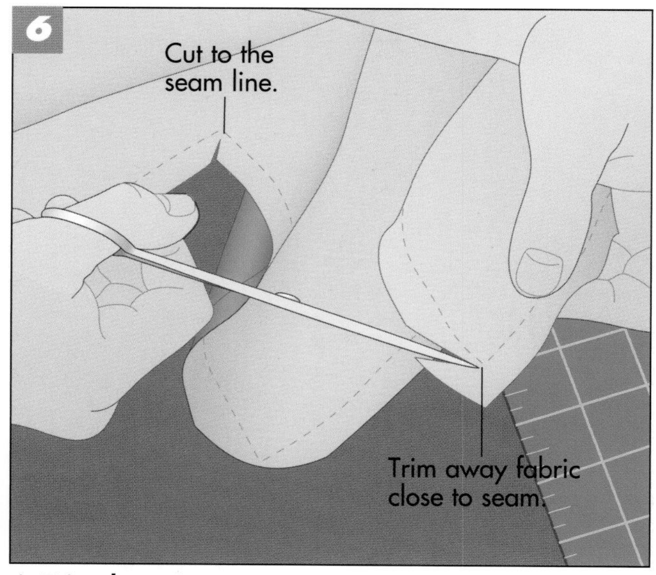

6. Trim the points.
Pin the roof to a side, with right sides facing and matching points. Stitch, using a ½-inch seam allowance. Cut the "Vs" to the seam line and trim away the fabric close to the stitching line of each point. Turn to the right side and iron. Stitch the roof to the side along the ironed guide line. Repeat to sew the other side to the roof.

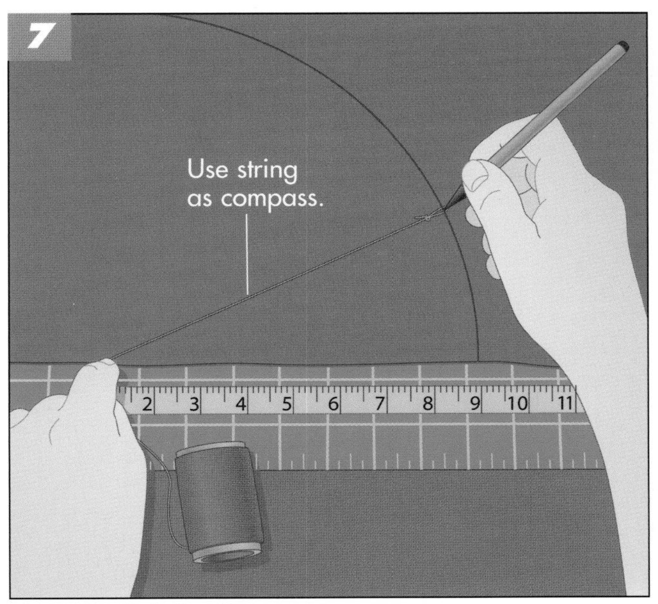

7. Mark arch for doorway.
Cut out the door opening, following the dimensions on page 99. Mark the 9-inch radius of the arch, using a string-and-pencil compass. Cut out the arch; use it as a pattern for the opposite door panel. Hem the puppet stage upper curtain by ironing ½ inch, twice, under two long sides of each curtain; stitch. Iron the lower edge under 1 inch, twice; stitch to hem.

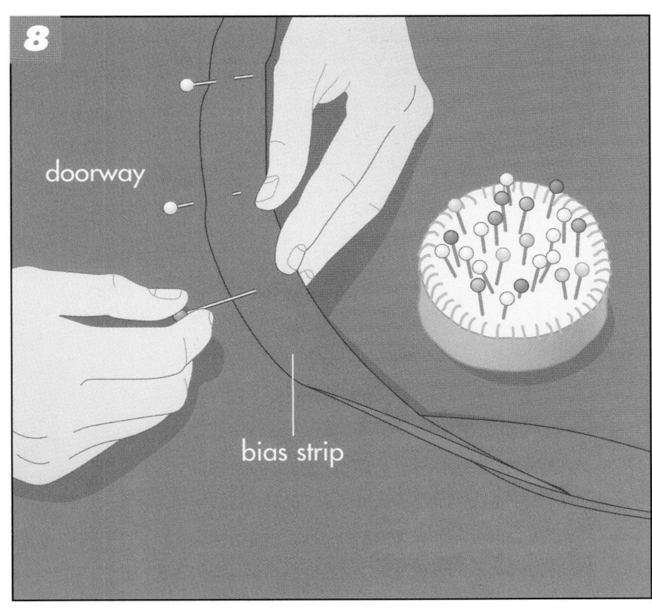

8. Make binding for doorway.
Cut 3-inch-wide strips on the bias from red fabric. Join the short ends to make two long strips. Iron each in half lengthwise, with wrong sides facing. Pin a bias strip to the front edge of each doorway, stretching the strip to lie flat around the curve. Using a ¼-inch seam allowance, sew along the edge. Press the strip to the back side. Pin in place, then topstitch.

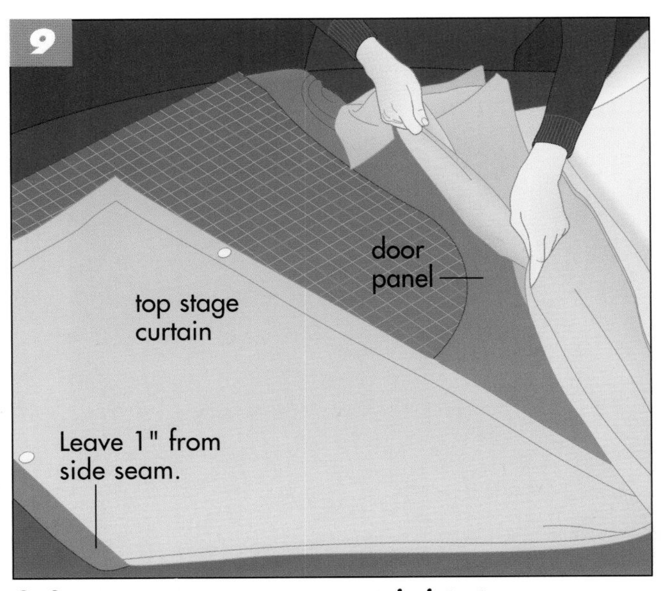

9. Sew puppet stage upper curtain into top seam.
Pin the upper stage curtain to the top edge of a door panel, with the outer edge 1 inch from the side. Pin, then sew the door panel to the top/side, working with one plane at a time. Match the center roofline to the peak of the door panel. Note: The top/side seam falls 2 inches below the corner of the door panel. To hem, iron the bottom edges under 1 inch, twice. Stitch, changing thread to match the fabric.

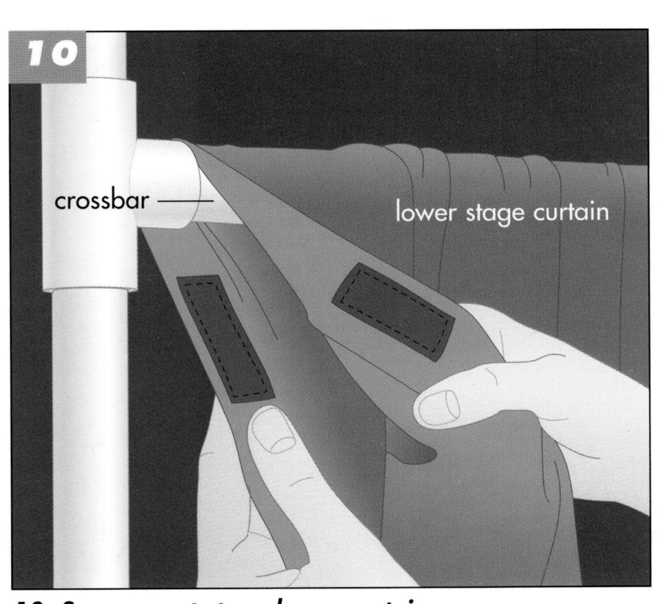

10. Sew puppet stage lower curtain.
Hem all sides of the lower stage curtain by ironing the edges under 1 inch, twice, and stitch. Lay the curtain over the crossbar and mark the center. Attach 2-inch-long hook and loop fasteners to each side hem 2 inches from the center mark. Secure the fastener strips to hang the curtain.

LAUNDRY MONSTER

Picking up dirty clothes is almost fun with this friendly laundry-eating monster. Hang it on a closet door (a simple child's hanger is built in) or on a bed frame. When its belly is full, you can tip the monster over and dump the laundry out through its mouth. Make additional monsters for storing pajamas, toys, or hats and gloves (see page 29).

You can make your monster from a wide range of fake furs or thermal fleece, choosing a monstrous combination of colors or coordinating with your child's room decor. If you use fake fur, select a thin lining material—it will make sewing easier.

To make a girl monster tie pigtails with bows. Other options include using rickrack or ribbon as hair. Simply pin the trim into the seam before sewing the monster top pieces together.

YOU'LL NEED

TIME: Allow 3 to 4 hours per bag.
SKILLS: Moderate sewing skills.
TOOLS: Sewing machine, scissors.
SUPPLIES: 1 yard of fake fur or thermal fleece, 1 yard of lining fabric (thermal fleece or cotton), ¼ yard of black thermal fleece for arms/legs, fiberfill, matching wide bias tape, ½ yard of ½-inch-wide white grosgrain ribbon for teeth, 1½ yards of 1½-inch-wide ribbon for girl monster bows, one pair of 1½-inch-diameter black plastic eyes, and one child-size hanger.

ABOVE: This endearingly monstrous laundry bag may inspire reluctant room cleaners to keep it well fed. Made of fake fur or thermal fleece and a child-size clothes hanger, this project goes together quickly. Involve your child in the fun of picking out fabrics and colors.

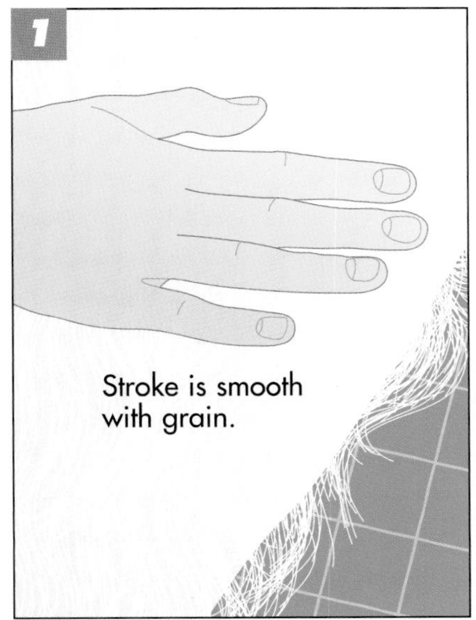

1. Find the grain of the fur. Enlarge the pattern (see page 100) to size. Find the grain of the fur by stroking it. If the fur feels smooth, then you are stroking with the grain. If it feels rough, then you are stroking against the grain. Note the direction of the grain and flip the fabric over.

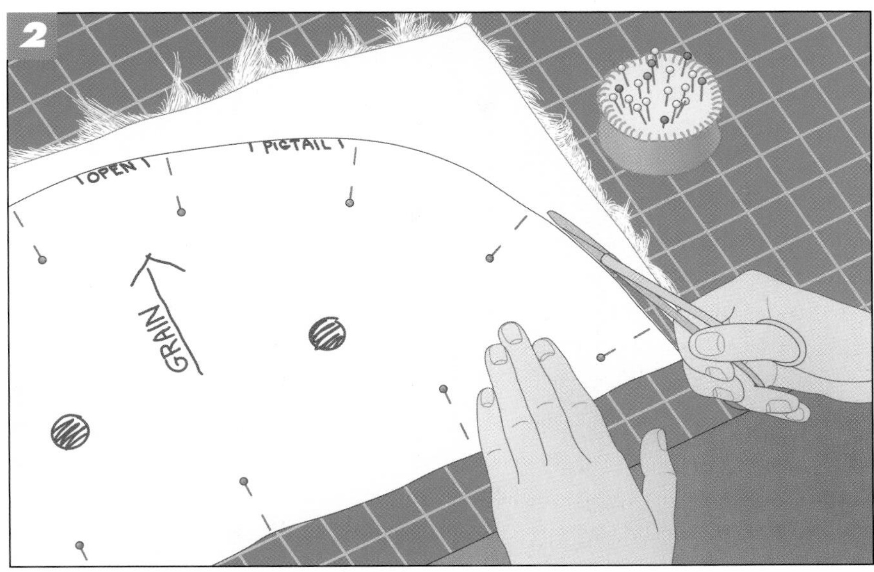

2. Attach pattern and cut material. Cut out the pattern pieces. Pin the patterns to the back of the fabric so that the arrow on the pattern points along the grain. Using the pointed tips of scissors, cut through only the fabric backing, doing your best to avoid cutting the fur fibers. Cut the head, belly, and back pieces from the fur and from the lining fabric. From thermal fleece, cut the arm and leg pieces.

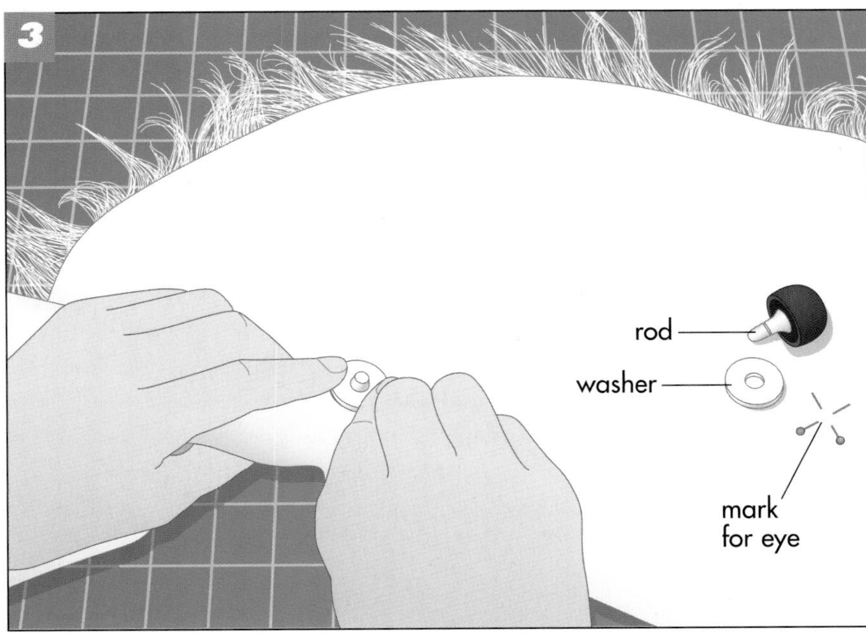

3. Fasten the eyes in place. Following the markings on the pattern as a guide, place crossed pins to mark each eye location. Using the tip of your scissors, poke a small hole through the fur. Insert the eyes from the fur side and snap the washer on the rod following the manufacturer's directions. Or, stitch a large button on the right side for each eye, using doubled thread.

EXPERTS' INSIGHT

WORKING WITH FAKE FUR

Fur can be pretty wild to work with. Here's how to tame it.

- Cut one layer of fake fur at a time. Use the points of sharp scissors to cut the fur from the fabric side. Try not to cut any of the hairs of the fur.
- After cutting the fabric backing, gently pull the pieces apart to disengage the hairs.
- Brush the fur away from the seam before joining the parts of the bag. After sewing, use a straight pin to pull out any fibers of fur that have been caught in the seam.
- To avoid clogging your sewing machine, remove the lint that fake fur leaves behind.

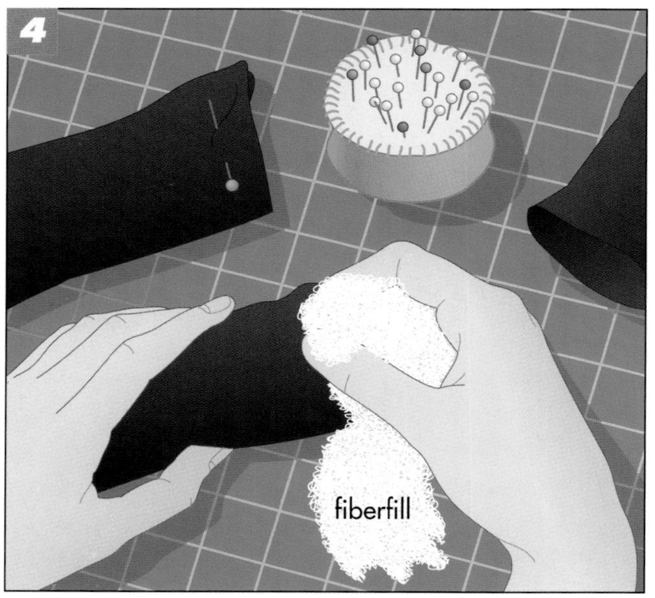

4. Sew arms and legs.
Pin pairs of arms and legs together, with right sides facing. Using a ½-inch seam allowance, sew together, leaving the top open. Turn each to the right side. Lightly stuff each limb with polyester fiberfill. Pin the opening shut. If you are making a girl monster, sew pigtails from the fur in the same manner. Turn the pigtails to the right side, but do not stuff.

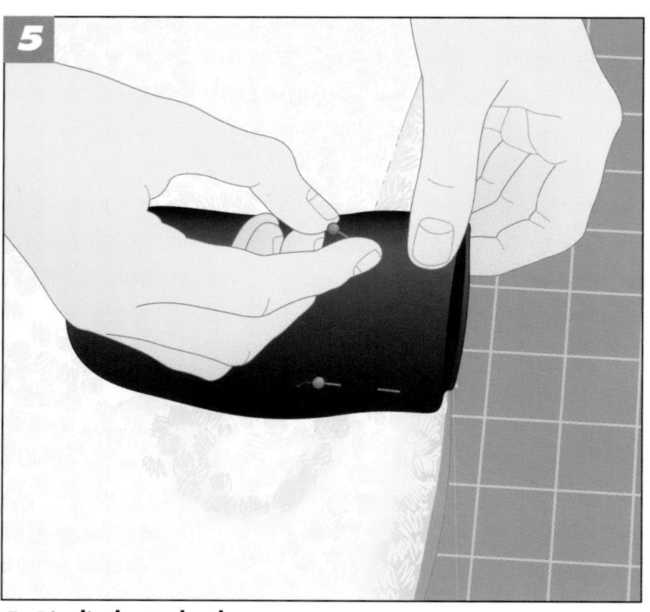

5. Pin limbs to body.
Baste the back lining to the wrong side of the body fabric. Pin the limbs in place on the body, following the pattern markings. Pin the pigtails in place for a girl monster. If you choose to add rickrack hair (see page 29), baste it to the top of the head now.

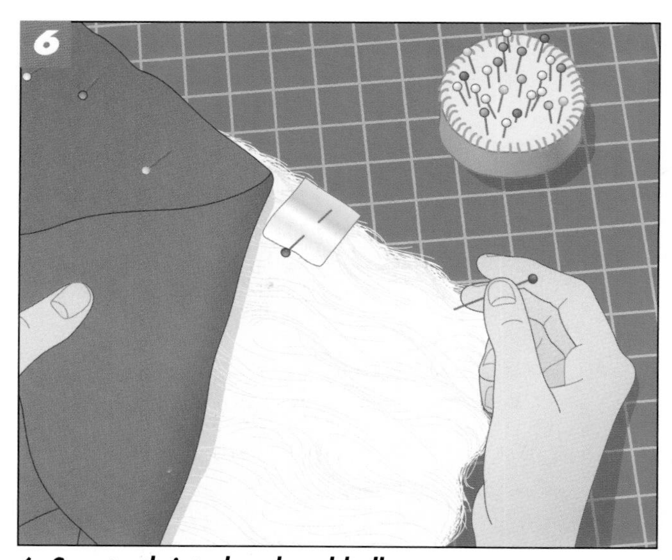

6. Sew teeth into head and belly seams.
For teeth, cut four 3-inch-long pieces of ribbon. Fold each in half and pin to the head at pattern markings, aligning raw edges. Pin the lining to the lower edge of the head with right sides facing. Using a ½-inch seam allowance, sew, catching the teeth in the seam. Turn to the right side and baste the raw edges. In the same manner, pin the bottom teeth between the belly pieces. Make tucks at pattern markings, folding the fur and the lining separately. Stitch, turn, and baste.

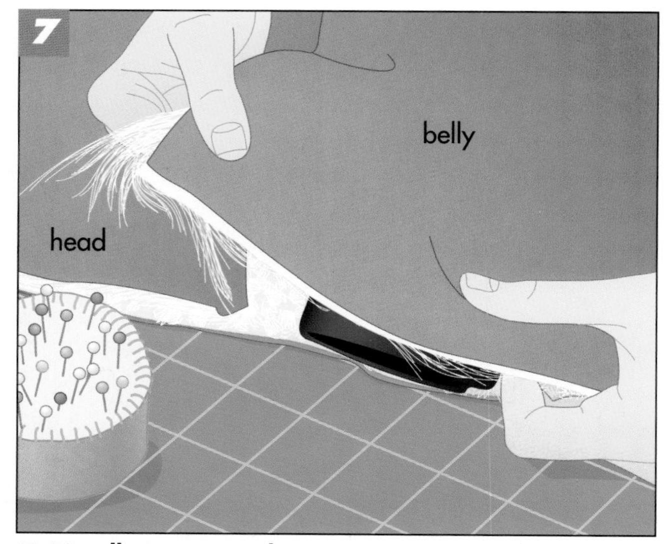

7. Pin all pieces together.
Pushing the fur to the inside, pin the head to the back with right sides facing. Pin the belly to the back, with right sides facing. Overlap the head as marked on the pattern. As you pin the belly, make tucks along the sides and bottom, at pattern markings.

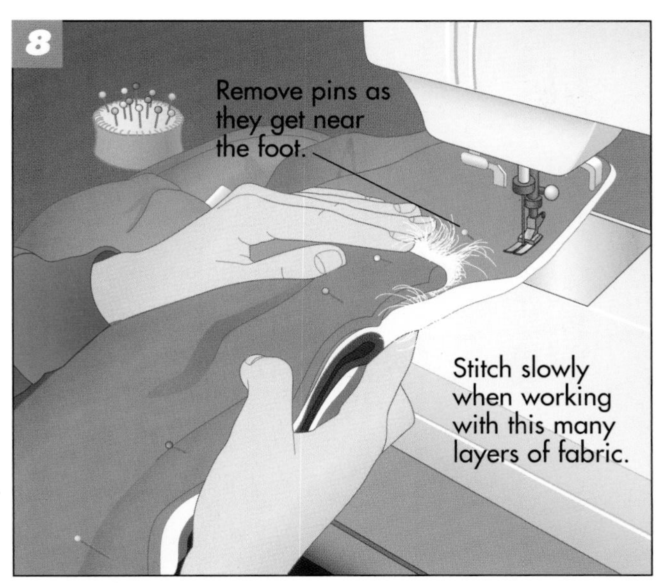

8. Sew the seams.
Using a ½-inch seam allowance, sew around the perimeter of the monster bag. Begin and end at the top of the head, leaving an opening for the hanger. Sewing through this many layers is difficult: Use a heavier needle in your machine and stitch slowly. Take out the straight pins just before you get to them—do not sew over pins.

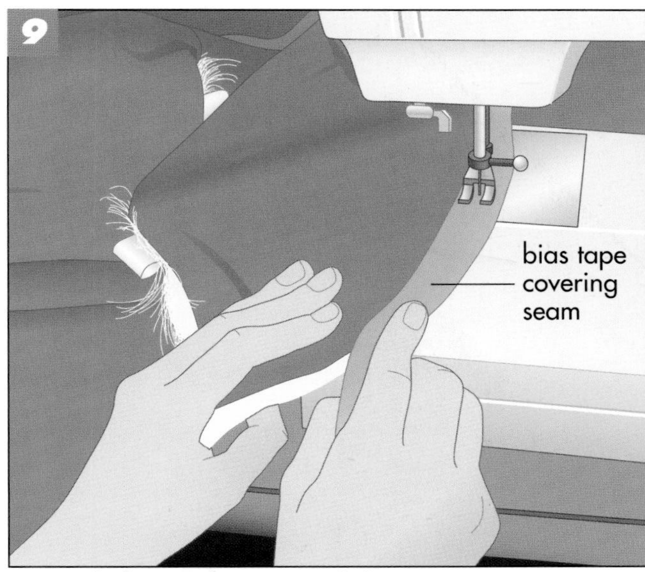

9. Finish the inside seam with bias tape.
Use a zigzag stitch to sew bias tape over the raw edges of the seam. Leave the opening for the hanger. Turn the monster bag to the right side. Place a child-size hanger through the opening at the top of the head. Tie ribbons into bows around the pigtails.

Other Uses for Monster Bags

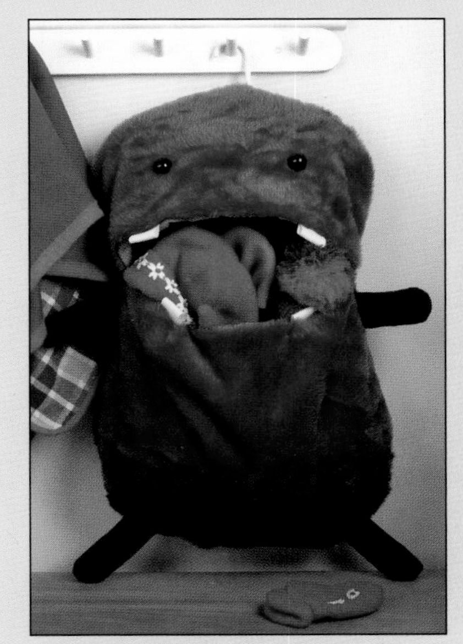

Hat and glove storage
A monster bag in a mudroom or entry will devour plenty of stocking caps and gloves.

PJ bag
Hang a monster bag on the bed frame for a place to store pajamas, robe, and slippers.

Toy storage
Hook a bag onto a door handle and pile your child's toys into the monster's maw.

MY MANNEQUIN

If mornings are a jumble of clothing confusion, here's a project that might calm things down. This mannequin board can be hung on the back of a closet door or be attached to a nearby wall. With it in place, your child can try out clothing options the evening before and hang up the final selection, avoiding panic in the morning.

To make this project, you'll need to buy a 4×8-foot sheet of ⅛-inch tempered hardboard. Have a home center cut the board for you. Not only will you save yourself the tricky task of making long, straight cuts, but you'll also find the cut-down board much easier to transport. Before heading to the home center, measure your door. Subtract 2 to 4 inches from the height so that the panel will clear the door stop and not catch on the carpet. Subtract 6 to 8 inches from the width to allow for the lockset and the stop along the hinges.

Two hooks that fit over the door top hold the panel. To attach it to a wall, find the studs (see page 34) and fasten it in place using 2-inch general-purpose screws with decorative washers (see page 35).

Tracing and painting is a great chance for parents and children to work together. For easy cleanup and airbrush effect, consider using latex spray paint. As your child grows, flip the board and create a new tracing and background.

YOU'LL NEED

TIME: About 4 hours to notch and paint the board.
SKILLS: Moderate carpentry skills.
TOOLS: Drill, ¼-inch bit, utility knife, ruler, sandpaper, paintbrushes, drop cloth.
MATERIALS: ⅛-inch tempered hardboard, plastic over-the-door hooks, primer, paint.

ABOVE: *Your child can mix and match clothing in advance and be ready for the morning with this handy mannequin board. Ideal for collaboration between parent and child, this fun-to-do project goes together quickly.*

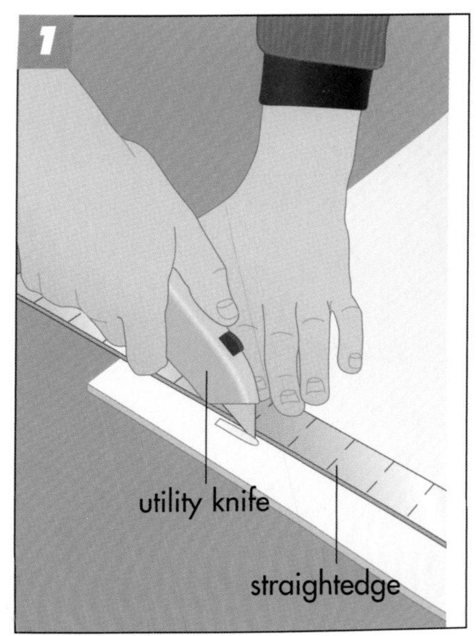

1. Cut hook holes.
With the ⅛-inch panel cut to size, make two slots for the plastic over-the-door hooks. (Try this first on scrap to confirm the distance from the top edge.) Mark for a slot ½ inch wider than the hook. Drill a ¼-inch hole at each end of the slot. Slice out the area in between.

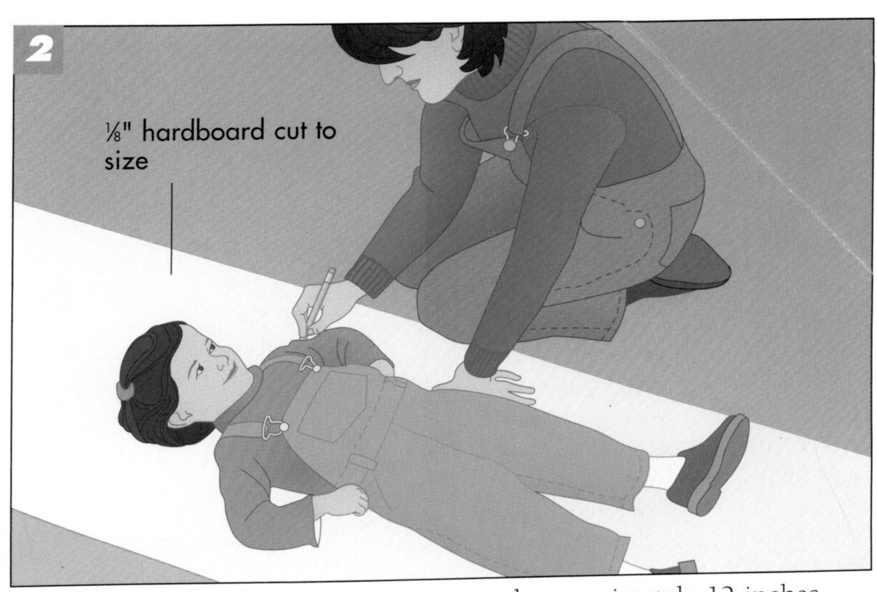

2. Sand, prime, and trace.
Sand off the rough edges of the panel with 100-grit sandpaper, and paint the panel with primer. Paint the background first. Sketch a horizon line and, using spray paint, fill in the major areas of color. Once the background is dry, have your child lie down on the panel approximately 12 inches from the bottom. Make a tracing. For a realistic rendering, stay as close to your child's outline as possible. For a more stylized rendering, capture the general shape only. Sketch in additional details on the mannequin and on the landscape.

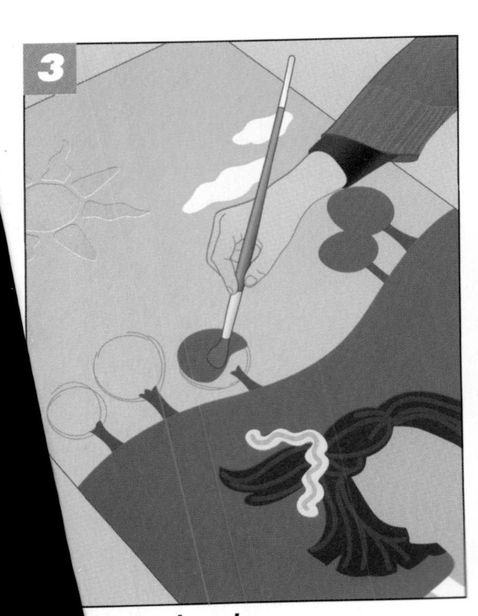

aint and seal.
g acrylic paints, color in the s and add details. If mixing for large areas, make sure to ore than enough to cover a. Add a drying deterrent le at art supply stores) for nding. Let it dry, then e entire panel with a satin lyurethane.

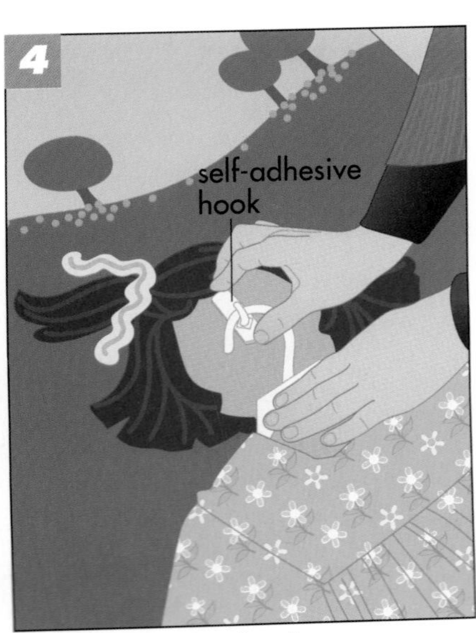

4. Attach clothes hooks.
After the panel is completely dry, position a piece of clothing on a hanger on top of the mannequin as if it were "dressed." Slide a self-adhesive hook under the hanger's hook and press it in place. Position another hook for shorts and pants.

5. Hang mannequin.
Slide the over-the-door hooks through the top of the panel and set the hooks over the top of the door. If mounting it on a wall, find wall studs (see page 34) within 12 inches of each edge. Fasten the board with 2-inch general-purpose screws (see page 35), using a level to plumb along one edge.

MAKE THE ART GALLERY SCENE

Creative kids will churn out more displayable art than even a large side-by-side refrigerator can accommodate. Here's a project that will give your young artist plenty of space to display art plus a blackboard for those more immediate creative urges.

You can adapt this project to suit the wall you want to use as a display area. Necessary supplies are simple: a wall-mounted piece of galvanized sheet metal that can hold artwork with magnets, a wall painted to be a blackboard, and a shelf for holding framed art. You can expand each section to suit your space. If you end your gallery mid-wall, a trim piece caps it off (see page 35).

Order the galvanized sheet metal from a heating and cooling contractor (see page 35). Molding for the ledge is readily available from your local home center. A paint or hardware store will have brush-on or spray blackboard paint. As the years go by, the blackboard can be painted over to match the wall color, but very likely there always will be posters and photos to display on the wall and new objects d'art to show off on the ledge.

YOU'LL NEED

TIME: About 2 hours to make the ledge, 2 hours to paint the blackboard, 2 hours to install the sheet metal.

SKILLS: Moderate carpentry skills.

TOOLS: Level, measuring tape, painter's tape, fine-toothed handsaw or back saw, miter box, screwdriver, sandpaper, white glue, drill, and nail set.

MATERIALS: Galvanized sheet metal, trim washers and 2" galvanized deck screws; blackboard paint; 1×3 clear pine, decorative ledge trim, bumper trim, 6d finishing nails, putty, primer, paint.

ABOVE: *Give a budding Rembrandt plenty of room for display with a gallery wall. Galvanized sheet metal applied to the wall allows use of magnets to mount treasured works of art. A shelf dis[...] and provides [...] used on the b[...] project can [...] the availab[...]*

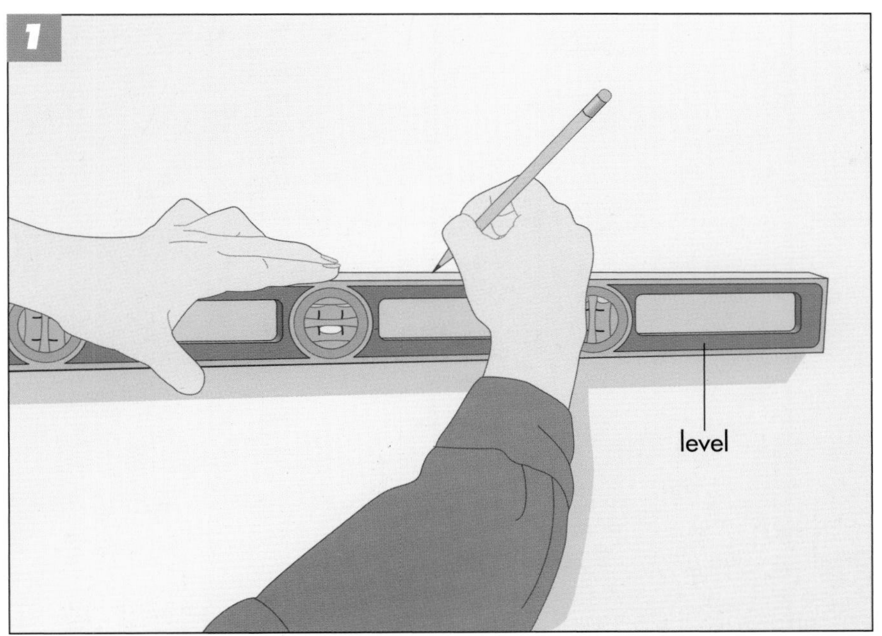

1. Strike a level line.
Measure 30 to 36 inches from the floor, and use a level to strike a line to indicate the topmost boundary of the blackboard. Extend the line along the wall. Use the level to mark a plumb line if your gallery will have a vertical boundary.

EXPERTS' INSIGHT

CHOOSING BLACKBOARD PAINT

If your blackboard area is small (16 square feet or less), try using spray blackboard paint. You'll get a factory-smooth surface without brush marks or the usual cleanup. However, guard carefully against over spray. Mask the area carefully (see Step 2) and cover adjacent areas with drop cloths. For larger areas, purchase paint in a can and roll it on using a roller sleeve with a nap of ¼ inch or less.

2. Paint the blackboard.
Mask the area surrounding the blackboard with painters' tape and newspaper. Cover the floor and anything within 10 or 12 feet to guard against over spray.

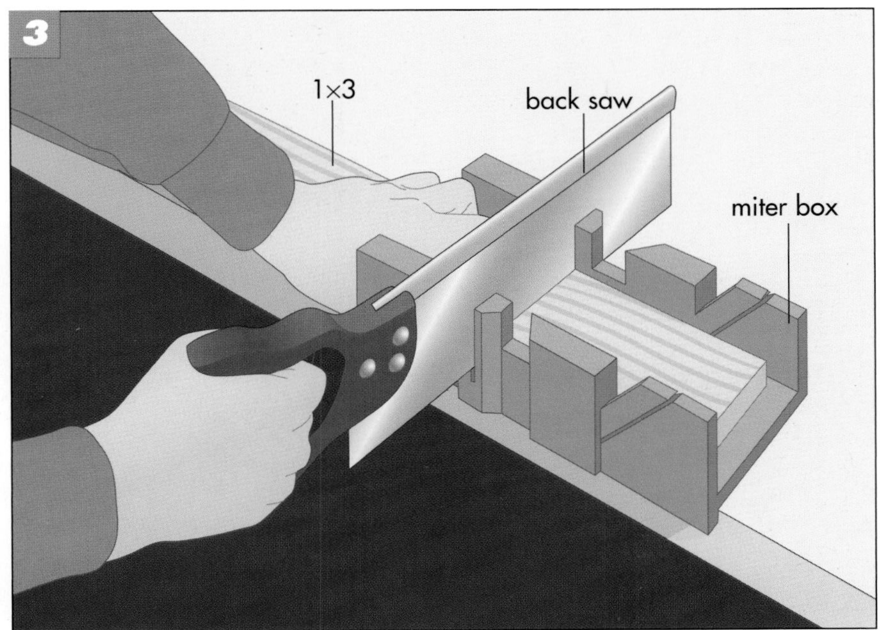

3. Measure and cut the shelf pieces.
Purchase clear 1×3 for the shelf and chair rail or picture-hanging rail for the shelf support. Buy a piece of screen bead or another thin decorative molding to act as a bumper along the shelf edge. Measure the length needed, and cut the pieces to size using a miter box and a fine-toothed handsaw or backsaw.

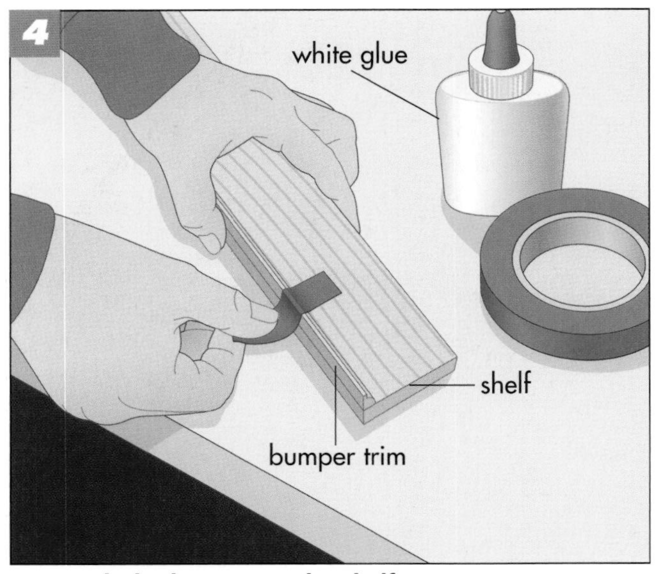

4. Attach the bumper to the shelf.
Lightly sand the cut edges of each piece using 100-grit sandpaper. Carefully spread a bead of white glue along the front edge of the shelf. Put the bumper in place and hold it with masking tape until dry.

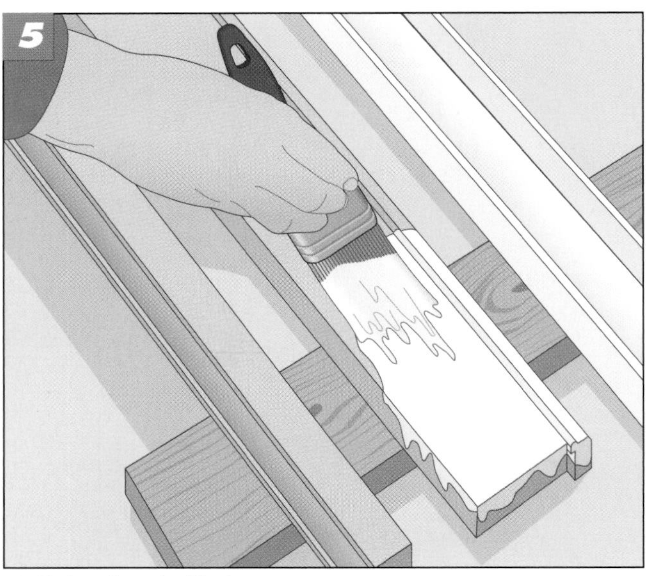

5. Paint the shelf pieces.
Before mounting the shelf pieces on the wall, prime and paint them. Lay down a drop cloth before painting. Set the pieces on scrap lumber placed every 2 or 3 feet.

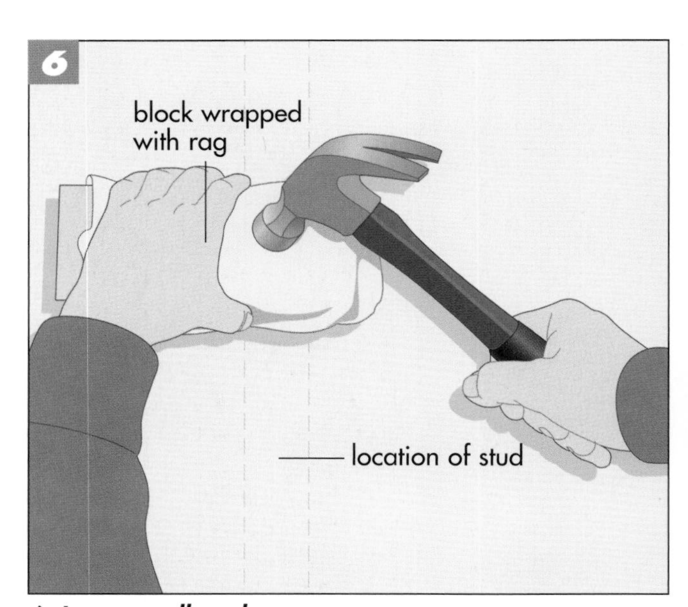

6. Locate wall studs.
To be sure the shelf and the magnetic display area are adequately supported, find the studs (vertical framing members) in your wall. To do so, cover a scrap of wood with a rag (to avoid damage to the wall) and slide it along the wall, tapping it with a hammer every couple of inches. A hollow sound indicates a wall cavity; a solid thud indicates a stud.

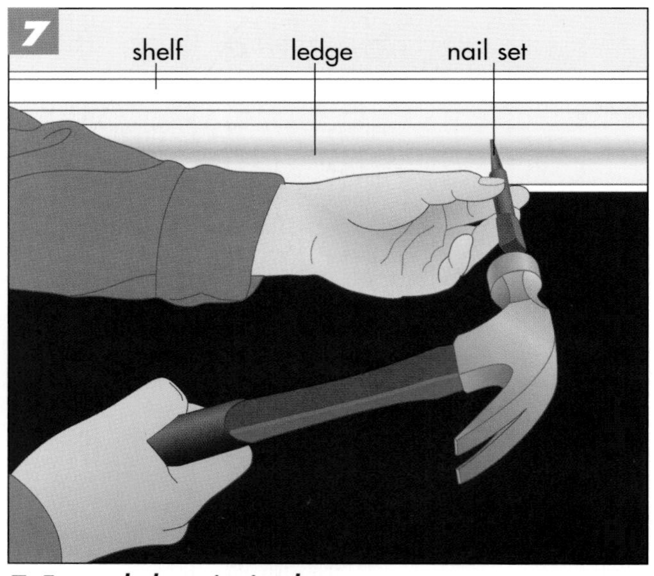

7. Fasten ledge trim in place.
Drill pilot holes at each stud, using a $\frac{3}{32}$-inch drill bit. Fasten the ledge in place along the horizontal line marked as the border of the blackboard. Then attach the edge trim with one or two 6d finishing nails.

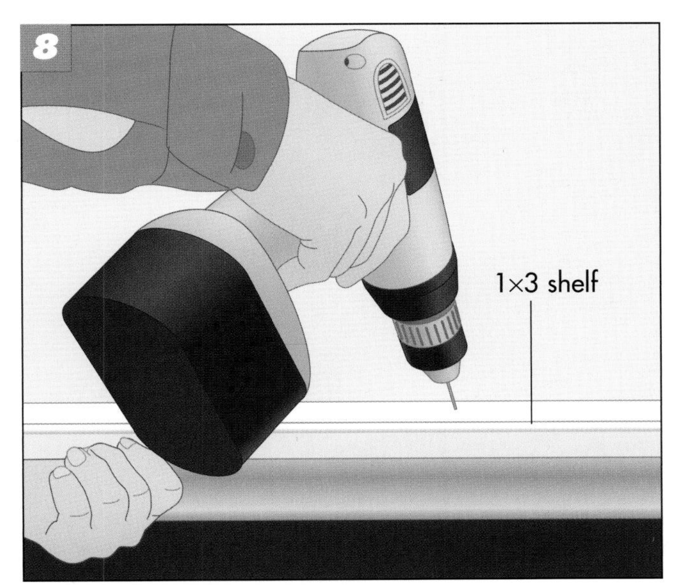

8. Attach the shelf to the ledge.

Apply a bead of white glue to the shelf ledge and set the shelf in place. Every 12 inches, use a 3⁄32-inch drill bit to drill pilot holes at an angle through the shelf and into the shelf ledge. Nail 6d finishing nails into the holes and punch the heads slightly beneath the surface with a nail set. Putty the holes and touch up with paint.

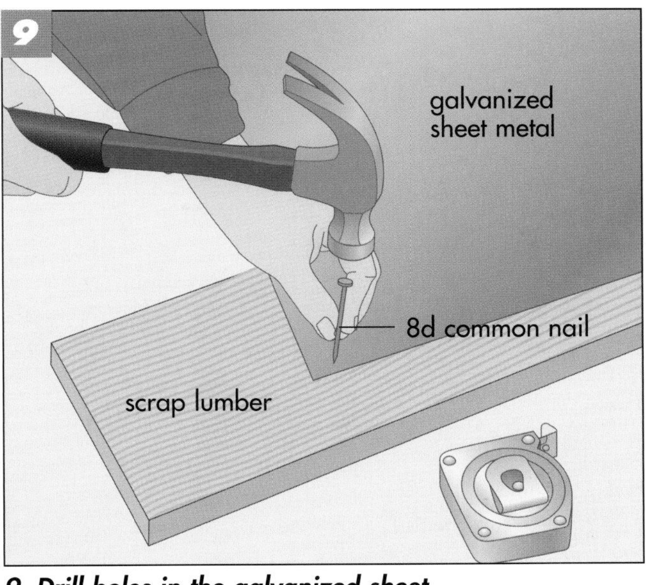

9. Drill holes in the galvanized sheet.

Set the galvanized sheet in place on top of the ledge and mark the location of the wall studs. Make marks 3⁄4 inch from the edge and every 12 to 14 inches along the edge. Mark 3⁄4 inch in at each corner. Lay the sheet over a scrap of wood and punch a starter hole in the sheet with an 8d to 16d nail or a nail set. Drill 1⁄8-inch holes.

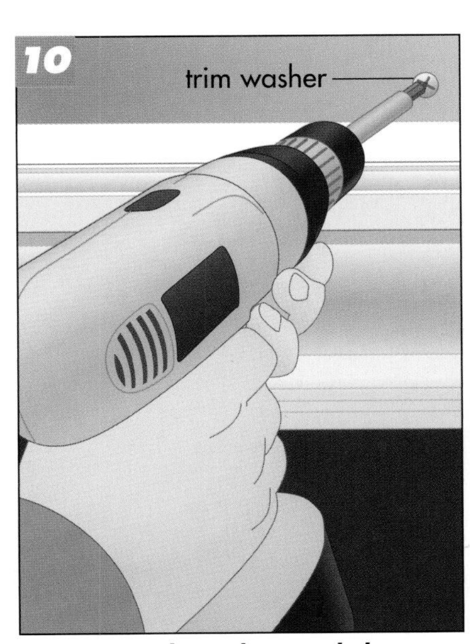

10. Fasten the galvanized sheet metal above the shelf.

Have an assistant hold the metal sheet resting on the ledge and flat against the wall. Place chromium-coated trim washers on 2-inch galvanized deck screws and fasten them in place with a cordless drill or phillips screwdriver.

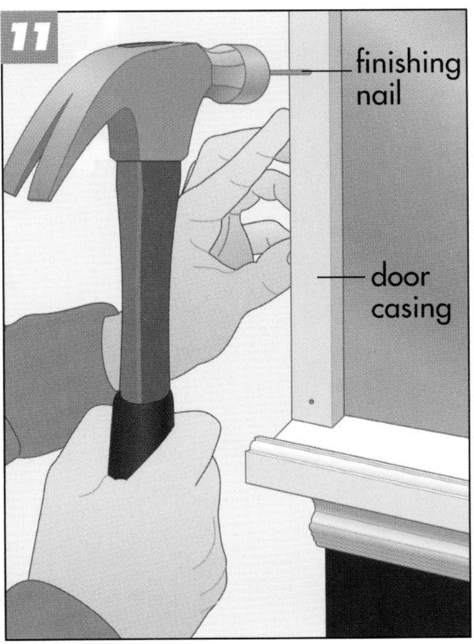

11. Add vertical trim.

To finish off your gallery mid-wall, add a vertical trim to finish the sheet metal edge with door casing trim. Cut it to length with a fine-toothed saw and a miter box (see page 33). Drill starter holes through the trim and metal with a 3⁄32-inch bit and fasten the trim with 6d finishing nails.

BUYING SHEET METAL

Check your phone directory for sheet-metal shops or heating and cooling contractors. Give them the measurements for the sheet you want and ask them to "roll" the edge. That means they will bend the edges back so the sheet will lie flat and the edges won't be sharp. Ask for 26-gauge galvanized sheet metal. A 4×3-foot piece will cost about $20 to $30.

VAN GOGH TO GO

Kids love to make large pictures. This art table gives them plenty of room to create with brushes, markers, and crayons.

Paper from a roll held by a dowel pulls across the table. Hold-down strips steady the paper. When artwork is done, the child can neatly tear it off for display, then pull through a new sheet.

This design accommodates a 24-inch-wide roll of paper, about 3 inches in diameter. (An 18-inch roll will also work.) Both sizes are commonly available at crafts and art supply stores. If you want to use a thicker roll—newsprint or butcher paper, for instance—raise the dowel so that it will fit.

Drop-in plastic bins ease the job of cleaning up. A round, deep container keeps water from spilling and doubles as storage for brushes and pencils. A large rectangular container holds paints and other art supplies.

Use stencils or hand-cut masking tape for this starry night motif, or involve your child in coming up with an original color scheme. For easy cleanup later, finish with a coat of polyurethane.

YOU'LL NEED

TIME: About 1 day to construct and paint.
SKILLS: Moderate carpentry skills.
TOOLS: Tape measure, hammer, nail set, compass, framing square, finish saw, miter box, saber saw, masking tape, drill, drill bits, #1 and #2 screwdriver bits, sandpaper, paintbrushes, pliers.

BELOW: *A child will have plenty of scope for creativity with this art table.*

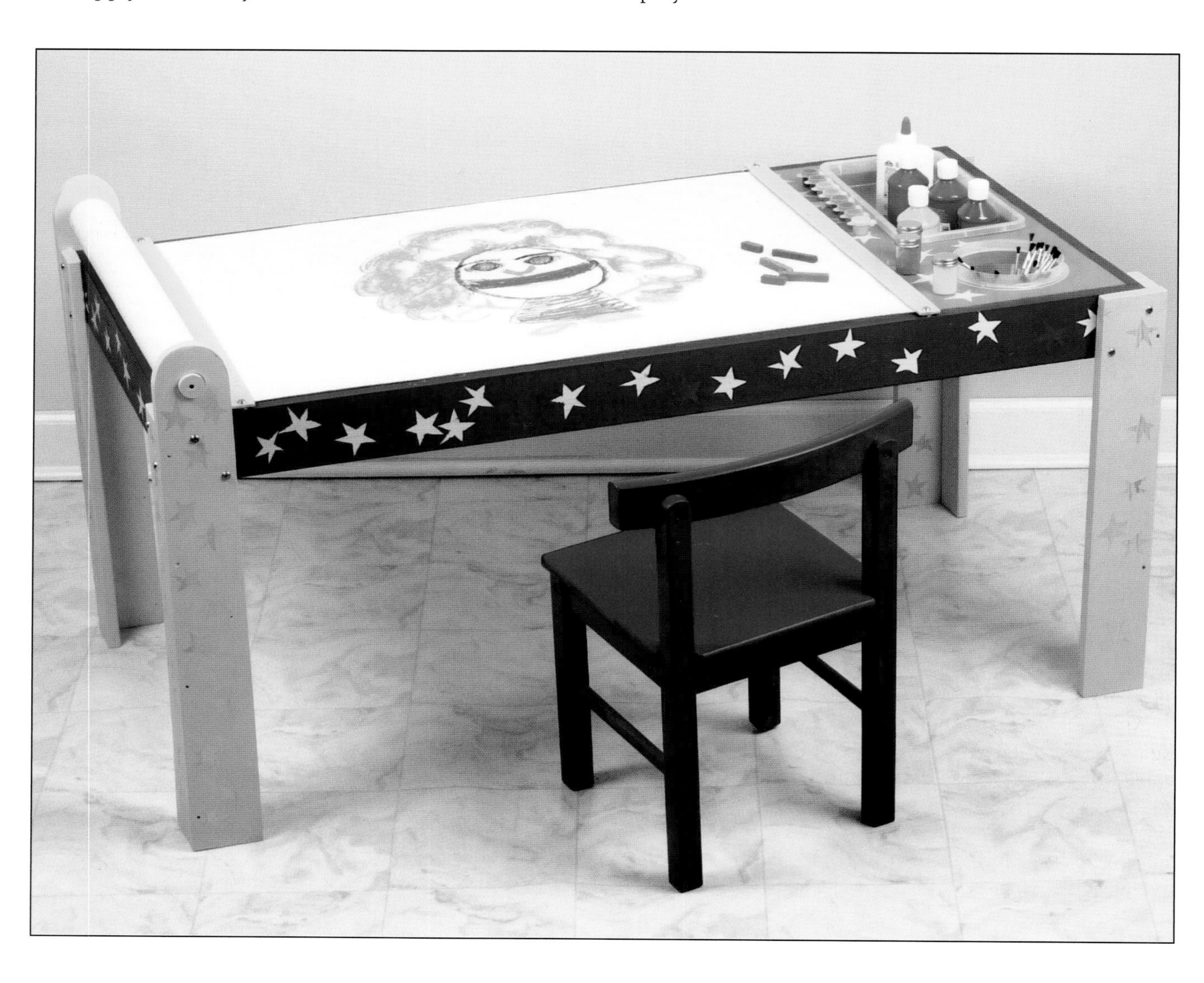

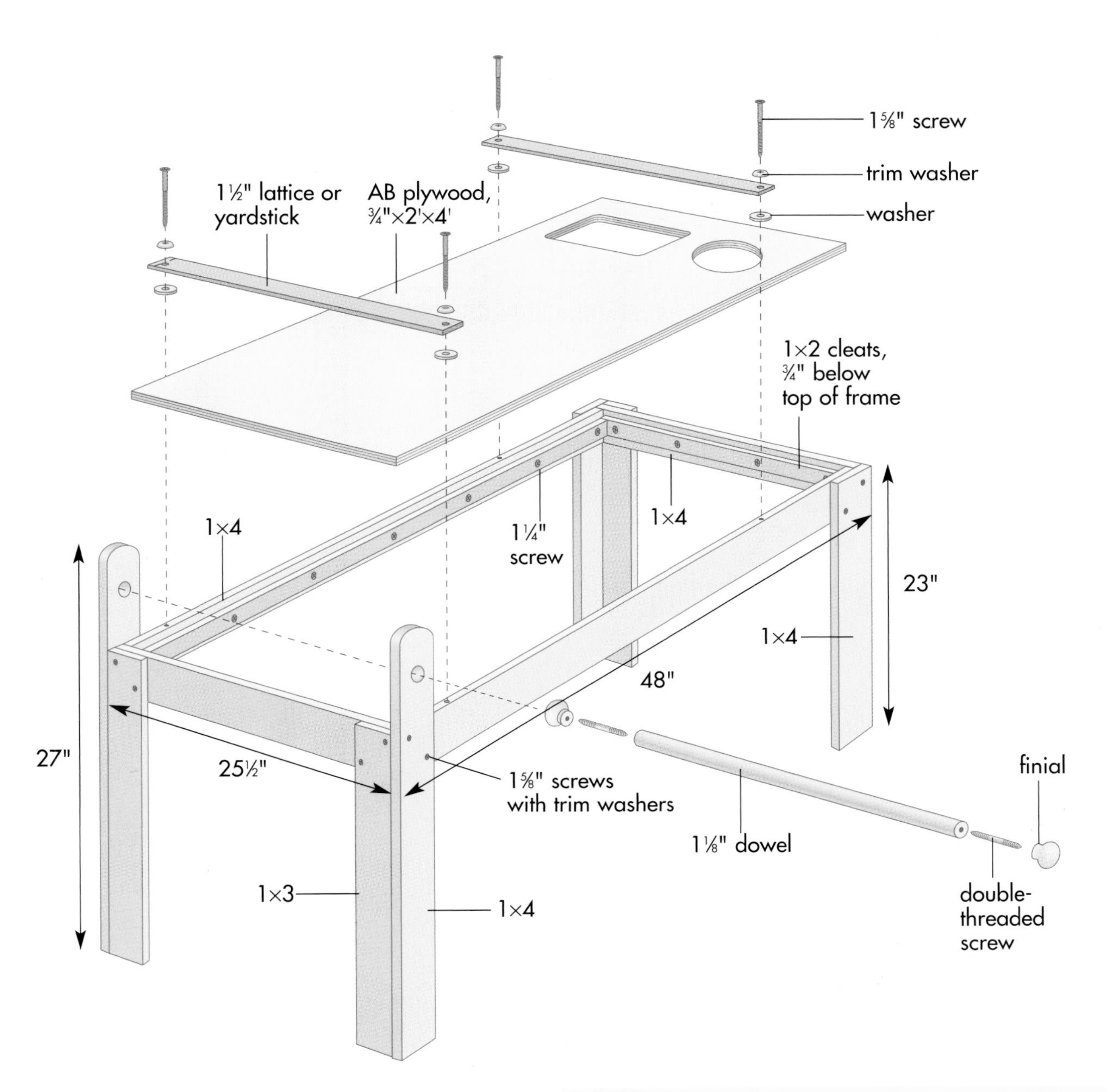

ABOVE: Purchase a 2-foot-by-4-foot sheet of plywood for the top. Pine plywood works fine for projects using paintbrushes or markers, but if the child will press hard with a pencil or pen, pine plywood will dent. Hardwood plywood, such as birch, holds up much better.

Make the dimensions of the legs longer or shorter to suit your child. (See page 41 for how to make adjustable table legs.) If you use rolls of paper thicker than 3 inches in diameter, make the leg/standards taller. The 1×4 side pieces may be slightly longer or shorter, depending on the exact size of the plywood sheet. If a 1⅛-inch dowel will not fit into your paper roll, buy a dowel of a different size.

MATERIALS

- One 2'×4' ¾" AB birch plywood, precut
- Four 8'-long 1×4s
- Two 8'-long 1×3s
- Three 8'-long 1×2s
- One 1⅛" dowel, 2' long
- Two finials
- One 5'-long 1½" lattice
- 1⅝" trimhead screws
- 1¼" #8 all-purpose screws
- 6d finishing nails
- 20 trim washers for #8 screws
- Two ¼" double-threaded screws
- 12 ¼" washers
- Wood glue
- Wood filler
- Two plastic bins
- Paint and finish

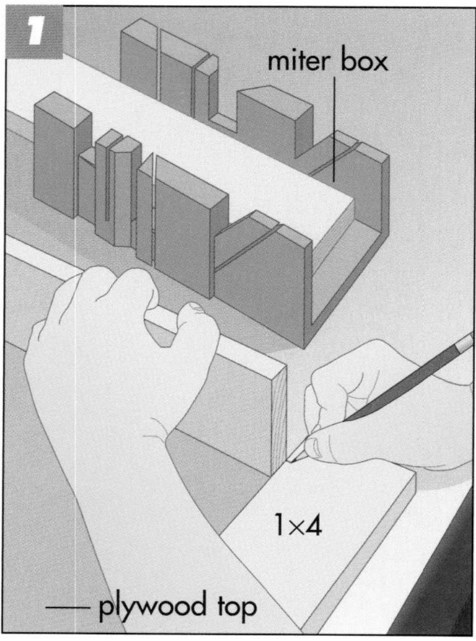

1. Cut the sides.
Plywood that's cut at a home center may be slightly less than 2 feet by 4 feet, and it might be out of square. So hold pieces of 1×4 in place and mark them for cutting. For the long pieces, take into account the thickness of the shorter pieces as shown.

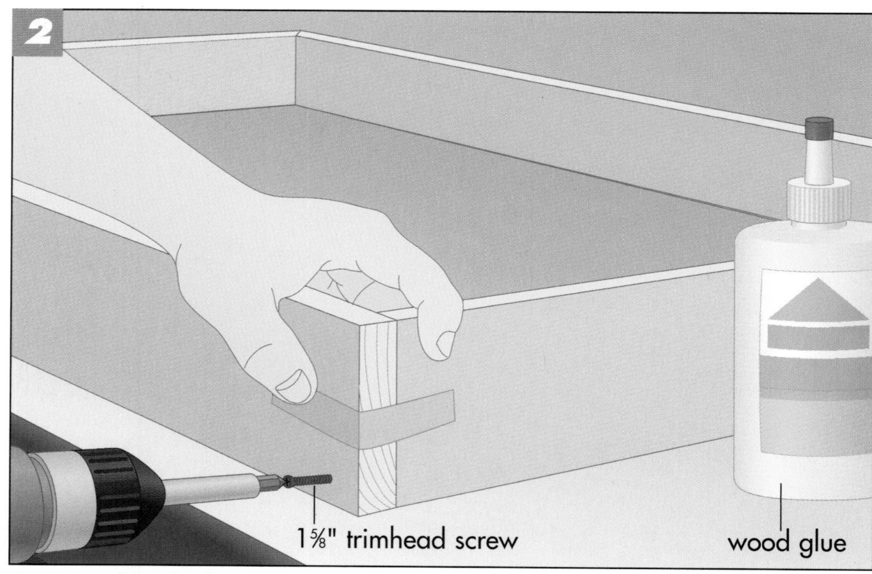

2. Assemble the frame.
On a flat work surface, set the side pieces in place around the plywood. Make sure they all fit precisely; you may need to recut a piece or two. At each corner, hold the two pieces together so their edges line up; a piece of masking tape may help with this. Equip a drill with a #1 phillips screwdriver bit. Drill two 7/64-inch pilot holes, squirt a bead of wood glue on the edge of one piece, and drive a 1 5/8-inch trimhead screw into each hole.

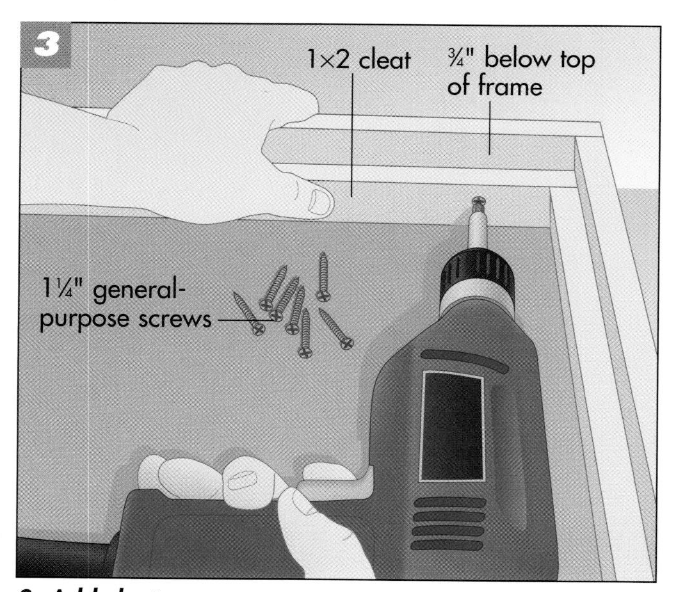

3. Add cleats.
Cut pieces of 1×2 for cleats; the plywood will rest on top of them when you turn the table right-side up. The cleats do not need to fit tightly. Use a piece of tape to mark a 7/64-inch drill bit so that you will not drill all the way through the cleat and the 1×4. Press down on each cleat so the plywood is flush with the top of the 1×4, and drill pilot holes every 8 inches or so. Drive a 1 1/4-inch screw into each hole.

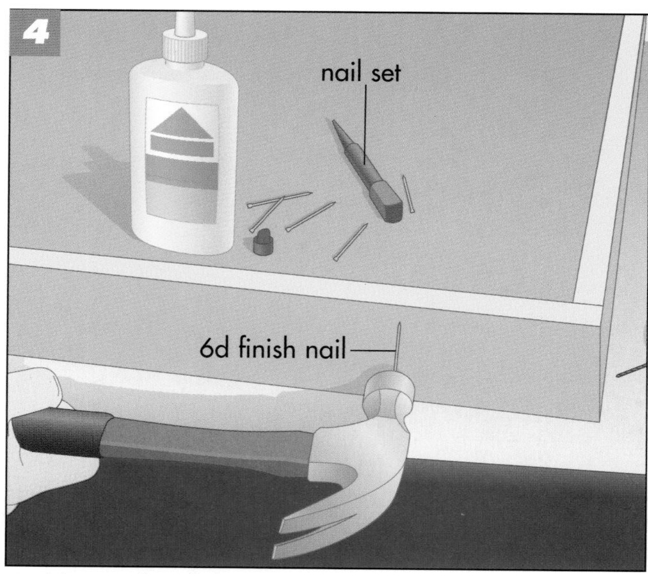

4. Glue and nail the top.
Turn the table right-side up. Check that the plywood is flush with the 1×4s. You may need to remove a screw or two, move the cleat, and drive new screws. Squirt a bead of wood glue all along the top of the cleats, and set the plywood into the frame. Drill 5/64-inch pilot holes through the 1×4 and into the plywood every 8 inches or so, and drive a 6d finishing nail into each hole. Use a nail set to pound the nailhead just beneath the surface.

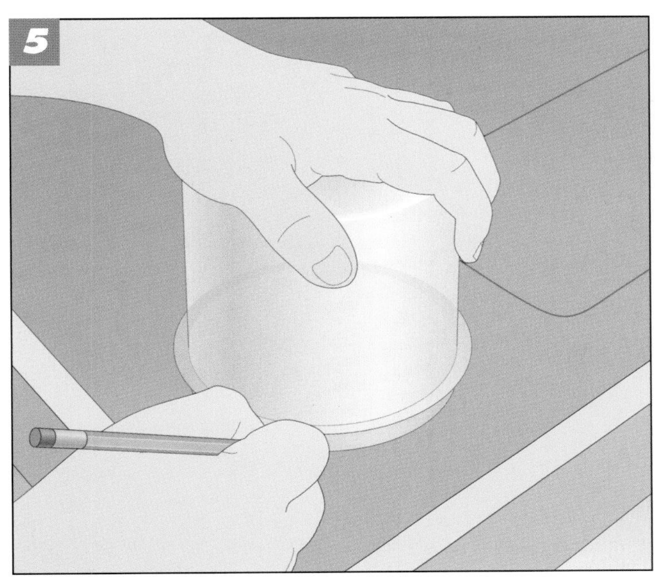

5. Mark for holes in the plywood.
Place your plastic bins upside down on the plywood, positioned where you want them to rest. Mark their outlines lightly with a pencil. Depending on the container, you may need to trace another outline, the actual cut line, inside the first outline. (Make sure the container's lip will rest outside the cut.)

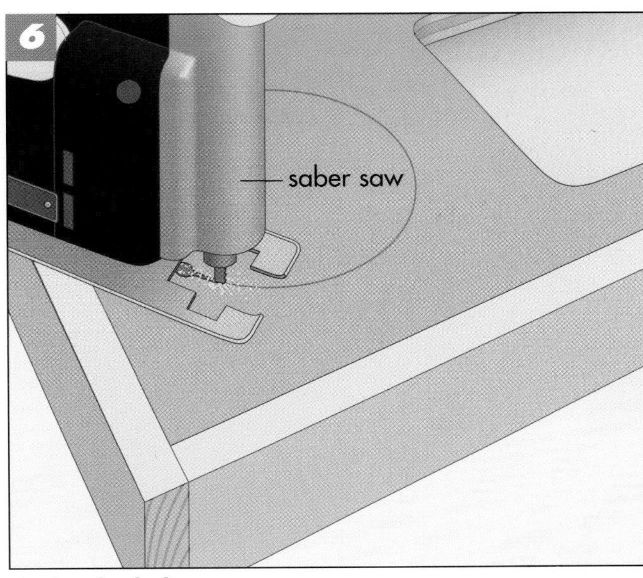

6. Cut the holes.
Erase the outer outline if it is not the cut line. Inside the area to be cut, drill a hole large enough for the saber saw blade to fit into. Cut slowly with the saber saw, continually blowing away sawdust as you go so you can see the cut line.

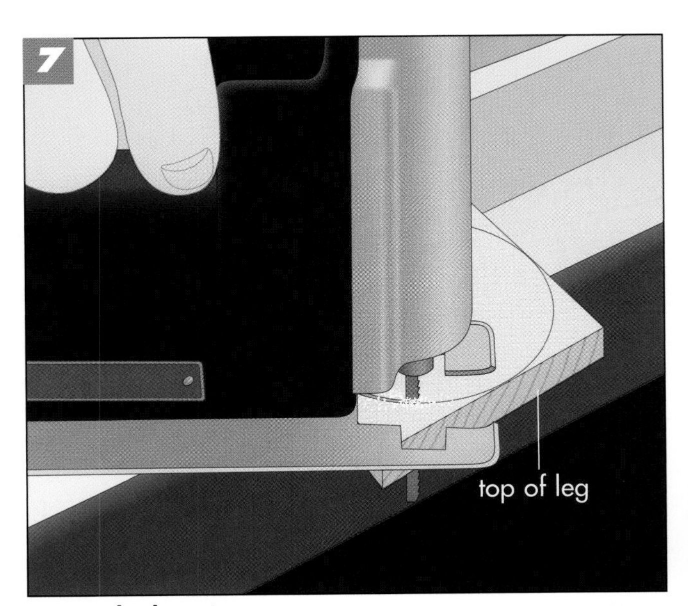

7. Cut the leg pieces.
Cut two 1×4s and four 1×3s to 23 inches, or the table height of your choice. Cut two 1×4s 4 inches longer than the other pieces—or longer, if you will use rolls of paper thicker than 3 inches in diameter. Mark one of the longer 1×4s for a curved cut, using a compass or by tracing around a cat-food can. Cut the curve with a saber saw.

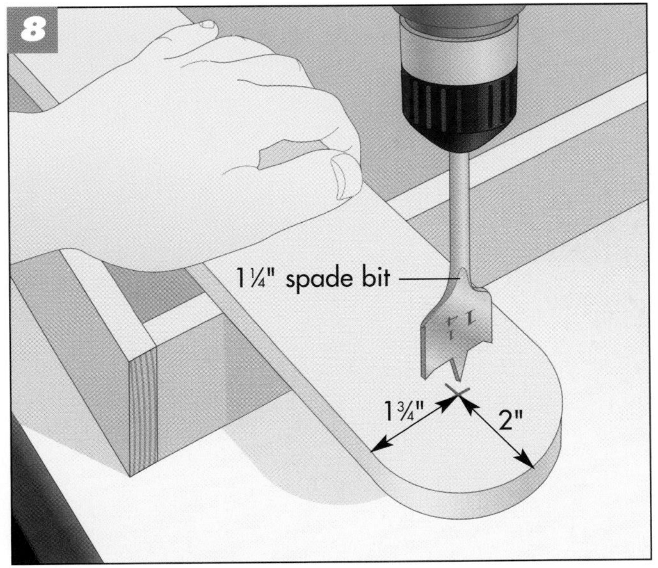

8. Drill a hole for the dowel.
Equip a drill with a 1¼-inch drill bit. (Adjust the size if you will use a larger or smaller dowel—the hole should be just slightly larger than the dowel.) Mark a spot in the center of the curve as shown.

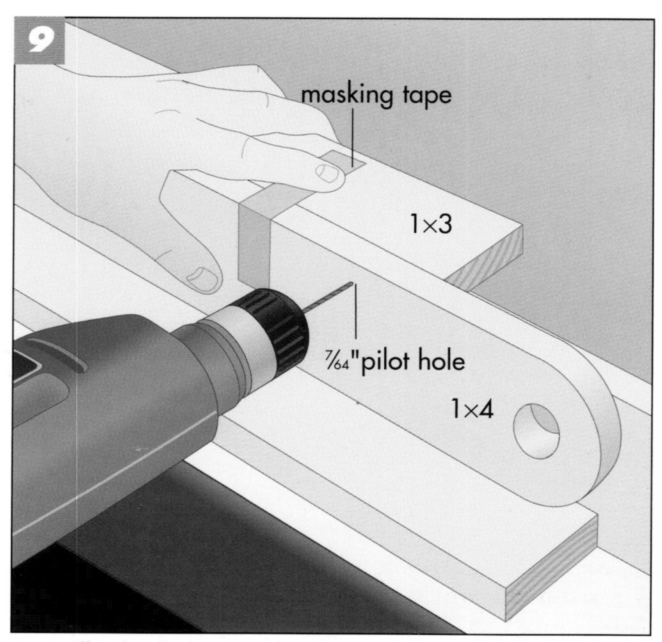

9. Drill pilot holes for the legs.
Turn the table upside down. Place a scrap piece of 1×4 or 1×3 on the work surface right next to it, and position the 1×4 and 1×3 so that their edges are flush with each other. Use pieces of tape to keep the pieces stable while you drive four 7/64-inch pilot holes through the 1×4 and into the 1×3.

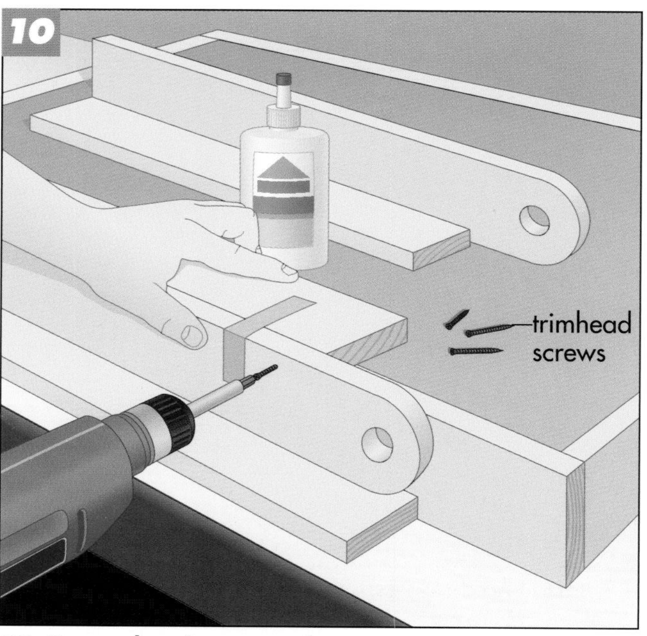

10. Screw the pieces together.
Squirt a bead of glue on the edge of the 1×3. Drive a 1⅝-inch trimhead screw into each pilot hole. Make sure every screw head is sunk slightly below the wood surface.

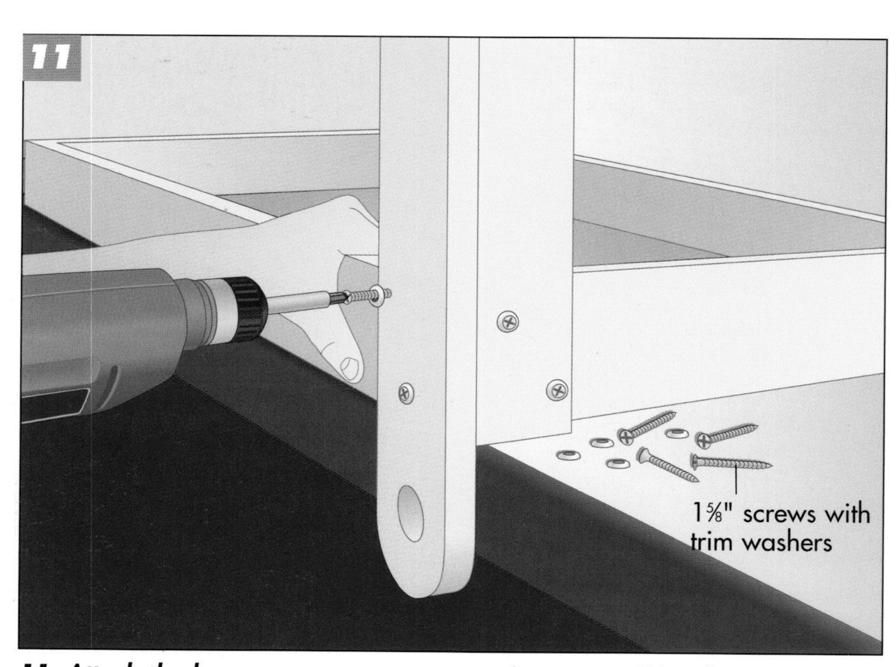

11. Attach the legs.
Keep the table upside down. Position a leg in one corner, and check that it is square to the frame. Drill 7/64-inch pilot holes in a pattern as shown, *above*. Slip trim washers onto 1⅝-inch #8 screws, and drive one into each pilot hole. When attaching a leg with a long piece, let the long piece hang over the work surface.

EXPERTS' INSIGHT

PAINT AND FINISH OPTIONS

You'll need to clean paint, marker, and crayon off this table, so choose a finish that is scrubbable. Oil-based paint forms a hard surface, and it's definitely easier to clean than even the highest-quality latex paint. If you want to see the wood grain, apply oil-based polyurethane, whether or not you stain the wood first. If oil-based products are prohibited in your area, choose the glossiest and most durable water-based products you can find—they should be designed for use on cabinets and other surfaces that must be scrubbed.

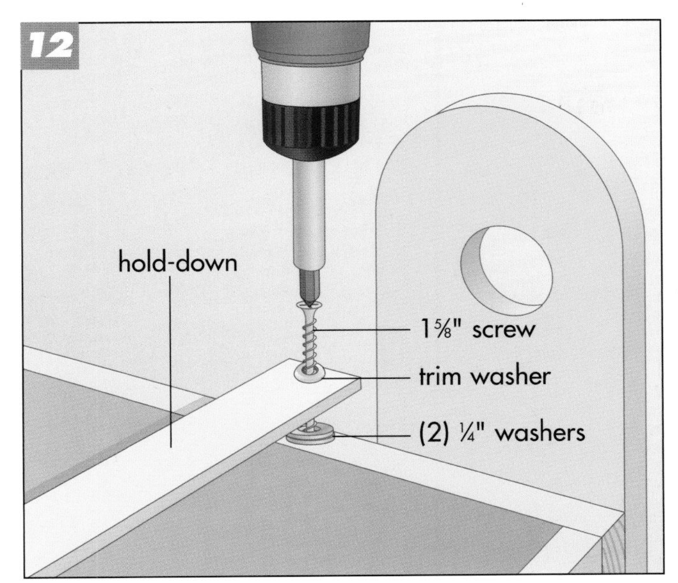

12. Install hold-downs.
Turn the table right-side up. Cut two hold-downs to the width of the table. Drill 3/16 holes ⅜ inch from either end of the pieces. Place one piece by the paper roll and drill 7/64-inch pilot holes into the centers of the 1×4s. At either end, place two ¼-inch washers over the pilot hole, place the hold-down strip on top, and drive a 1⅝-inch screw with a trim washer. Do the same for a hold-down at the other end of the table.

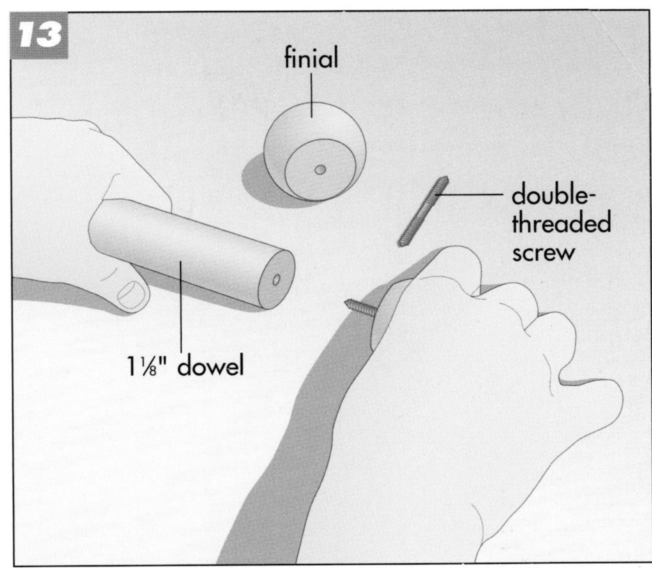

13. Assemble the paper holder.
Cut a dowel so it will extend beyond the brackets by about ¼ inch. Drill a pilot hole into the center of the dowel ends, and into the center of each finial. With a pair of pliers, screw a double-threaded screw halfway into each finial, then twist one on the dowel. Slide the dowel through a hole, through the paper roll, and through the other hole, and attach a finial at the other end. To change a roll of paper, unscrew a finial.

Adding Adjustable Legs

If you need to raise the table because your kids have grown, add "stilts" to the legs. Hold a 1×3 against the inside of the 1×4, and drill ¼-inch holes, spaced 2 inches apart, through both pieces. Clamp a stilt to a leg using ¼-inch bolts and wing nuts.

14. Sand, fill, and paint.
Erase any pencil lines, and fill all holes with wood filler. Sand all the rough edges smooth, and apply the finish of your choice.

FANTASY CANOPY

Gauzy and dreamlike, this canopy bed will make any young girl feel like a princess. The canopy frame is made of standard 1-by lumber painted gloss white. Yards of pink and white netting delicately decorated with strings of beads cover the canopy.

The canopy frame fits over a twin bed with room to spare for blankets and a quilt or duvet. The canopy stands on its own, so no bolting to the steel bed frame is required. If you have a bed of different dimensions, simply measure the width and length of the box springs and add 3½ inches to each of the horizontal members of the canopy frame (see schematic drawing, opposite).

The canopy shown combines coarse netting and fine netting (known as tulle). Both are available at fabric stores.

BELOW: *The tapered design of the canopy complements most furnishing styles and supports the cloudlike layers of netting.*

YOU'LL NEED

TIME: About 1 day to complete the canopy frame; about 4 hours to sew the canopy.
SKILLS: Moderate carpentry and beginner sewing skills.
TOOLS: Circular saw, saber saw, miter box, handsaw, drill, ¼-inch bit, square-head bit for trimhead screws, adjustable wrench, clamps, glue, tape measure, square, shaper, sanding block, sewing machine, rotary cutter or scissors, measuring tape.

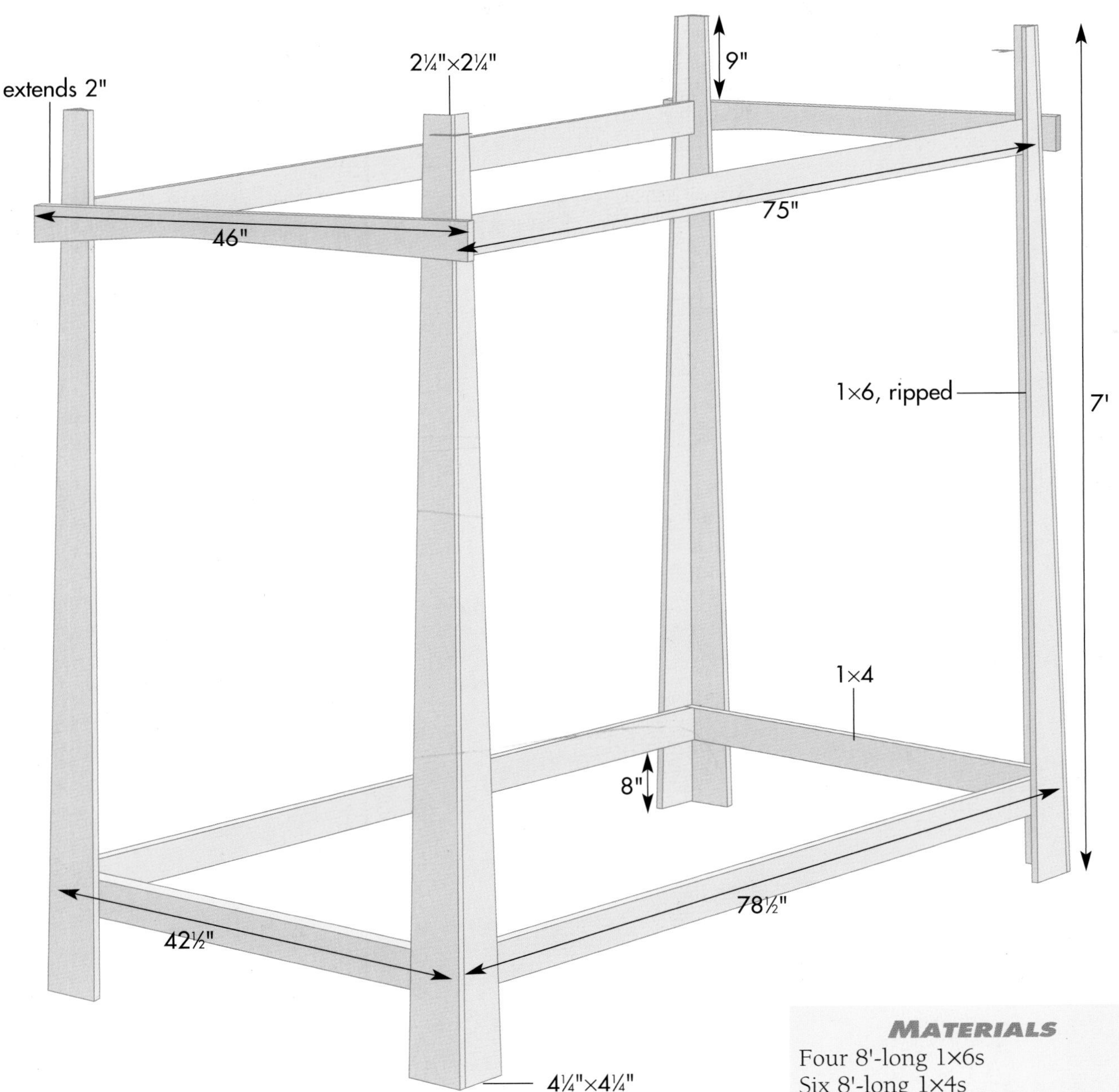

ABOVE: *This simple canopy is made from readily available pine lumber. The posts are made from single 1×6s ripped diagonally and joined edge to edge for strength. The end sections are glued and fastened as permanent units; the horizontal bars attach to each end section with carriage bolts and cap nuts.*

To ease reassembly, mark each upright and the crosspieces that attach to it to ensure that the bolt holes will line up.

Cutting the tapered posts (see Step 4, page 44) is best done with a circular saw. If you are more comfortable using a saber saw, it will do the job, but be prepared to spend more time smoothing the edge (see Step 5, page 45).

MATERIALS

Four 8'-long 1×6s
Six 8'-long 1×4s
Eight ¼"×2" carriage bolts, washers
Eight ¼" nylon cap nuts
50 1¼" trimhead screws
8 to 12 5-yard lengths of netting
Two yards of 3"-wide satin ribbon
Five yards of ½"-wide grosgrain ribbon
20 yards of ⅛"-wide ribbon
(300–500) beads
Primer, semigloss paint

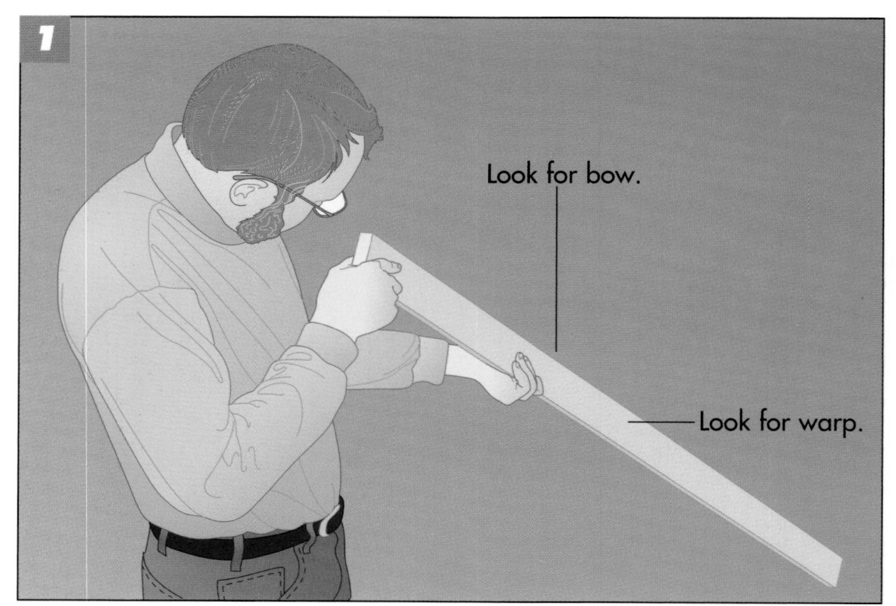

1. Select boards.
At your home center, ask for #2 grade pine lumber, a designation that means the wood will have tight, crack-free knots. Sight down each piece of lumber to check that it is warp- and twist-free. Check the ends for splits. Be picky, watching out for loose knots, gouges, and splinters. Though more expensive, clear pine, birch, and poplar also are readily available and would be ideal for this project.

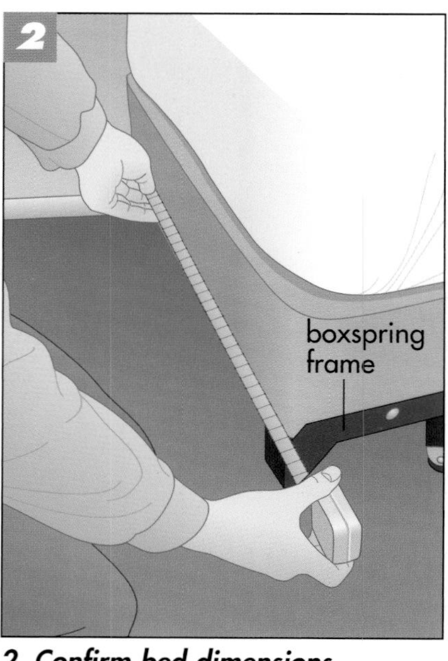

2. Confirm bed dimensions.
Measure the steel frame that holds the box springs. The headboard end of the frame is widest; measure that and add at least 3½ inches to allow for bedding. Measure the length of the box springs and add 3½ inches.

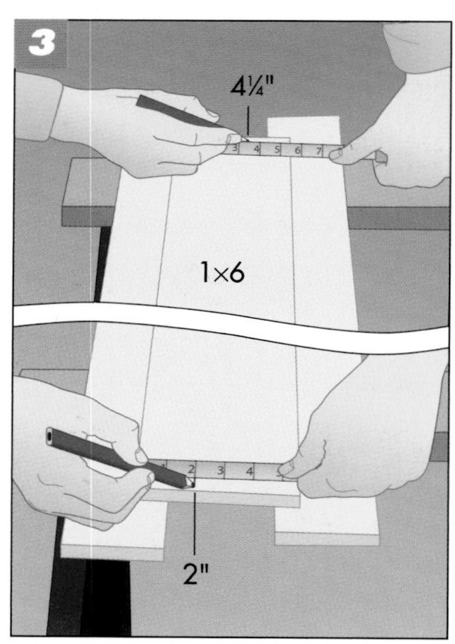

3. Mark the two sides of each post.
With a handsaw or circular saw, trim square one end of an 8-foot 1×6, removing any splits as you do so. Then mark and cut the board to 84 inches (7 feet). Mark the ends as shown.

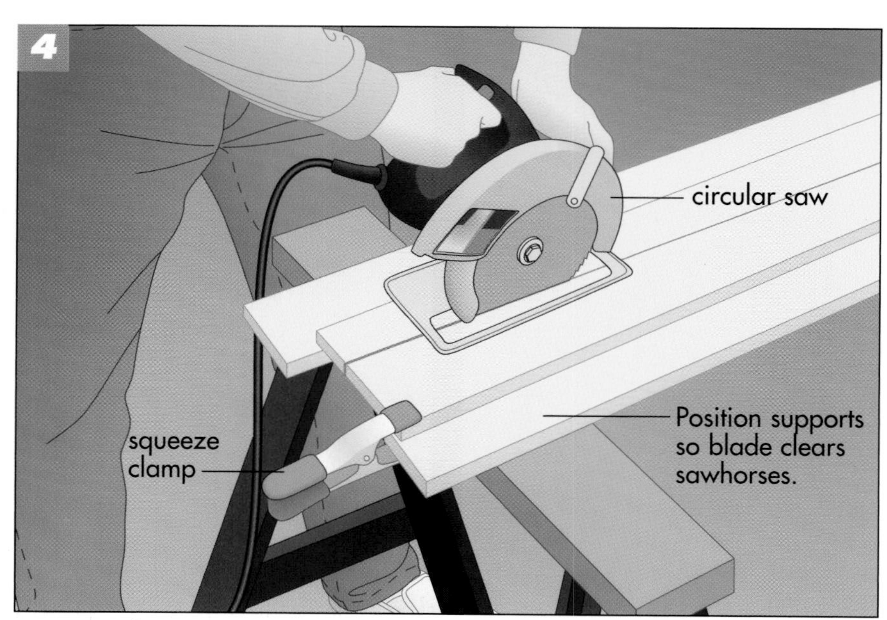

4. Rip each post.
With a straight board, mark a diagonal line from end to end, joining the marks made in Step 3. Separate the support boards by 2 to 3 inches. Position the 1×6 so your saw blade will pass between the 1×4 supports. Clamp the 1×6 in place. This setup will keep your work stable and help prevent your saw blade from binding. Before you plug in the circular saw, check that the blade is ⅛ inch lower than the thickness of the lumber. (See page 105 for how to rip with a circular saw.)

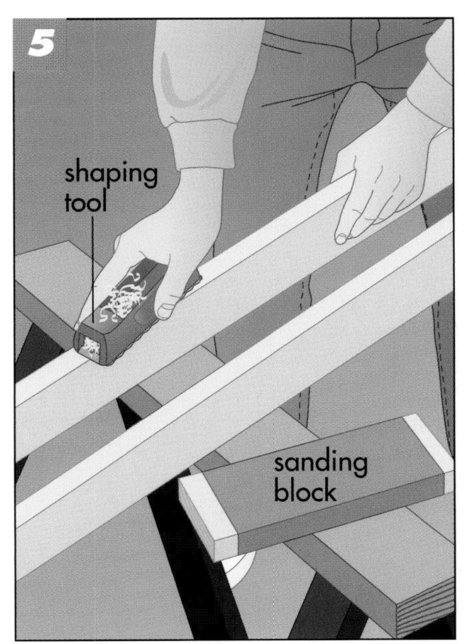

5. Smooth the edges.
With a shaping tool or a plane, smooth the newly cut edge of each post side. Slightly round the edges that won't be glued and fastened together. Sand the edges.

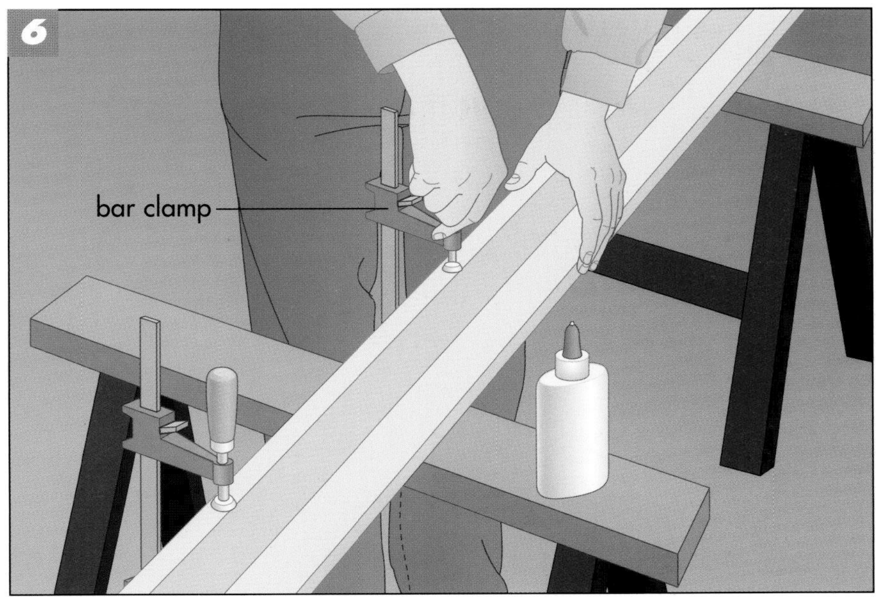

6. Clamp and glue each post.
Note that one piece has been cut wider than the other. Do a dry fit, joining the "factory" edges (the smoothest, fresh-from-the-home-center edge of each) so the wider piece overlaps the other. The resulting post should have sides of about 2¼ inches at the top and about 4¼ inches at the bottom. Apply white glue and clamp the two together. Clamp firmly, but don't tighten the clamp so much that it dents the wood.

EXPERTS' INSIGHT

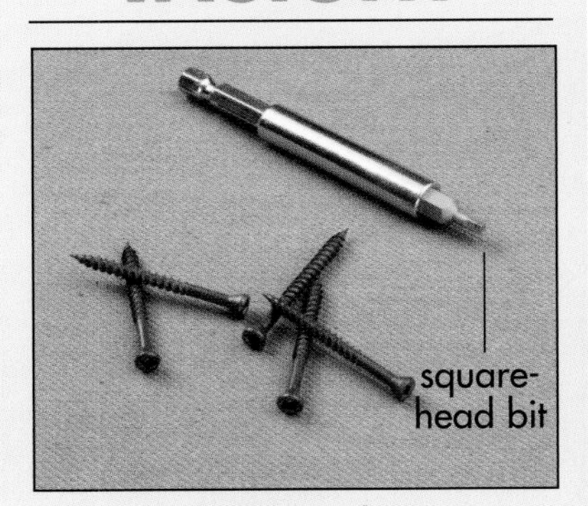

USE TRIMHEAD SCREWS

Trimhead screws, available at most hardware stores and home centers, have the holding power of an all-purpose screw without the unsightly head. Buy a square-head bit to install them. Drill a pilot hole first (use a ³⁄₃₂-inch bit for trimheads) to eliminate splits.

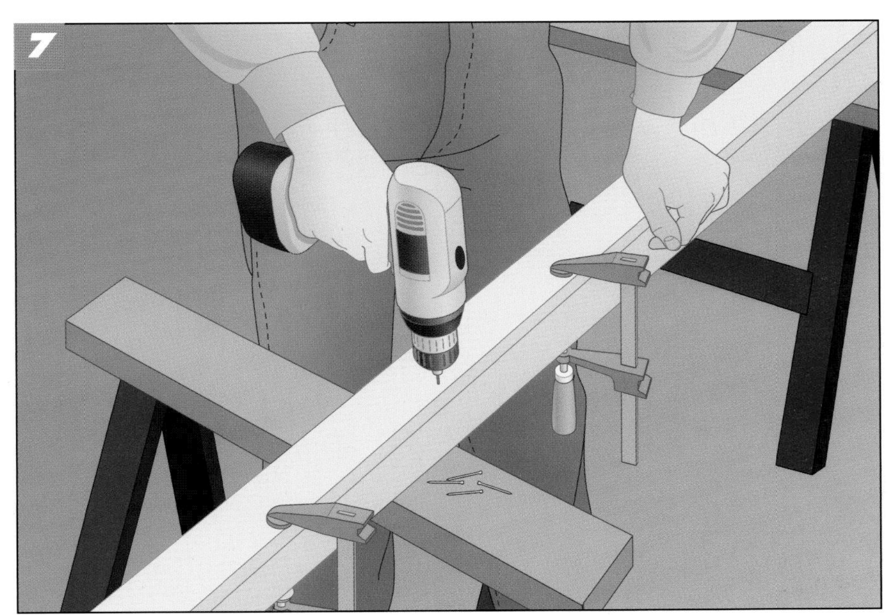

7. Fasten with trimhead screws or finishing nails.
Every 12 inches and ⅜ inch in from the post edge, drill a ³⁄₃₂-inch pilot hole and fasten in place a 1⅝-inch trimhead screw. Allow the screw to pull itself just beneath the wood surface. Or, drill pilot holes with a ¹⁄₁₆-inch bit and fasten with 4d finishing nails. Punch the head of the nail slightly beneath the surface with a nail set.

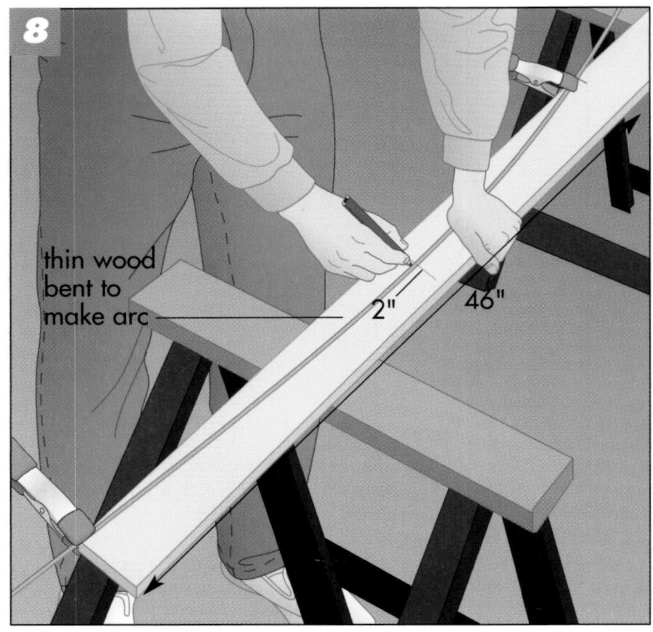

8. Mark and cut each arched crosspiece.
Trim square a 1×4 and mark it at 46 inches. Using a thin piece of wood (thin trim or a piece of lattice works well), bend an arc so that at its apex, the crosspiece will be 2 inches wide. Mark along the arc and cut with a saber saw. It's difficult to cut a smooth arc; you may want to practice on a couple of pieces of scrap lumber first. Smooth and sand the piece.

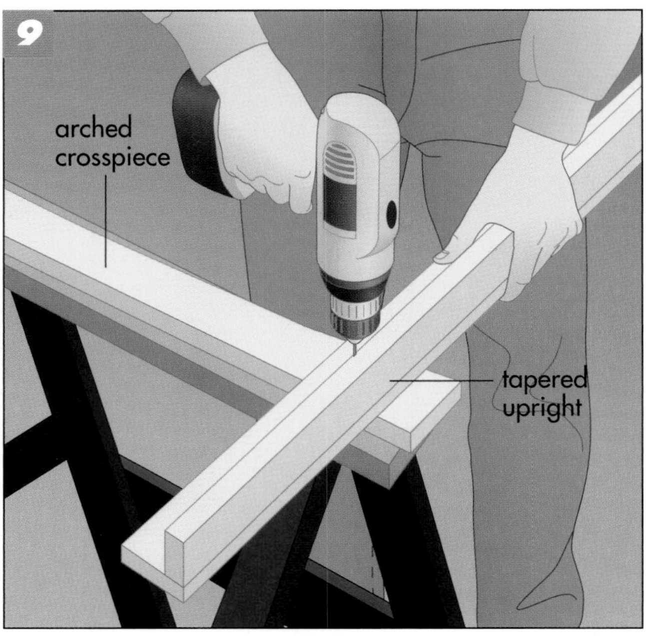

9. Assemble each end section.
Following the dimensions shown on page 43, glue and then fasten the pieces together using 1¼-inch trimhead screws, two at each joint. Fasten from the inside out so that the fasteners will not show.

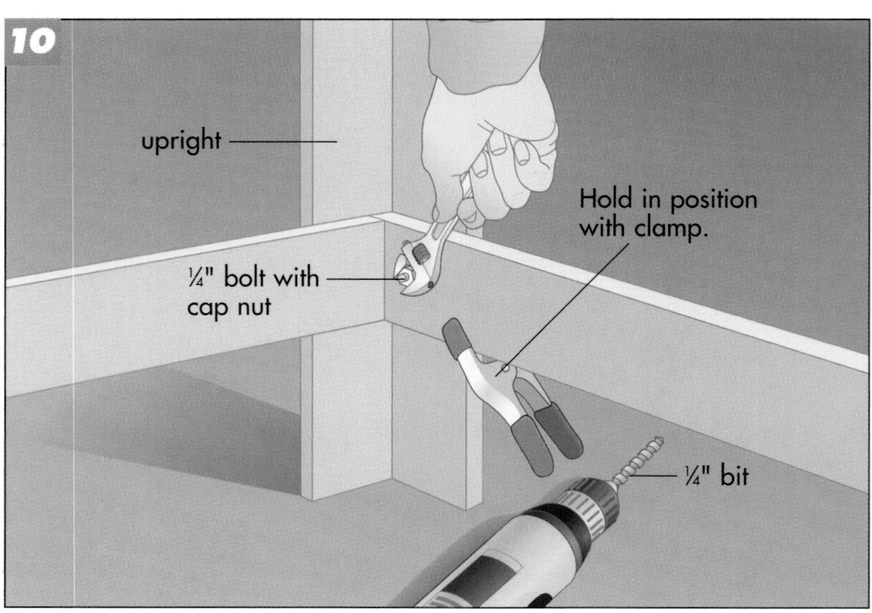

10. Assemble the complete frame.
Cut horizontal pieces of 1×4 to length (see dimensions on page 43). Have two assistants hold the end sections upright and clamp one lower horizontal piece in place. Drill a hole using a ¼-inch bit, and fasten the piece in place with a 2-inch carriage bolt and a cap nut. Disassemble the frame. Lightly sand and paint or stain it.

ADD BEADS

To coordinate the new canopy bed with the rest of the room, tie strings of beads onto a Japanese paper lantern, glue beads to a lampshade, or sew strands of beads onto curtains.

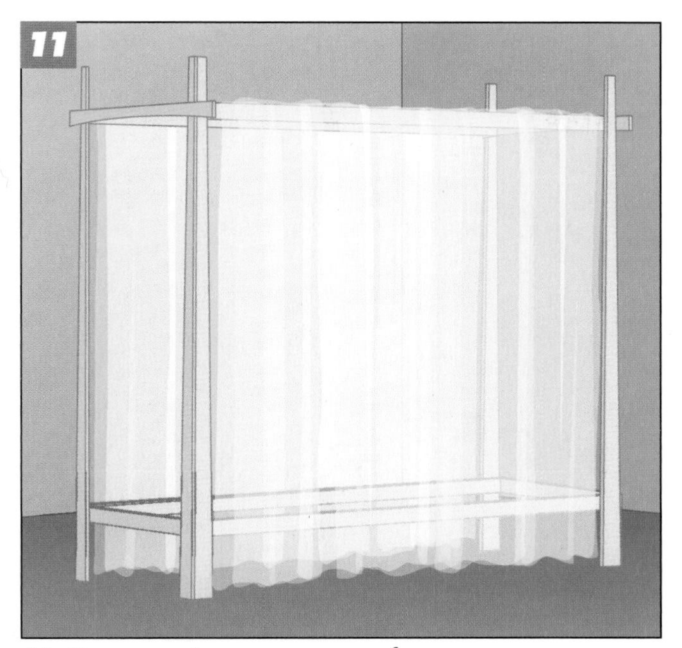

11. Drape netting over canopy frame.
Arrange all the lengths of tulle and netting over the frame. Use coarser netting for the bottommost layer. Layer colored lengths between layers of white until you have a pleasing combination. Pin layers together along the top of the frame. Trim any excess fabric so the netting will be just off the floor.

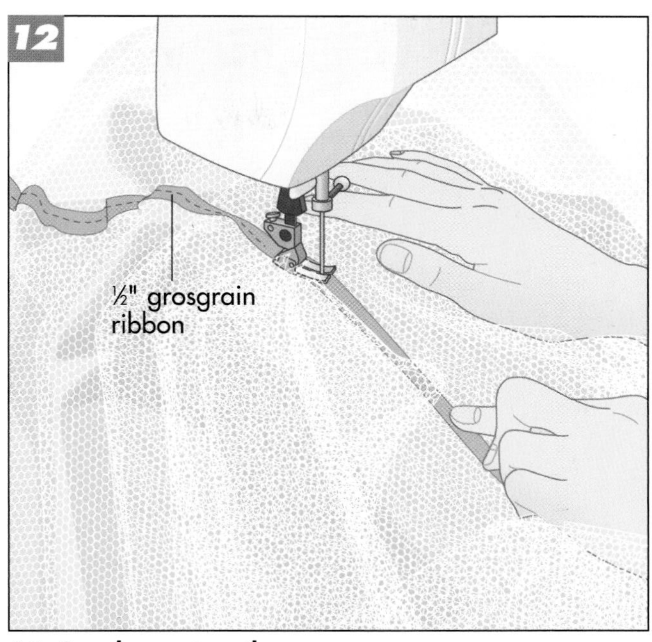

12. Sew layers together.
Pin ½-inch grosgrain ribbon onto the layers of tulle, working down both sides of the frame. Remove the canopy from the frame. Join the layers together, sewing a seam down the center of the ribbon.

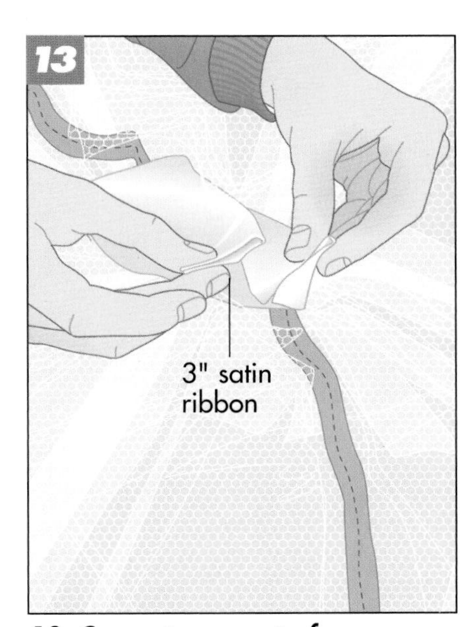

13. Connect canopy to frame.
Make loops using four 12-inch lengths of 3-inch satin ribbon. Fold under the raw edges of the grosgrain ribbon. Sew loops to the underside of each corner. Slip the loops over the posts of the canopy bed to hold the netting in place.

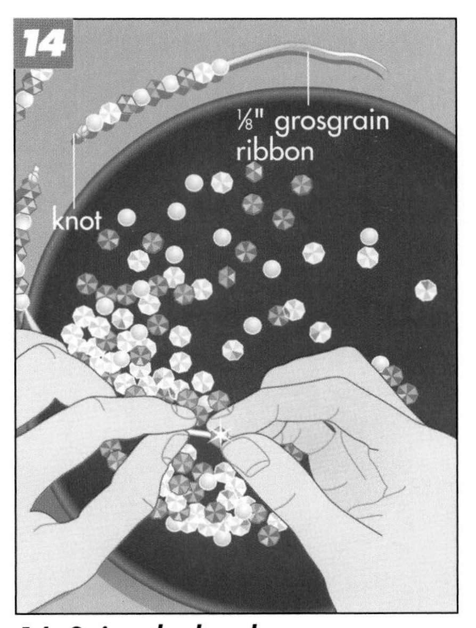

14. String the beads.
Cut 12-inch lengths of ⅛-inch grosgrain ribbon. Tie a knot at the end to secure. String on at least 10 beads. Secure with a knot, leaving at least a 5-inch tail. Make at least 30 strands for a subtle shimmer, 100 for a fantasy of beads.

15. Thread end of ribbon through the netting.
Double-knot the ribbon, and trim off any excess. Place beads on both sides and the ceiling of the canopy. Space them randomly throughout the net canopy.

HANDY HEADBOARD

Books, stuffed animals, a radio, and framed pictures can be close at hand with this attractive headboard. This pedimented project is not only a focal point for a kid's bedroom, it also conserves wall space by combining the features of a bookshelf and a bedside table. Made of prefinished shelving material readily available at home centers and lumberyards, the project involves simple saw cuts and assembles easily.

The shelving material used in this project comes in pieces 8 feet long and 11¾ inches wide. Top, bottom, and front edges are coated with a hard white coating—only the rear edge shows the raw particleboard core. One drawback of this material is that it cannot be painted. However, the doors, hardboard backing—even the pediment—offer an opportunity to add an accent color. (See page 50 for paintable material options.)

The doors adorned with kid-friendly pulls use concealed hinges that keep the appearance clean and allow for adjustment if the final opening is slightly out of kilter.

RIGHT: *This handy and attractive headboard storage unit offers plenty of shelf space for books and toys. The self-supporting headboard is about 12 inches deep.*

YOU'LL NEED

TIME: About 2 days.
SKILLS: Moderate carpentry skills.
TOOLS: Tape measure, framing square, clamps, fine-toothed saw, miter box, circular saw, speed square, hammer, nail set, variable-speed drill, drill bits, boring bit, phillips screwdriver.

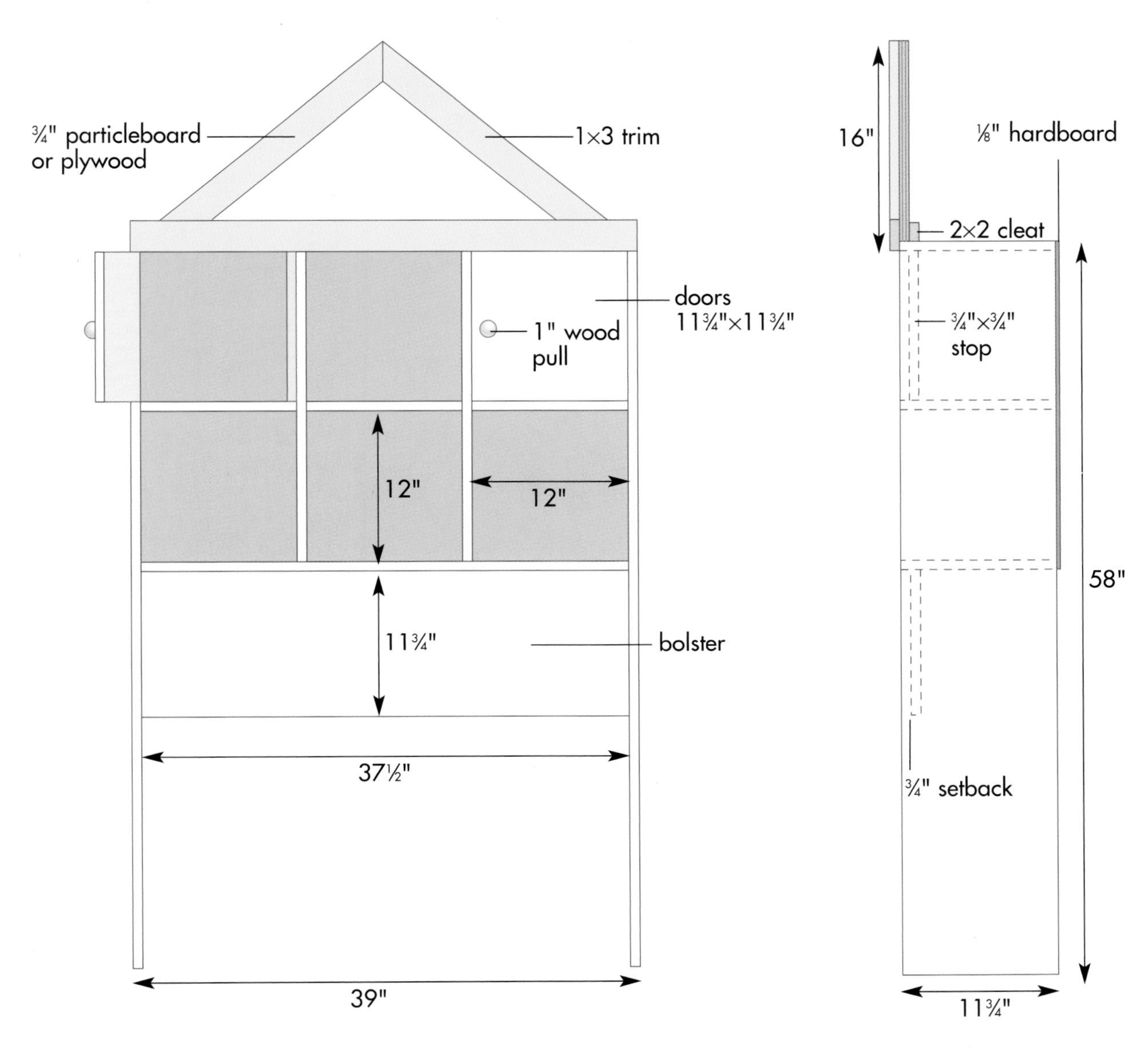

MATERIALS

Four 8'-long 1×12 shelving
One 8'-long 1×3
One 4'×4'×¾" particleboard
One 4'×4'×⅛" hardboard
One 4' 2×2
50 2" trimhead screws
Ten 2½" all-purpose screws
3d finishing nails
4d common nails
Four concealed hinges
Two 1" wood pulls

Although sheet goods or 1×12 lumber (see page 50) can be used to make this headboard, for ease of cutting and hauling, the project is designed around prefinished, precut shelf standards. These standards have a hard white coating, don't need priming and painting, and are easy to clean; however, they are available only in white. (Medium-density fiberboard standards are a paintable option—see page 50.) Most of the joints in this project are fastened with 2-inch trimhead screws; they hold well and are barely visible even if the holes are left unfilled. (Let the screw pull itself into the wood about 1⁄16 inch, as if you were "setting" a finishing nail.) You can heal rough or slightly gapping joints with a thin bead of white bathtub caulk.

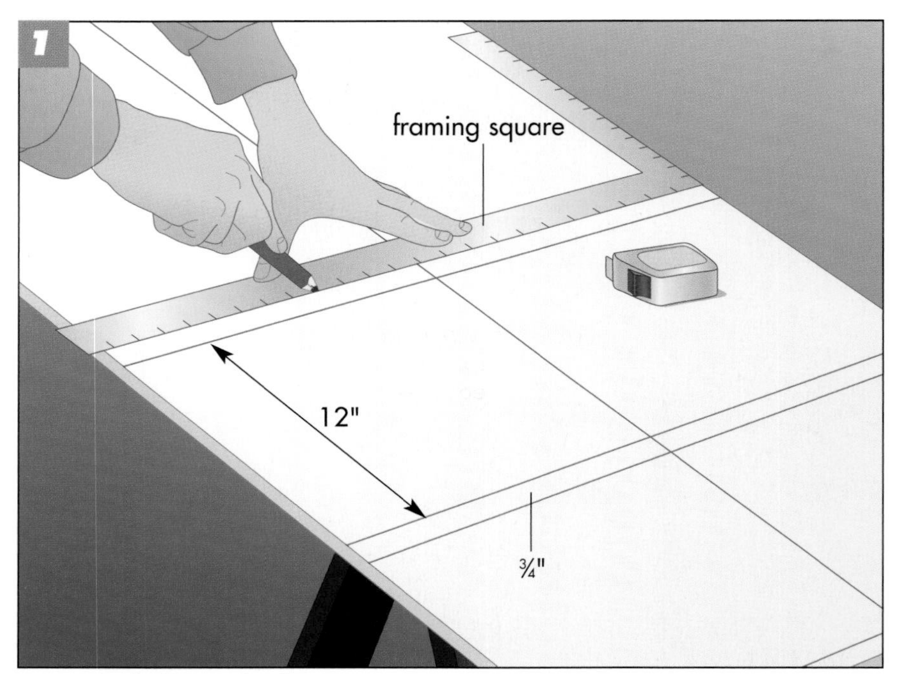

1. Mark shelf standards.
Set two 8-foot lengths of shelving side by side on sawhorses, making sure the ends line up with each other. Using a framing square (above) or a drywaller's T square (see page 64), measure and mark the location of each shelf, marking the line across both standards at once. Allow ¾ inch for each shelf, 12 inches between shelves. Mark both sides of each piece.

ALTERNATIVE MATERIALS

Medium-density fiberboard (MDF) shelving can be painted; has smooth, void-free edges; and cuts easily. Plywood and particleboard sheet goods are less expensive, but are difficult to cut into strips. Some grades have voids in the edges that must be filled. Standard #2-grade (tight knot) 1×12 lumber is prone to warps and will have some gouges and splits but is usable if you select carefully.

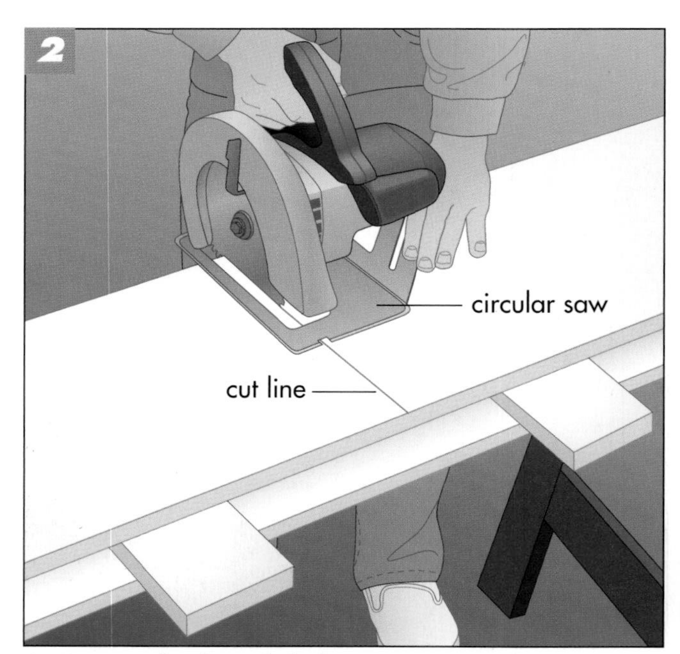

2. Cut standards and shelves.
To keep your saw from binding, lay a piece of shelving on the sawhorses and place on it four scraps of wood, two on each side of the cut line. Using a circular saw with a thin-kerfed, carbide-tipped blade, cut the shelves and standards.

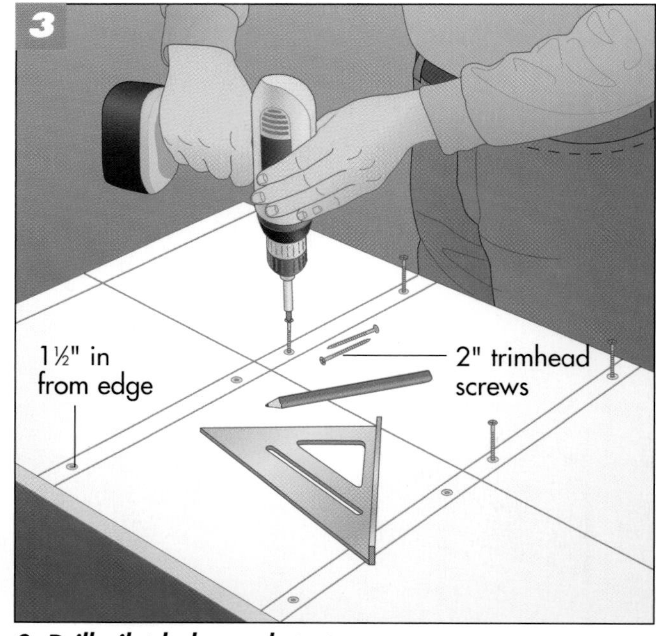

3. Drill pilot holes and start screws.
With a ³⁄₃₂-inch bit, drill pilot holes, locating them as shown. Start 2-inch trimhead screws (see page 45), and screw them in until they just pierce the other side of the board.

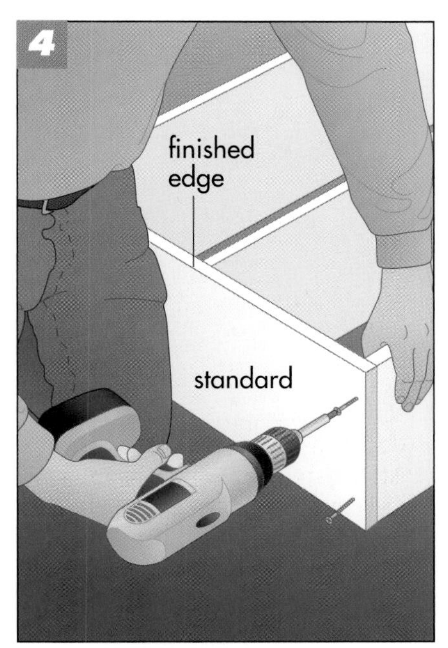

4. Assemble the shelves.
On a clean floor, lay one standard on edge. Have a helper hold each shelf in place, finished edge up. Drive the started screws into the shelves. Repeat the process with the second standard.

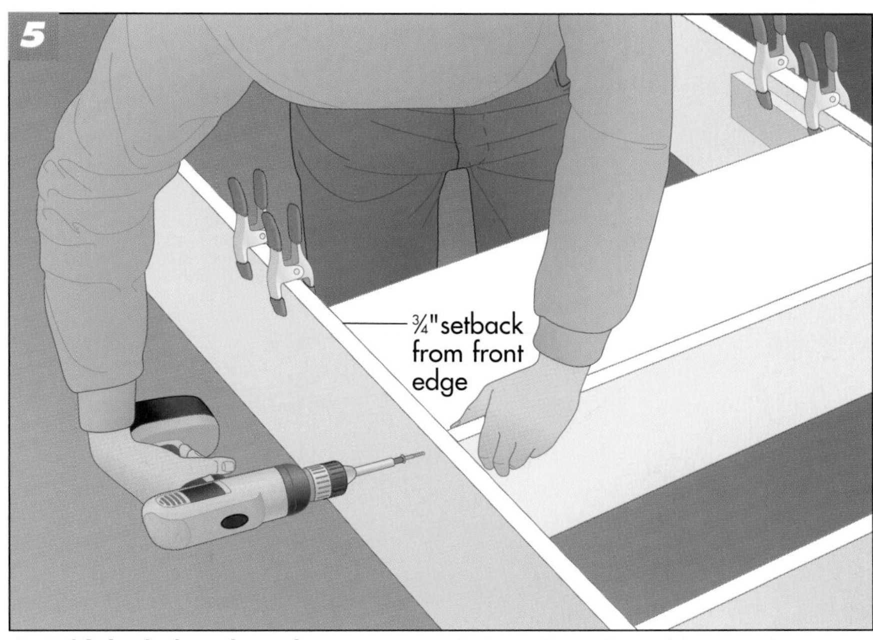

5. Add the bolster board.
The bolster board sets back ¾ inch from the front edge of the headboard. Use a scrap of shelving to mark the setback. Position the bolster board. Hold it in place with a 1-by clamped to each standard. Drill pilot holes and fasten the bolster with three 2-inch trimhead screws on each side.

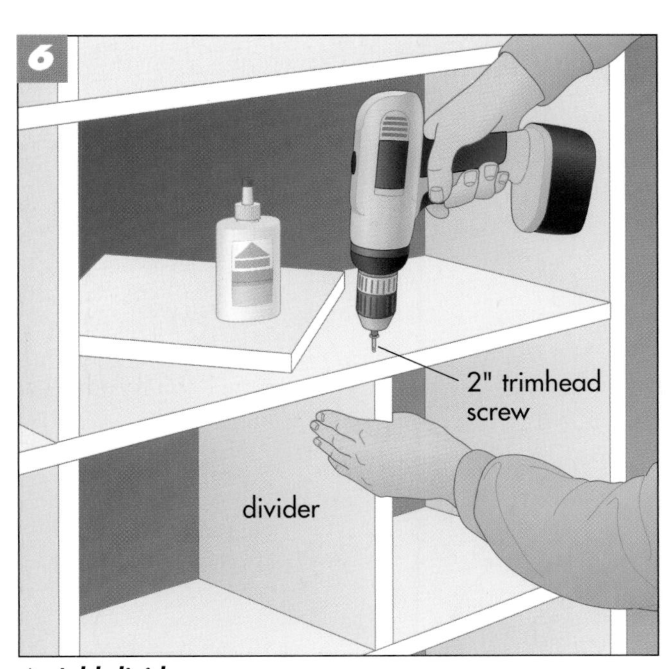

6. Add dividers.
Measure between shelves and cut to size each pair of dividers. Beginning with the bottommost pair, drill pilot holes and fasten with trimhead screws. Fasten the bottom pair from above and below; fasten the others only from above. Glue the bottom edge of those dividers.

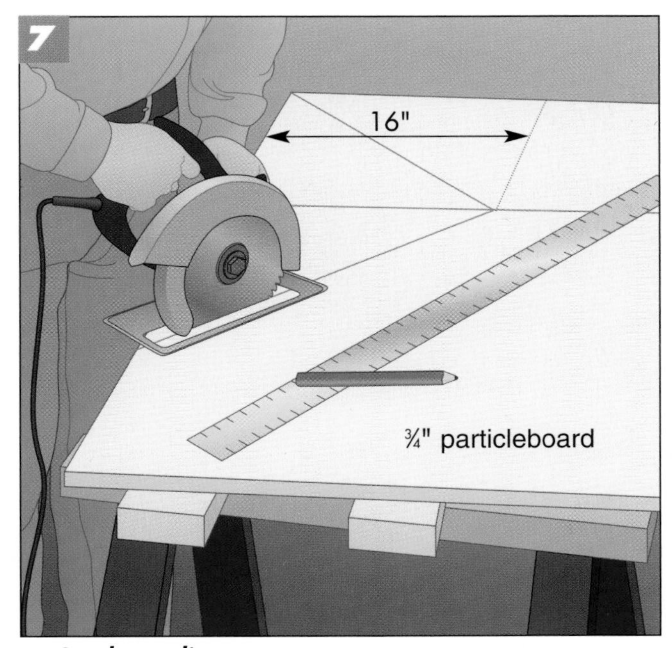

7. Cut the pediment.
Lay out the pediment as shown above, making the base 39 inches wide. Halfway along the base (18½ inches), mark a perpendicular line. Mark for the apex of the pediment at 16 inches, and strike lines from that point to each outside corner of the base. Cut out the pediment with a circular saw.

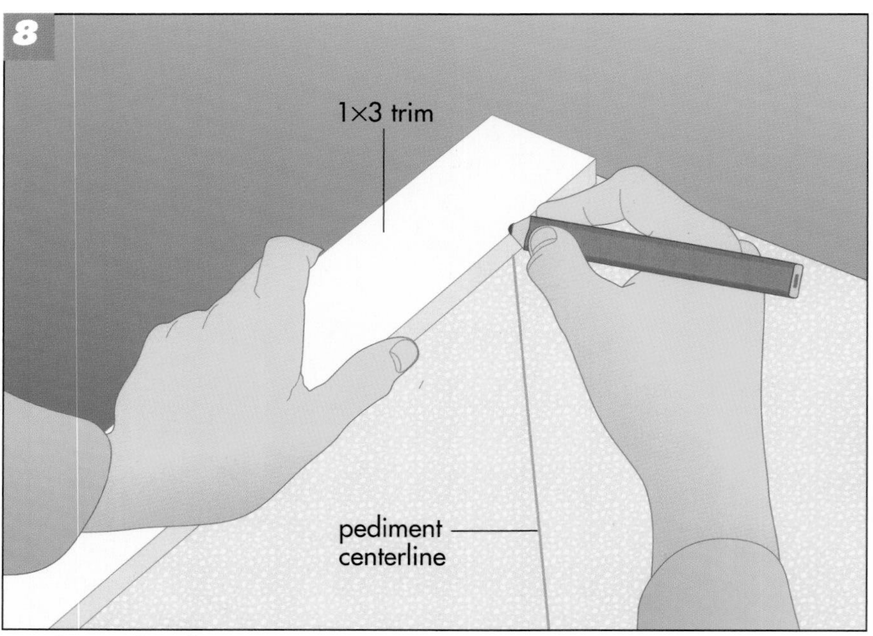

8. Glue and nail trim.
Cut a piece of 1×3 the width of the base of the pediment. Mark it to overhang the bottom edge of the pediment by ¾ inch. Glue and nail it in place, using 3d finishing nails. Rough-cut pieces of 1×3 for the diagonal pieces of pediment trim. Hold each in place and mark it for an angle cut. With a fine-toothed handsaw or circular saw, cut the joint at the apex of the pediment first, then mark and cut the others.

EXPERTS' INSIGHT

CURING GAPITUS

If the joint has a small gap, try this trick. Clamp both pieces firmly. With a fine-toothed handsaw, cut down into the gap. You'll remove a bit of wood from each side. Loosen the clamps and push the boards together. If some gap remains, repeat the process.

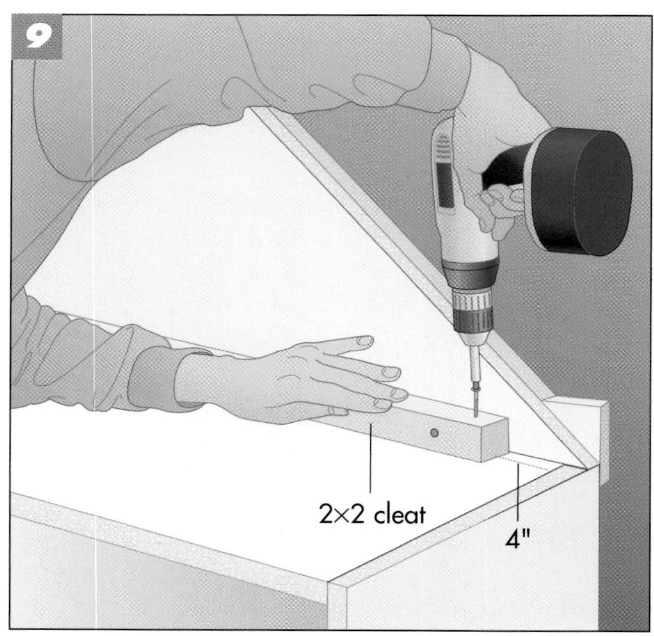

9. Attach cleat for pediment.
Attach a 31-inch 2×2 cleat to the back of the pediment, centered so it cannot be seen from the sides. Drill pilot holes and fasten it with 2-inch trimhead screws. Set the pediment in place atop the headboard and fasten it with 2-inch trimhead screws. Prime and paint the pediment and ¾×¾-inch stop.

10. Attach pediment from the front and add stops.
Fasten the pediment from the front of the headboard using four trimhead screws, one at each standard and one at each divider. Hold the ¾×¾-inch stop along the upper dividers, mark, and cut them to size. Use four 4d finishing nails to fasten each in place, ¾ inch from the outside edge of the divider.

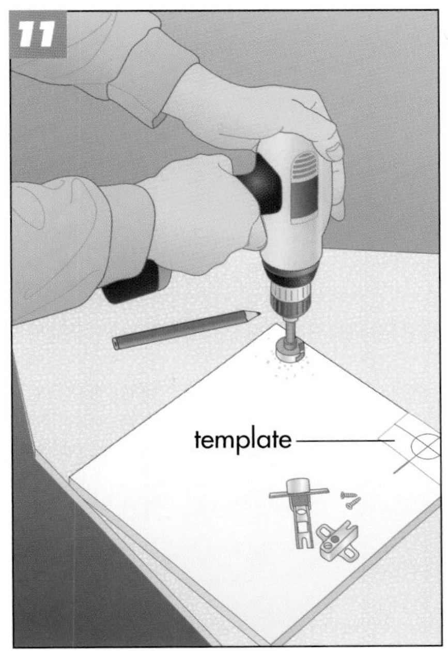

11. Bore holes for hinges.
Cut 11¾×11¾-inch doors from ¾-inch particleboard. Using the template provided with the hinges, bore holes for each hinge and for the screws holding the hinge.

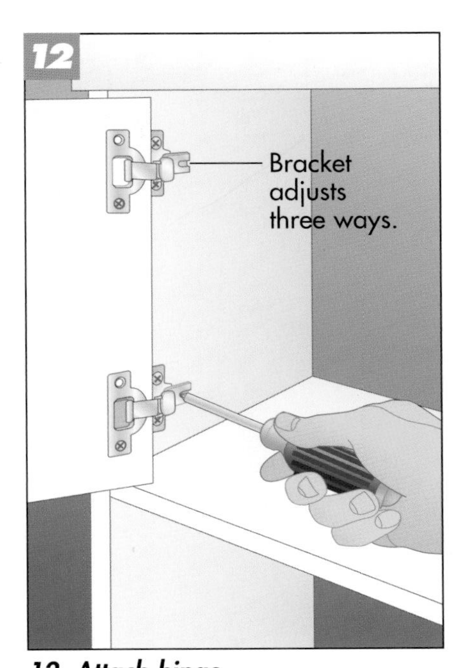

12. Attach hinge.
Use the template to install the other half of each hinge, then slide the door hinges in and tighten their mounting screws. Adjust until the door closes smoothly.

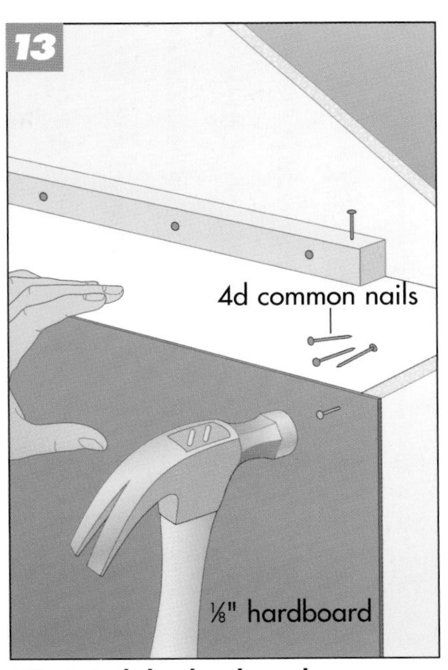

13. Attach backer board.
Cut a piece of ⅛-inch hardboard ¼ inch narrower than the headboard unit and long enough to overlap the bottommost shelf. Check the headboard for square, and nail it.

Transform the Headboard into a Dollhouse

When made without doors, this headboard becomes a spacious six-room dollhouse, complete with its own gabled roof. The headboard offers plenty of room for an expanding collection of furniture and miniature figures.

- Use wallcovering samples, gift wrap, or fabric as wallpaper. (Cut the material to size and check the fit. Then apply strips of double-sided tape to the back walls, and fasten the wallcovering in place.) Or, paint the backer board different colors for each room.
- Fabric scraps, thermal fleece, or felt works well as carpeting for floors. Or, try paint effects.
- Even if most of the headboard is dedicated to the dollhouse, one or two bays can be used to hold a night light or for jewelry storage.

STORAGE BY THE CORD

This woodsy storage unit is a perfect home for soft toys—especially those from the forest. Made of durable cardboard tubes (known as Sonotubes) that are used as forms for pouring concrete piers, this project can expand or contract to fit into any room. Simply stack the logs, which are slices of tube covered with fabric, as high and wide as you need. Stiffening solution lets you mold the cloth in barklike ridges. Paint mimics the color of bark and moss. The logs are lined with poster board and bolted together.

YOU'LL NEED

TIME: About 1 day, including drying time.
SKILLS: Moderate carpentry skills.
TOOLS: Handsaw, clamp, drill, adjustable wrench, measuring tape, scissors, pail, sewing machine, hot-glue gun.

MATERIALS

⅔ yard cotton muslin per log
½ yard dark green thermal fleece
Scraps of light and medium green thermal fleece
One 16-oz. container of stiffening solution per 4 logs
Waxed paper and clothespins
Poster board
6"-, 8"-, and 12" Sonotubes
Two to four 1"×¼" machine bolts and nuts per log
Brown, black, and green paint
Assorted insects and reptiles

BELOW: *These fabric-covered logs call out for finishing touches, such as thermal fleece vines and plastic insects and reptiles.*

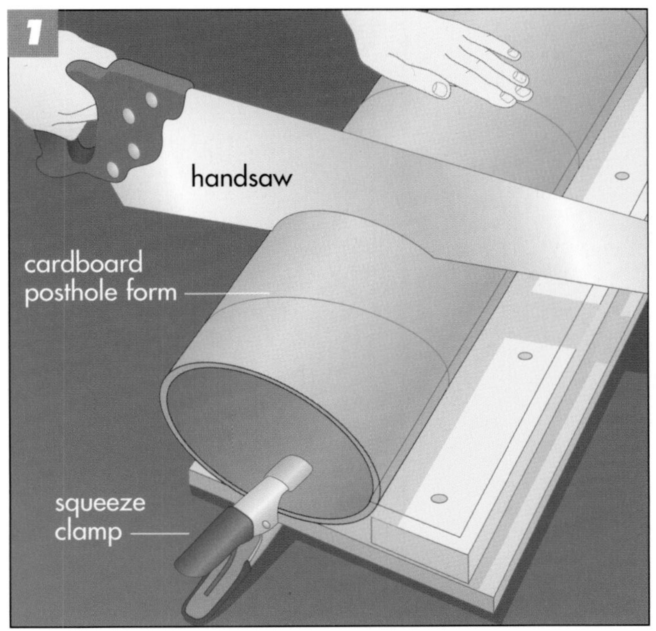

1. Cut cardboard tubes.
Buy 6-inch, 8-inch, and 12-inch pieces of Sonotube (tubes used to form concrete in postholes). Make a cutting jig by fastening a 2×4 to a 3- to 4-foot piece of board or plywood. Using a handsaw, cut tubes to 14- and 16-inch lengths. Stack sections to determine the size of woodpile that suits your storage needs.

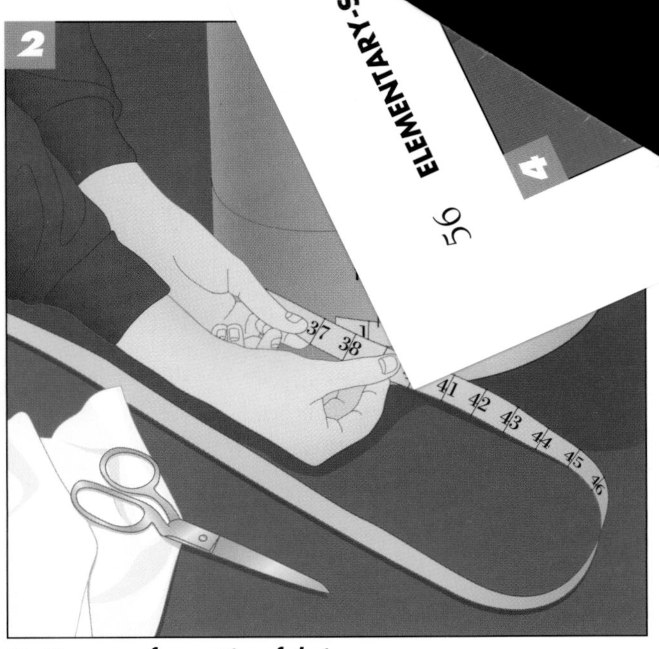

2. Measure for cutting fabric.
Measure the circumference of each tube and add at least 12 inches to that measurement for the width. Add 5 inches to the length. Cut fabric rectangles to size, and store each in its corresponding tube.

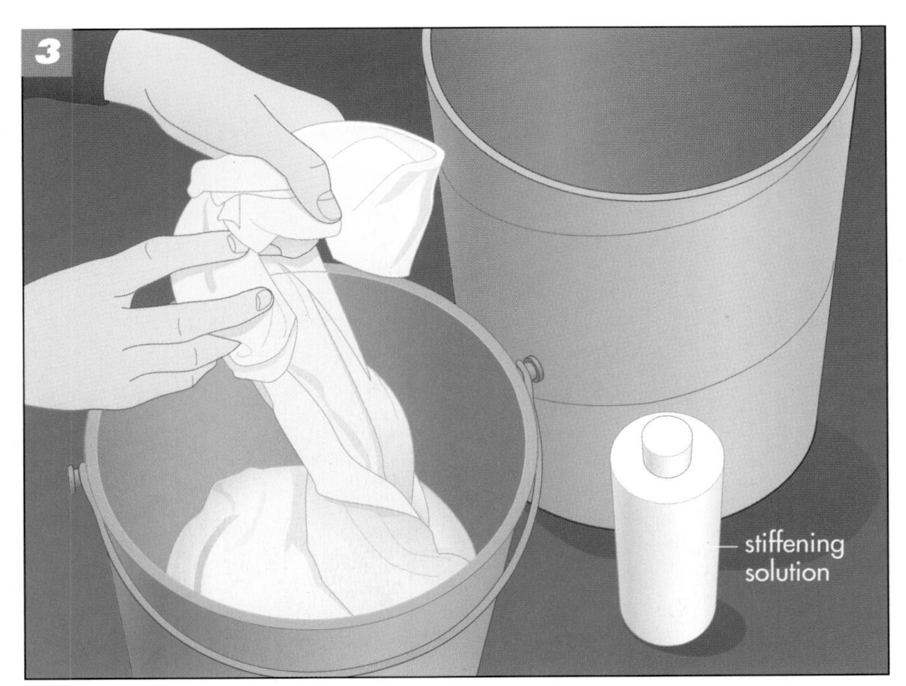

3. Mix up stiffening solution.
Determine what proportion of stiffening solution and water works best for your fabric (see box, *right*). Mix a thick paste: 1 part water to 2 parts stiffening solution works well. Soak the fabric for one tube in the mixture until it is completely dampened.

Stiff Solution

Test your stiffening solution on a small piece of fabric. Start with 1 part water to 2 parts solution. A greater proportion of solution will create a faster drying time, while a higher proportion of water will allow for greater flexibility.

It may take teamwork to crumple the fabric before it stiffens. Although this is a fun project to do with children, the stiffening agent is a glue product, so it is important to cover your work space with drop cloths and to have helpers wear clothing that can get messy.

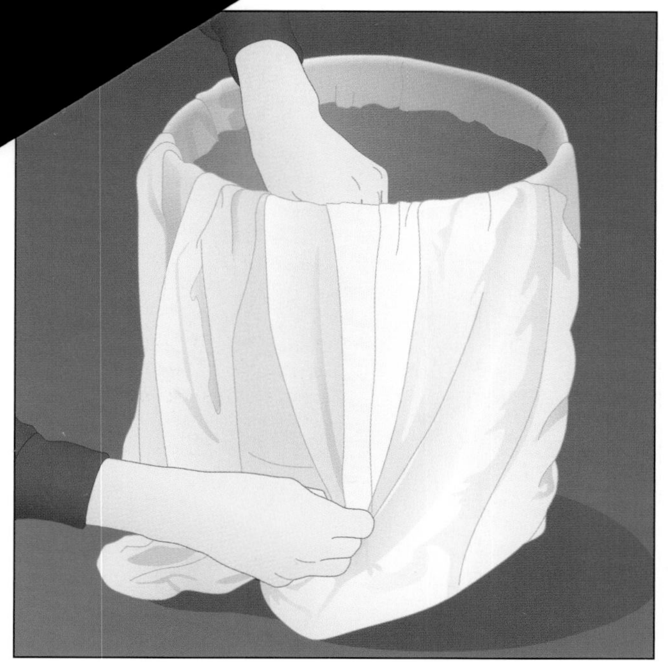

4. Crinkle the fabric.

Wrap the saturated fabric around the tube, overlapping the raw edges of the fabric 2 inches. Fold and crinkle it to resemble tree bark. Fold the excess fabric into the open ends of the tube.

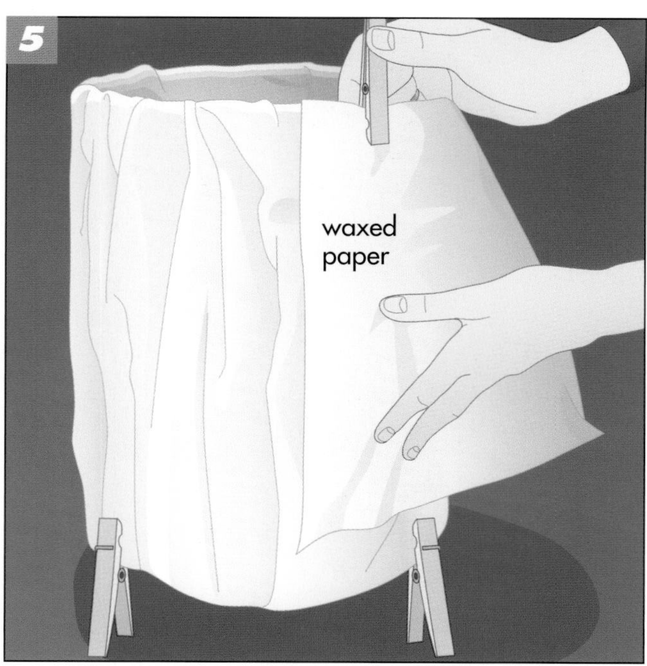

5. Wrap with waxed paper.

Stand the tube on end, using clothespins to raise it above the floor. Pin waxed paper around the fabric in order to hold the fabric to the tube. Let it dry completely (8 to 24 hours). Repeat for each tube.

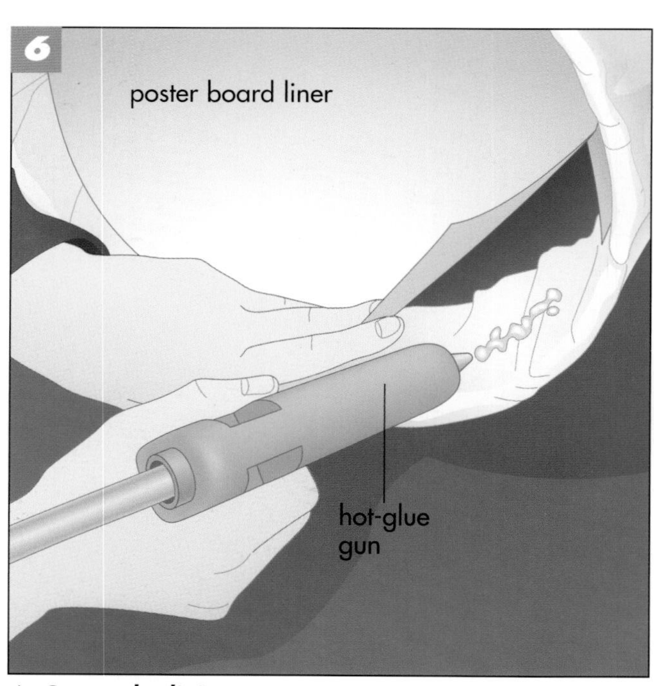

6. Create the lining.

Measure the inside dimensions of each tube. Add an inch overlap to the circumference. Cut the sheets of poster board in those dimensions to make lining to overlap the raw edge of the stiffened fabric. Attach the poster board to the fabric with a hot-glue gun.

7. Paint the logs.

Paint the logs (inside and out) with a base coat or two of brown paint. Using very little paint so the brush is nearly dry, stroke brown, black, and green over the fabric to create a barklike pattern and spots of moss.

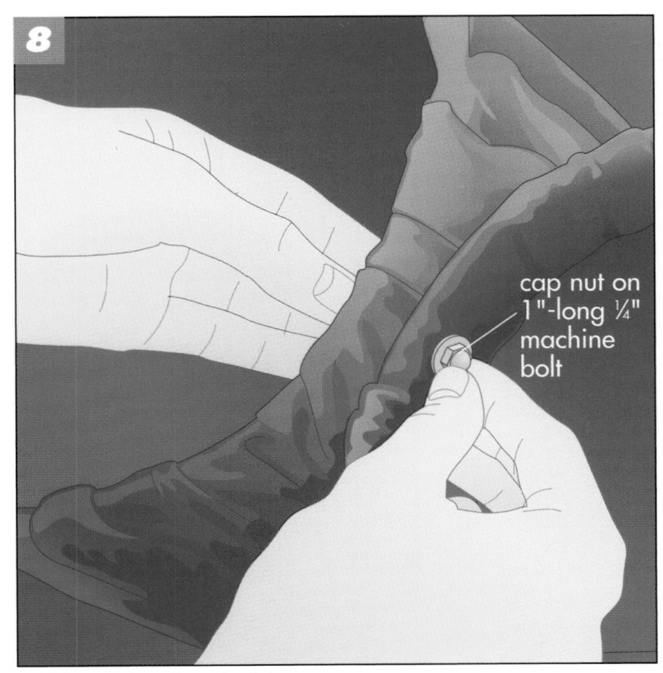

8. Construct the shelving.
Starting with the bottom layer, attach tubes together using 1/8-inch machine bolts, washers, and cap nuts. Drill a 5/16-inch hole for each bolt. Add bolts near the front and back end of each tube where it touches another log.

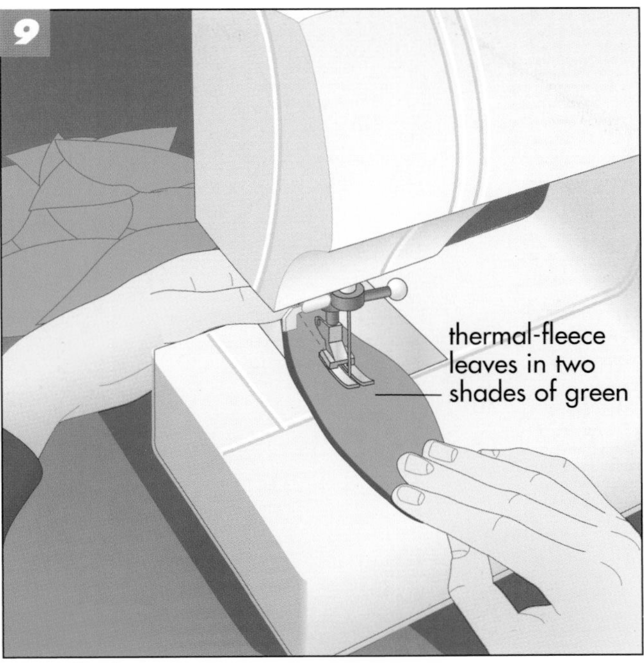

9. Make leaves.
Cut simple leaf shapes out of various green shades of thermal-fleece fabric. Cut two pieces of the same shape for each leaf in contrasting shades. Pin pairs together and sew down the center of each leaf to secure. Make about 35 leaves.

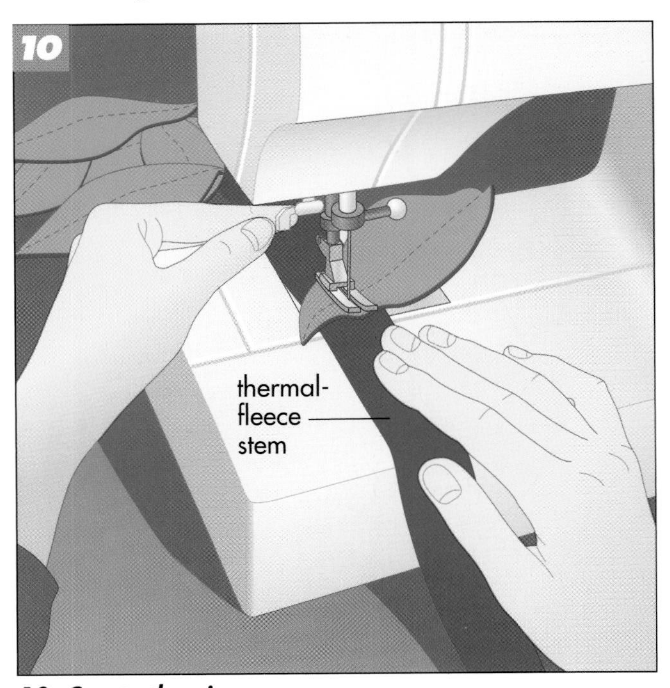

10. Create the vine.
Cut 4-inch-wide strips of dark green thermal fleece across the width of the fabric. Join the ends to make a long strip. Fold the strip in half lengthwise and join with a 3/8-inch seam. Sew leaves to the strip at irregular intervals.

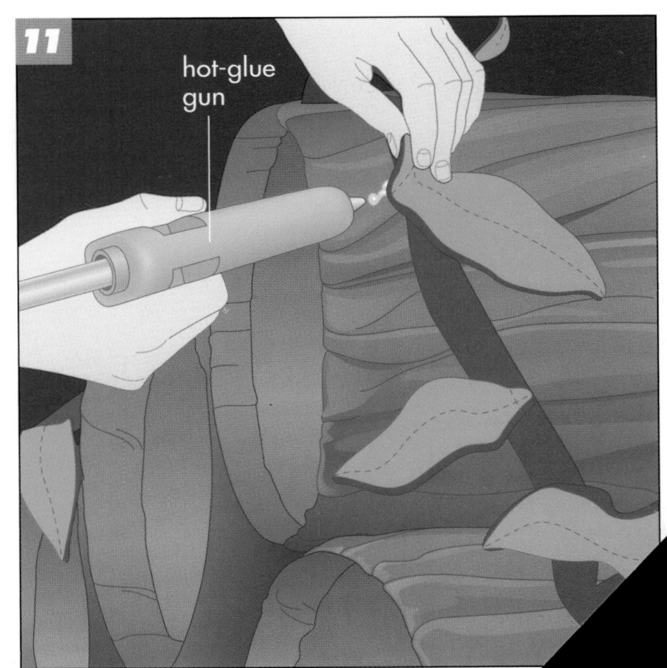

11. Add final decorations.
Glue the thermal-fleece vines to the wo
a hot-glue gun. To complete the outd
plastic ants, spiders, snakes, and li

IT'S A JUNGLE IN THE CLOSET

Patterned on the dense foliage of a tropical rain forest, this creative closet doorway lets kids plunge in anywhere to reach their clothes. When they have what they want, the forest closes behind them. Made of thermal fleece or felt strips topped by a fleece-covered plywood jungle canopy, this project adjusts to any size door opening—a kid-friendly substitute for bifold doors and an eye-catching addition to a young naturalist's bedroom.

YOU'LL NEED

TIME: About 1 day to make a doorway for a 64×80-inch closet opening.
SKILLS: Moderate sewing and carpentry skills.
TOOLS: Saber saw, handsaw, tape measure, framing square or drywaller's T square, hammer, staple gun, screwdriver, variable-speed drill, sewing machine, scissors, straight pins.

MATERIALS

4×8 sheet of ¼-inch plywood
Two 6"-long 2×4s
One 8'-long 1×6
6'-long piece of 2" lattice
3"-long, 1⅝" all-purpose screws
8d nails
Thermal fleece or felt: 30×90" of light green for canopy, 2½ yards of brown, and 5 yards each of 3 shades of green
30×90" hi-loft batting
Matching sewing thread

RIGHT: This colorful doorway adds a wild touch to a room while it tames the unsightly interior of a closet.

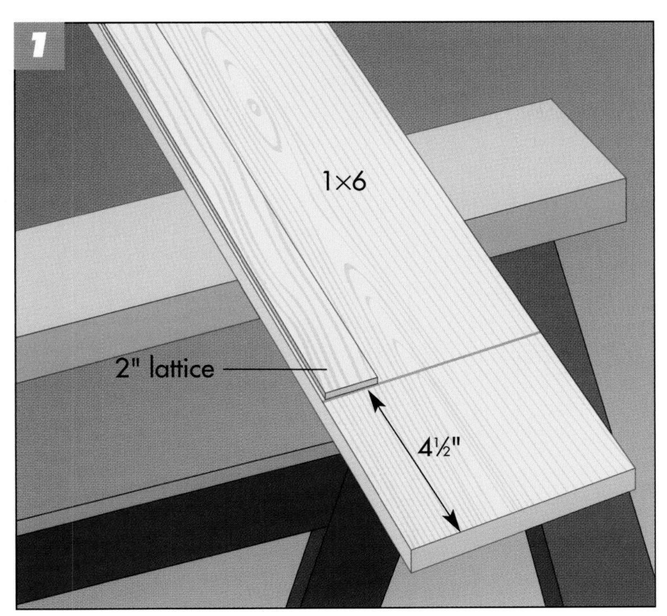

1. Measure and cut.
Cut two 6-inch-long 2×4s. Fasten each vertically on either side of the topmost piece of closet molding (see Step 11). Measure from the center of a 2×4 to the floor to determine the length of the strips. Measure across the closet opening from the outside edges of the 2×4s for the width of the jungle door. Cut a 1×6 to this dimension. Mark 4½ inches from each end. Cut lattice to fit inside this dimension.

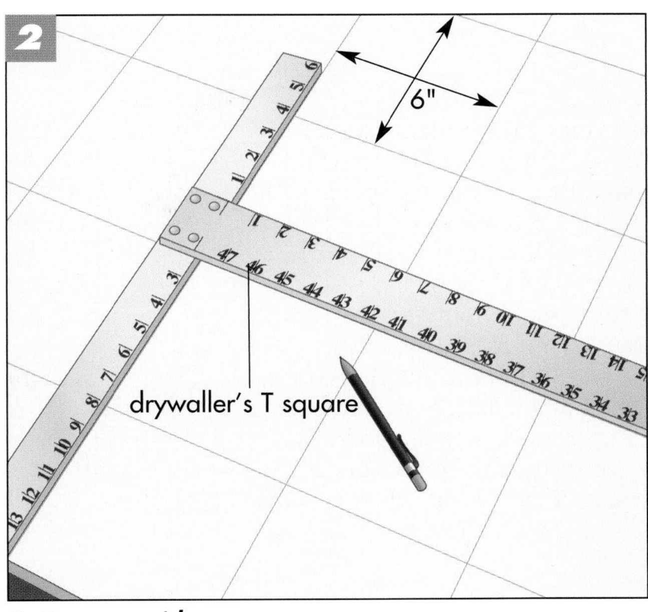

2. Draw a grid.
Have your home center trim the 4×8-foot plywood to 2½×8 feet. There should be little or no charge for this service, and the resulting piece will be easier to work with. Draw a 6-inch grid on the plywood. Use a T square or a framing square to keep your lines at right angles.

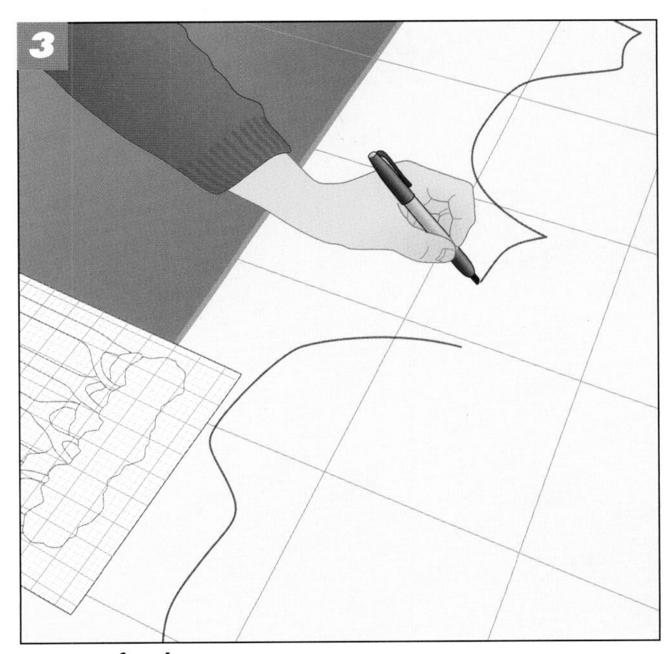

3. Transfer the tree canopy pattern.
Determine what size tree canopy you need for your closet door. Adjust the pattern on page 101 as needed. Sketch the tree canopy pattern on the plywood. (This does not need to be precise; just capture the general shape.) Use a marker to make a bold cut line.

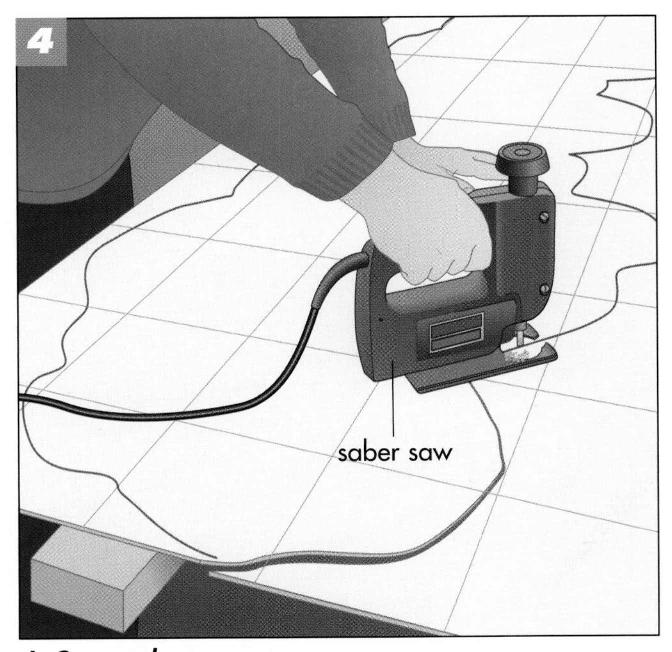

4. Cut out the tree canopy.
Set the plywood sheet on two 8-foot-long 2×4s resting on sawhorses. Cut out the shape with a saber saw. Move the plywood as you work to avoid cutting into the supports. Sand the edges with medium-grit sandpaper to remove any splinters.

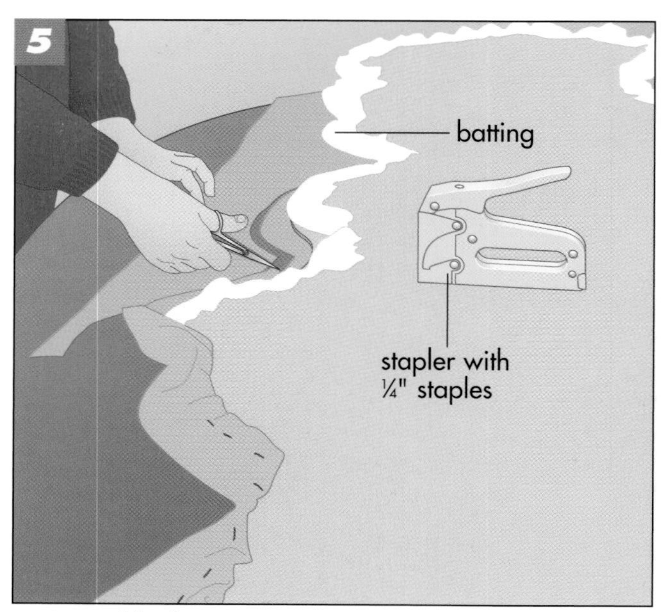

5. Assemble the tree canopy.
On a clean floor or tabletop, lay the green fabric face-down, then the batting, then the plywood shape. Cut the batting 2 inches larger than the plywood; the fabric, 3 inches larger. For a tight fit, clip the fabric almost to the plywood edge at each inside curve. Pull the batting to the back side of the canopy and staple, then stretch and staple the fabric in place.

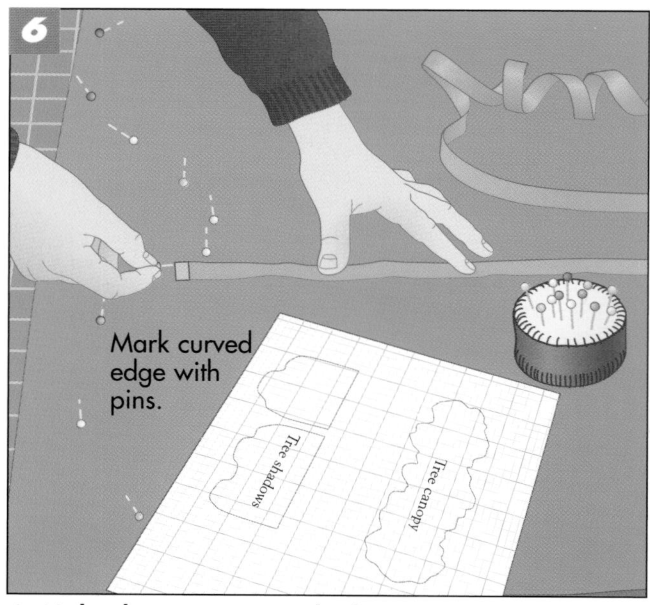

6. Make the tree canopy shadows.
Referring to the pattern on page 101, cut rectangles from medium green thermal fleece or felt. Measure from the top straight edge, and place pins along the curved edge. Cut out along the pinned line. Use each as a pattern to cut a second one (as in Step 7, below). Pin pairs together with wrong sides facing, and sew around the perimeter, using a ⅜-inch seam allowance.

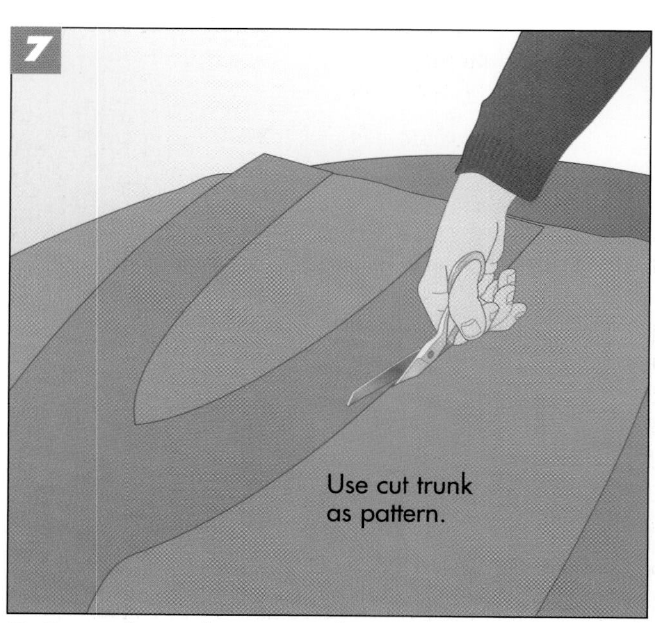

7. Cut and sew the tree trunks.
Determine how many tree trunks you want. Enlarge the trunk patterns on page 101, making them the length you need. Cut two pieces from brown thermal fleece or felt for each tree desired, using one as a pattern for the other. Pin pairs together with wrong sides facing, and sew around the perimeter, using a ⅜-inch seam allowance.

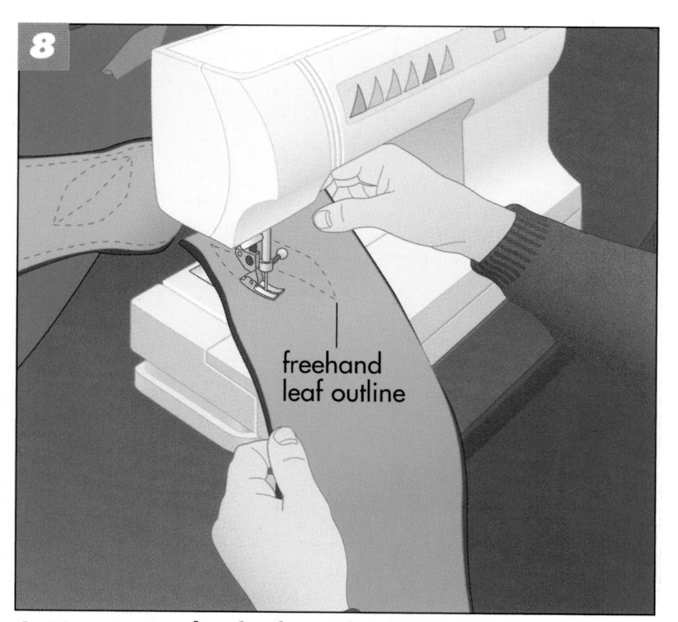

8. Hang strips for the forest backdrop.
Calculate the number of 5- and 6-inch strips needed to cover the lattice and the 1×6. Cut thermal fleece or felt in a variety of greens to 5- and 6-inch-wide strips to your determined length. Join pairs of strips in the same manner as tree trunks. As an optional touch, sew leaf shapes into the lower half of each strip.

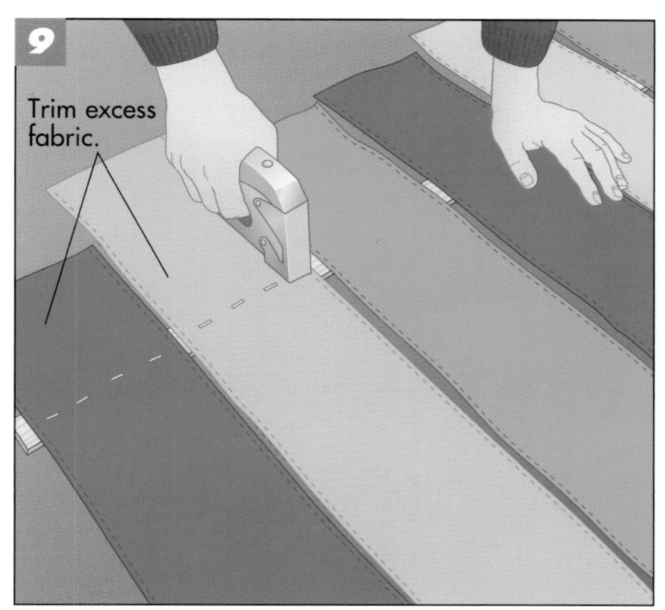

9. Staple strips to lattice.
Lay the lattice on the floor, and mark the background strip length with masking tape. Arrange the back row of strips on the lattice and staple to secure. Trim away the excess fabric. Lay the 1×6 on top of the lattice and arrange the front row of strips, alternating the openings. Add the tree trunks and staple to the 1×6. Place, then staple the tree shadows on top.

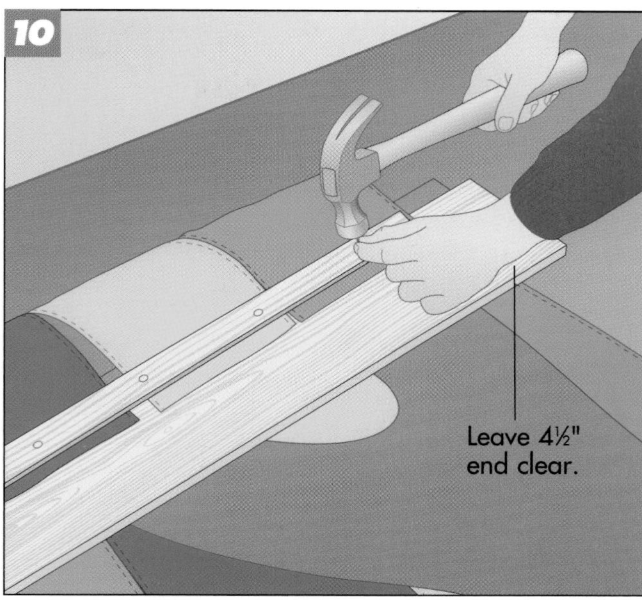

10. Attach lattice to 1×6.
Turn over the 1×6 and the lattice to the back side. Place the lattice along the lower edge of the 1×6, positioning one end at the mark 4½ inches from the end (see Step 1, page 59). Nail the lattice to the back of the 1×6 to assemble the forest backdrop.

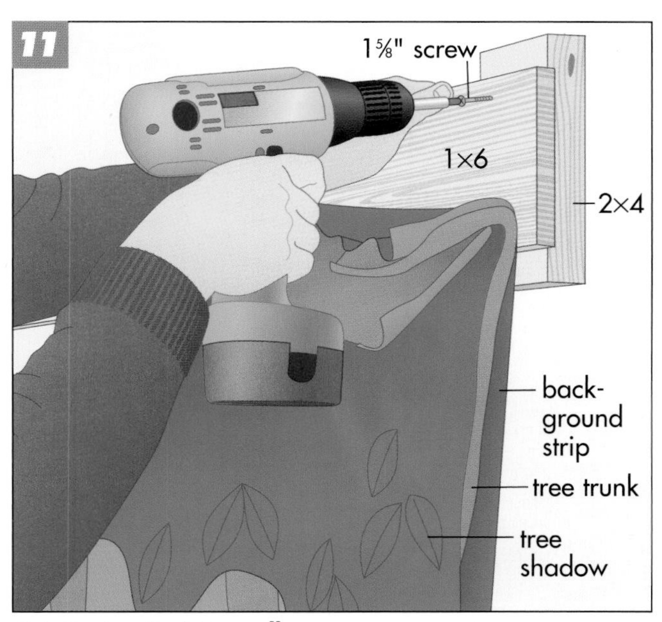

11. Fasten 1×6 to wall.
Pound a small nail 1 inch from the bottom of each 2×4 on which to rest the 1×6. Have a helper hold the assembled 1×6 in place. Check that the strips are the desired distance above the floor. Fasten the 1×6 to the 2×4s using 1⅝-inch all-purpose screws. Use one to hold the board in place until you are satisfied with placement; secure with two screws at each end.

12. Secure the canopy.
With a helper, arrange the treetop canopy on top of the 1×6 and nail through the canopy into the 2×4s and the 1×6, using 8d common nails. (Note: All-purpose screws won't work.) Use green fabric scraps to make leaves and vines (as in Steps 9–11, page 57). Glue or stitch the leaves to the canopy to cover the nails. Add a monkey, birds, or snakes, as desired.

DREAMY DOUBLE-DECKER

Patterned on London's famous double-decker buses, this bunk bed will carry kids to dreamland in style. And with spacious windows on the front and sides and a ladder at the rear, it has plenty of play potential, too.

This bunk bed can be cut out completely with a saber saw; but if you are comfortable using a circular saw, it will speed the job. (See page 105 for how to handle a circular saw and how to make the plunge cuts needed for the bus windows and ladder steps.)

You'll need a large work area for building the bus. The sides are made of two pieces; if you assemble it outside the bedroom, it may not fit through the doorway. Plan to assemble the project—and perhaps apply the final coat of paint—in the bedroom.

BELOW: *This bunk bed is made of medium-density fiberboard (MDF), but the project can also be made from plywood or standard particleboard (see box, page 64, for the advantages and disadvantages of each).*

YOU'LL NEED

TIME: About 3 days to build the bus; another day to paint.
SKILLS: Moderate carpentry skills; ability to transfer a complex pattern.
TOOLS: Saber saw, circular saw, variable-speed drill, drywaller's T-square or framing square, tape measure, coarse wood file or belt sander, sanding block, finish saw, miter box, screwdriver, drill.

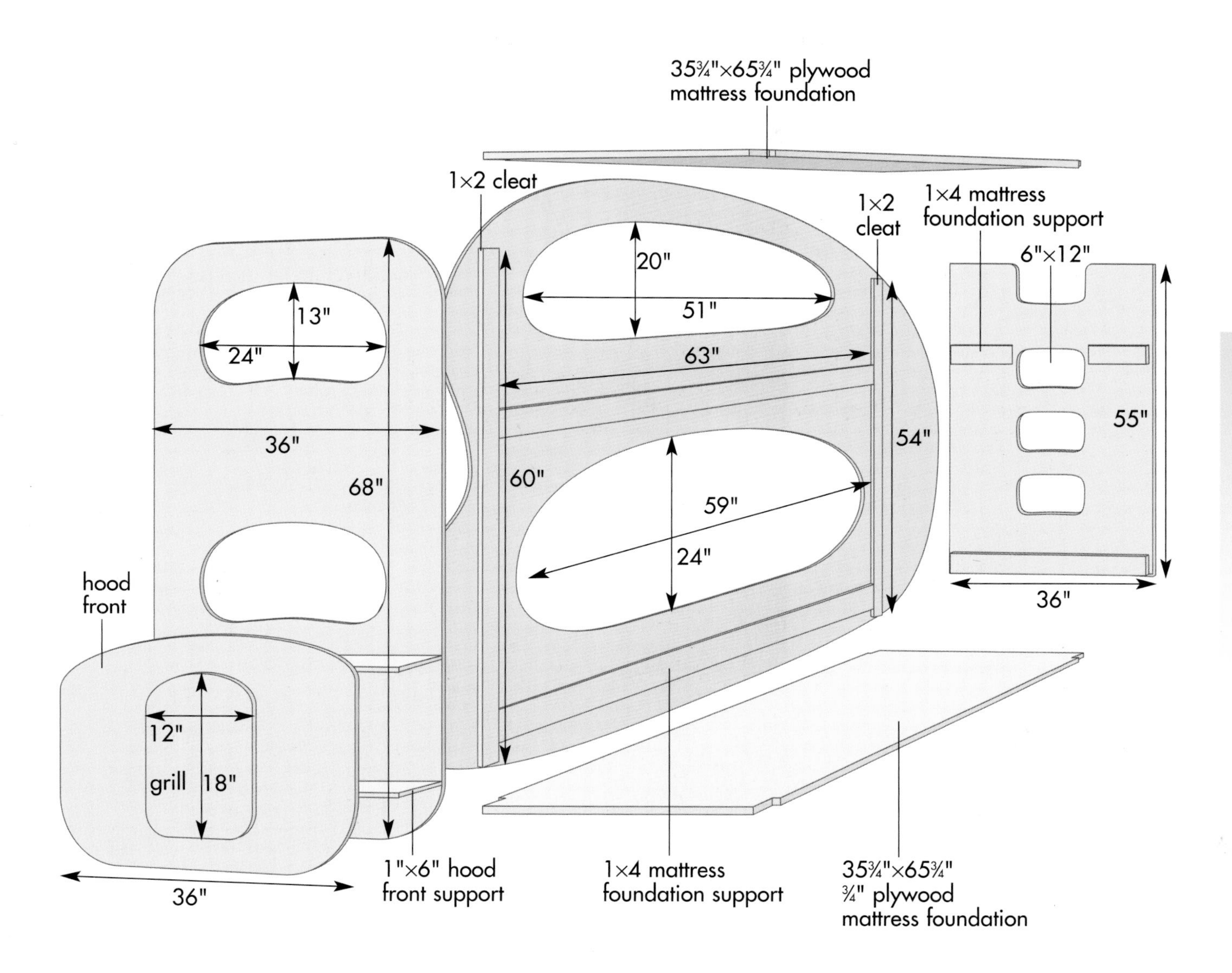

ABOVE: *The shell of the bus, reinforced by 1×4 supports for ¾-inch plywood mattress foundation and 1×2 vertical cleats, can be made of any ¾-inch sheet goods. Glue all cleats and fasten them every 6 inches with 1¼-inch all-purpose screws. Round all exposed edges with a coarse file and sandpaper, with a belt sander, or with a router that has a "roundover" bit. Where sheet goods abut each other, use a "factory" edge where possible for a clean joint. A coat of primer and three coats of gloss latex enamel finish the project. (Better quality paint pays off in better coverage.) To avoid having to paint in corners and crevices, prime and paint two coats before assembling the bus.*

MATERIALS

Five 49"×97" ¾-inch MDF
Two 4×8 ¾ sheets of plywood
Two 12'-long 1×2s
Two 12'-long 1×4s
1⅝" trimhead screws
1¼" all-purpose screws
2" all-purpose screws
3" all-purpose screws
Carpenter's glue
Primer
Red, white, and black enamel
6" transfer lettering

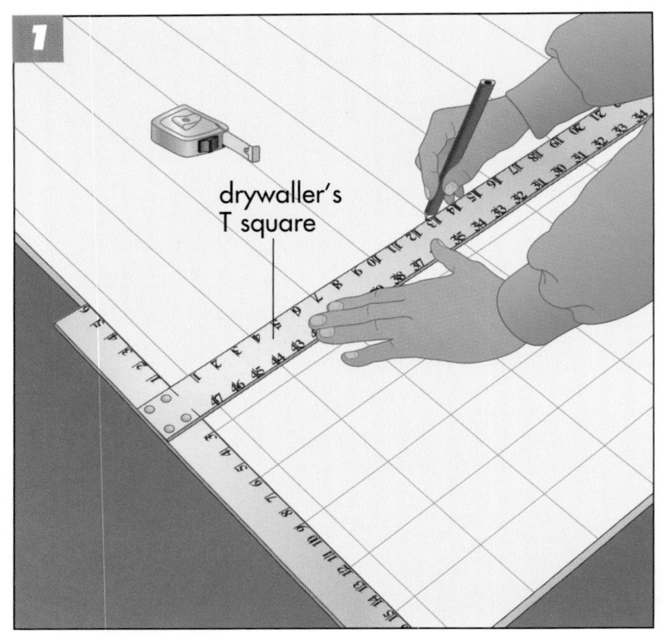

1. Mark grid with 3-inch squares.
Begin by marking the sheet goods with a 3-inch-square grid in order to transfer the pattern found on page 102. A drywaller's T square makes the job easy. If you don't have one, make marks every 3 inches along both sides of the board and, with a helper, use a straightedge to mark lines across the width and length.

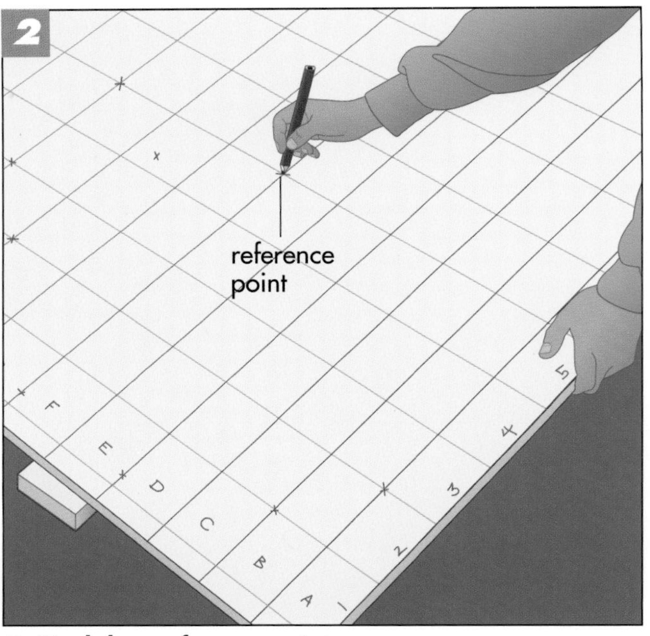

2. Mark key reference points.
Write numbers from left to right along the 8-foot length of the board, and letters along the width, just like those on the pattern. In particular, mark where the outline of the pattern hits a grid intersection. Mark these clearly as a guide to sketching the outline of the bus parts. Double-check your marks.

Sheet Goods

This project calls for ¾-inch sheet goods. Consider these options:

- Medium-density fiberboard (MDF) is easily cut and shaped, and it has edges without any voids. On the downside, it is heavy and does not come in the standard 48- by 96-inch sheet good size, but 49 by 97 inches. (Cabinetmakers like the extra inch to allow for the ⅛-inch kerf a saw blade eats up). The size can be a problem if you try to slip sheets of MDF into a van.
- Standard fiberboard is cheaper but less strong. It has voids in the edges that must be filled before painting.
- Solid-core plywood is pricey, but its edges have no voids and it can be shaped.

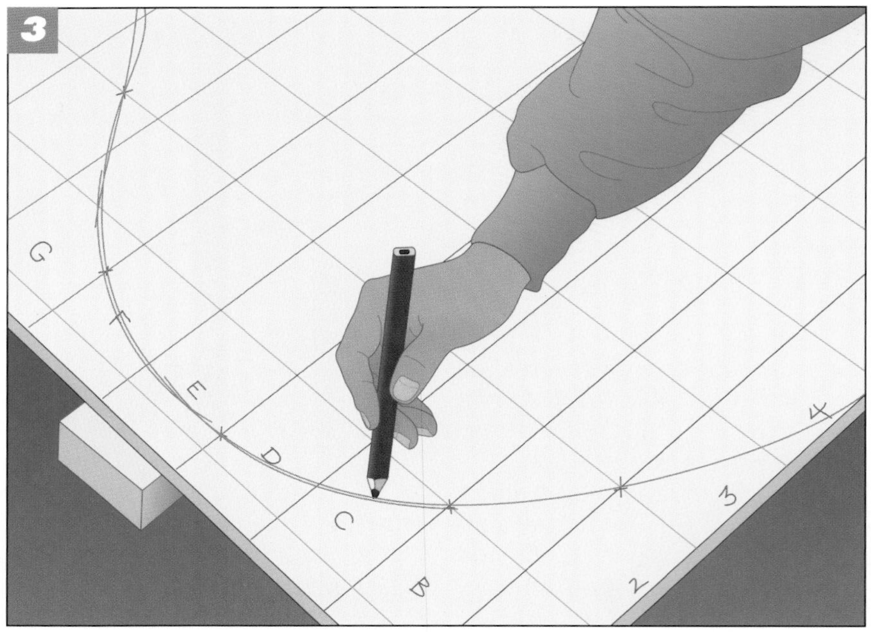

3. Sketch the bus.
Using the grid as a guide, lightly freehand the outline of bus body side. Use your whole arm to make smooth curves (see box opposite.) Be sketchy at first, and then bear down as you find the right curve. Try for smooth curves, even if you vary a bit from the pattern.

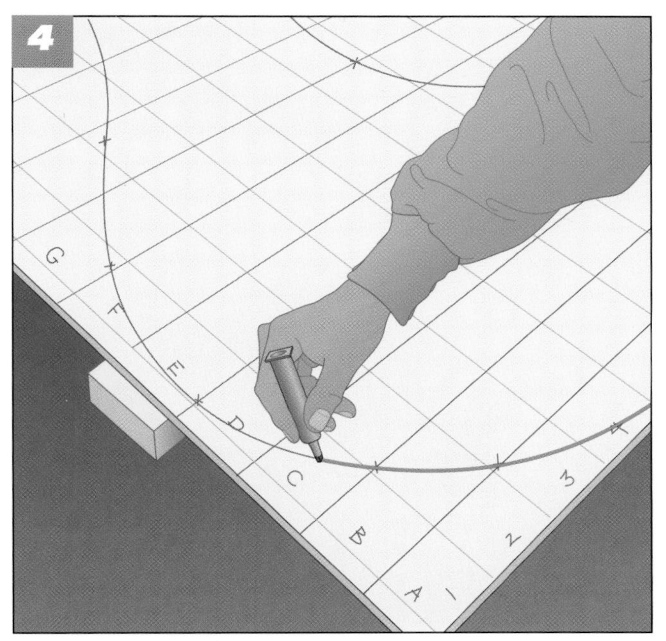

4. Clearly mark the cut line.
As a final check, confirm overall dimensions with a tape measure and make any needed adjustments. Use a marker to clarify the cut line.

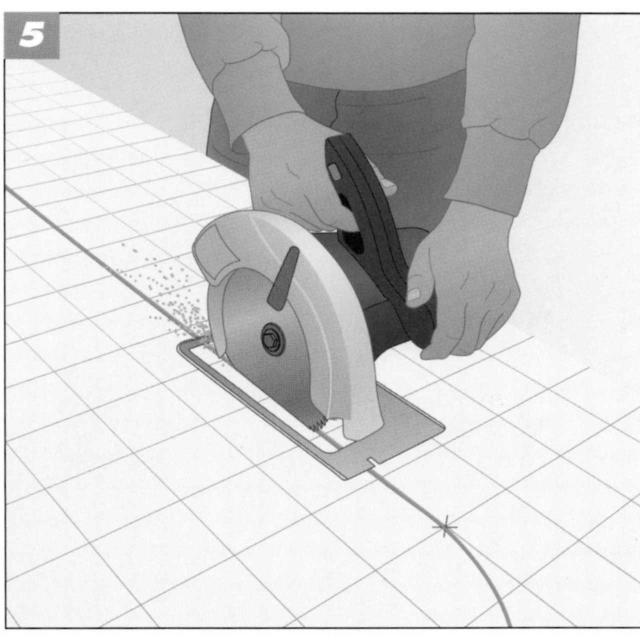

5. Make long cuts with circular saw.
Though these cuts can be made with a saber saw, the cut will go slowly and it will be difficult to hold a straight line. If you are comfortable using a circular saw, use it to make a plunge cut (see page 105) to cut out the straight sections of the windows.

EXPERTS' INSIGHT

SKETCHING THE BUS

This is a free-form project whose cartoonlike look depends on easy, fluid curves. The location, length, and height of the windows are all important, as are the overall length and height of the project; but otherwise, you have some latitude in sketching the bus onto your sheet goods. Follow these tips:

- Use a carpenter's pencil.
- Begin by sketching lightly, using your whole arm.
- If things go badly, erase your sketch with an all-purpose liquid household cleaner.
- Keep the big picture in mind. Stand back often to get the overall effect.

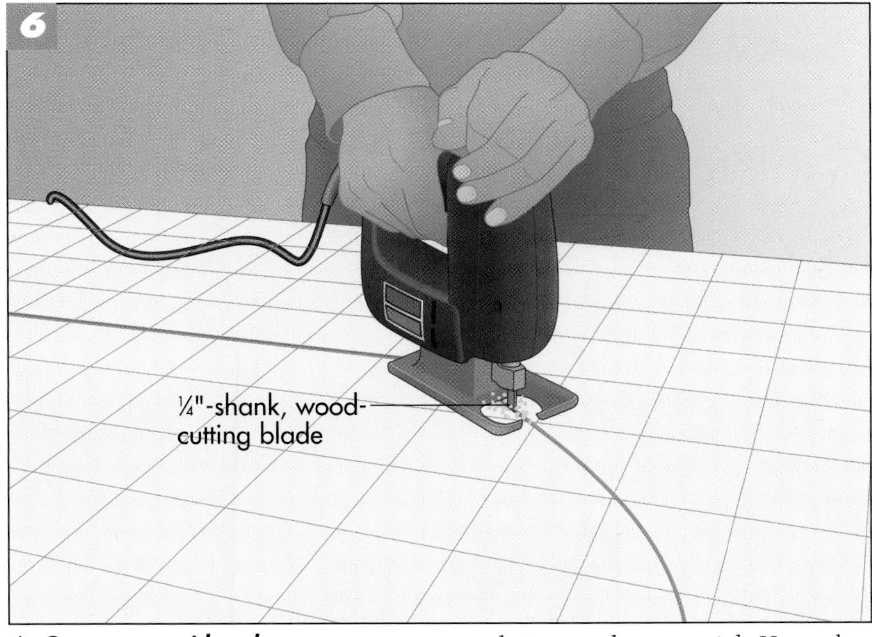

6. Cut curves with saber saw.
Fit the saber saw blade into the cut made by the circular saw, or bore ½-inch access holes. Let the saw come to full speed before you push it into the material. Keep the cut as smooth as possible, even if you wander off the cut line slightly. Don't force the saw; let the blade do the work.

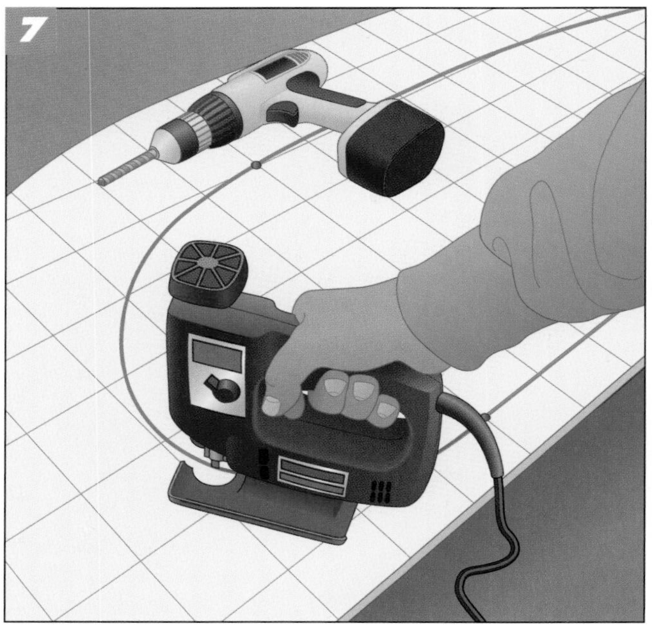

7. Sketch and cut top half.
Mark the lower half (about a 3×8-foot area) of a 4×8 piece of ¾-inch sheet goods with a 3-inch grid. Mark reference points and sketch one of the upper side sections of the bus. With a circular saw and a saber saw, cut out the piece.

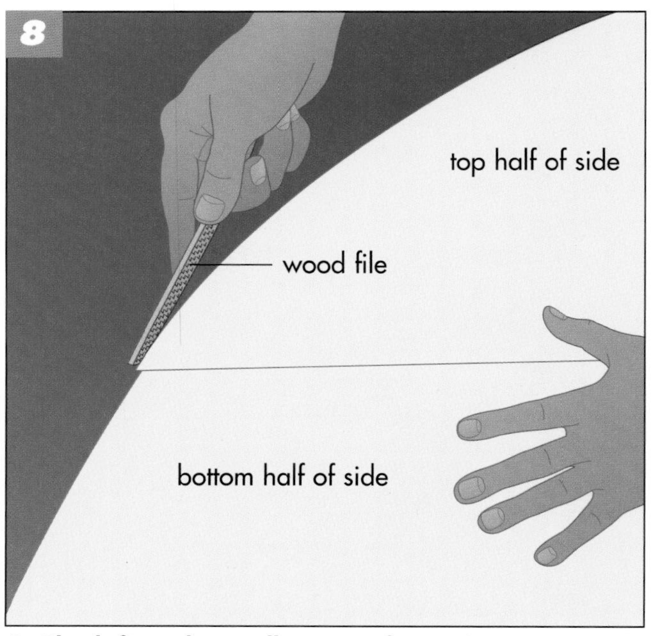

8. Check fit and overall curves of two pieces.
Lay the top and bottom side pieces on the floor and check that their corners match up. Use a wood file, belt sander, or the saber saw to make any adjustments. Mark the pieces so you'll remember how they go together.

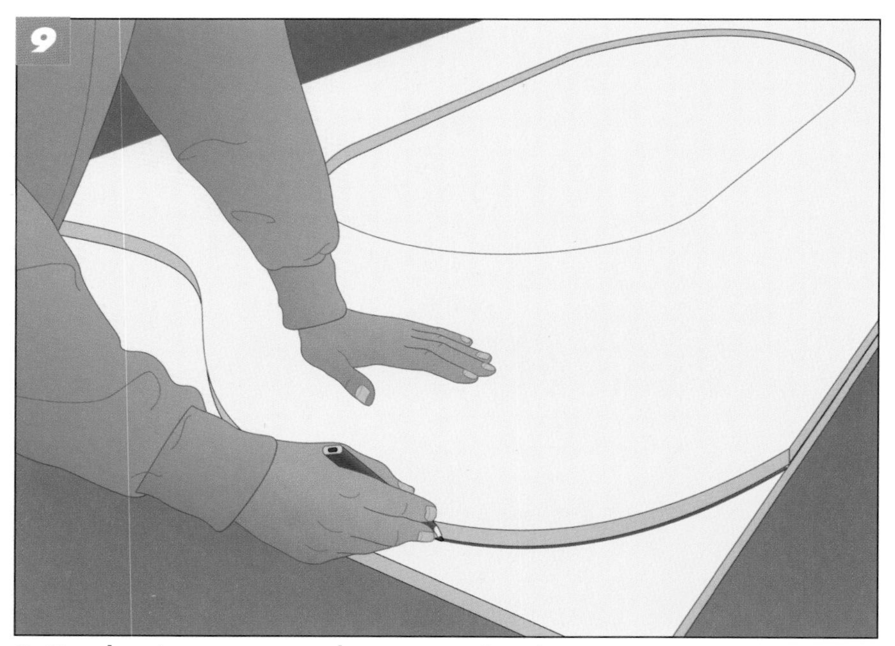

9. Use the pieces as a template.
Now that you've got the two pieces of one side cut, use each as a template for cutting the opposite side pieces. Check that the straight edges line up. Trace around the pieces and cut them. Then lay them on the floor to check how they match up (see Step 8).

TOOLS TO USE

Kid-friendly, smooth, rounded edges are important in this project. Here are two tools you can rent to make the job easier:

- A belt sander is ideal for smoothing curves and taking off the sharp edge. You'll have to buy disposable sanding belts. You can purchase them from the rental outlet, or save a little money by obtaining them at a home center.
- A router equipped with a ¼-inch "roundover" bit cuts a smooth, uniform rounded edge. It can save you hours of sanding, and it will give the project a pleasingly professional look.

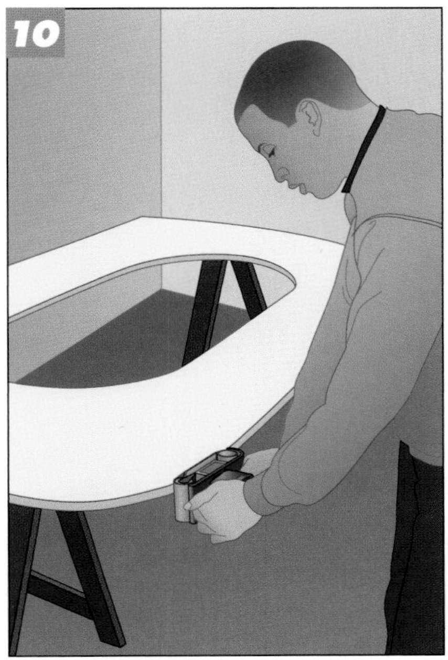

10. Smooth the shape.
Use a belt sander to smooth out imperfections in the cutting. Be careful: A belt sander can take a big bite if you bear down too hard. Move it back and forth, slowly working down any high points.

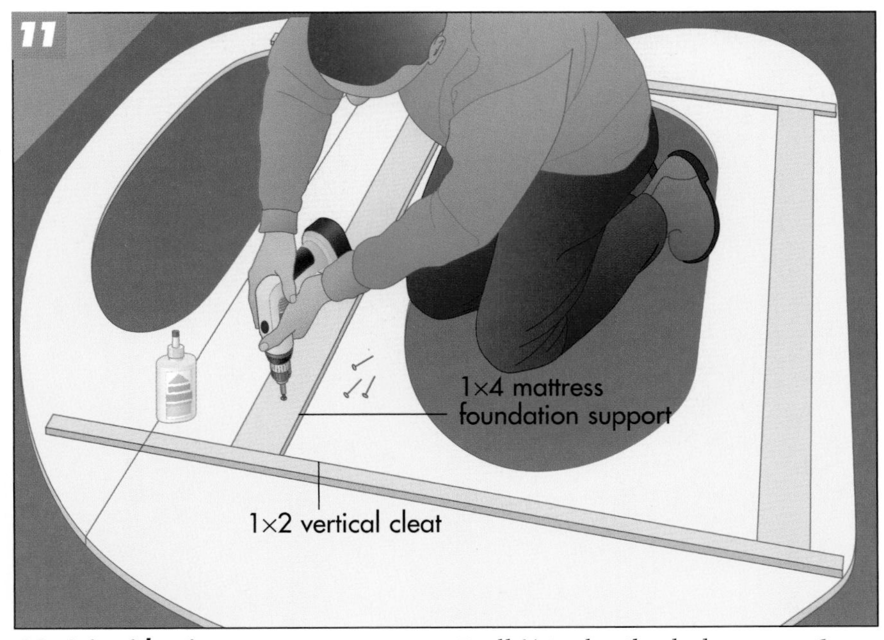

11. Join side pieces.
Cut the 1×4 mattress base support and the 1×2 vertical cleats to the dimensions shown on page 63. Drill ⅛-inch pilot holes every 6 inches. Then apply carpenter's glue and fasten the pieces in place with 1¼-inch all-purpose screws.

12. Fasten the thin edge.
Carefully drill two ⅛-inch pilot holes about 24 inches apart through the thin lower edge of the upper window. Glue it with carpenter's glue and fasten with 3-inch all-purpose screws.

13. Sketch and cut front piece.
Using a circular saw, trim a 4×8 sheet to a rectangle 36×68 inches. Mark a 3-inch grid and sketch out the front section of the bus. Cut out one window and use it as a template for the second window. Cut the rounded corners using a saber saw.

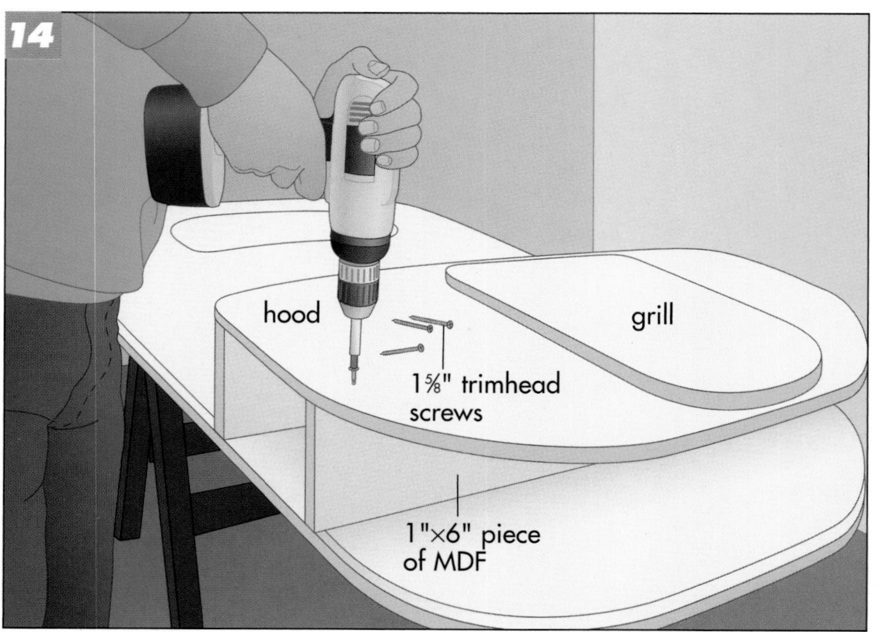

14. Build the hood section.
Cut a rectangle 36×24 inches. Use the bottom of the front section (Step 13) as a template for marking the bottom of the grill section. Mark a row of 3-inch squares along the top edge, and transfer the curve to the hood. Cut the hood section using a saber saw. From leftover scraps, mark and cut out the grill and two 6×36-inch supports. Glue and fasten the pieces as shown, *above*, with 1⅝-inch trimhead screws.

MEASUREMENTS

CHOOSING MATTRESSES

The double-decker bunk bed is built around youth-sized mattresses, 33 by 66 inches, a size that will accommodate elementary-school-age children and keep the project from taking over the bedroom. Most mattress outlets can fabricate or special-order this size. For a more affordable option, stop by an upholstery shop and select one of the many high-density foams that can be cut to your specifications. If you want to use twin-sized mattresses (39 by 75 inches), see the pattern on page 102 for where to add length and width to the bus.

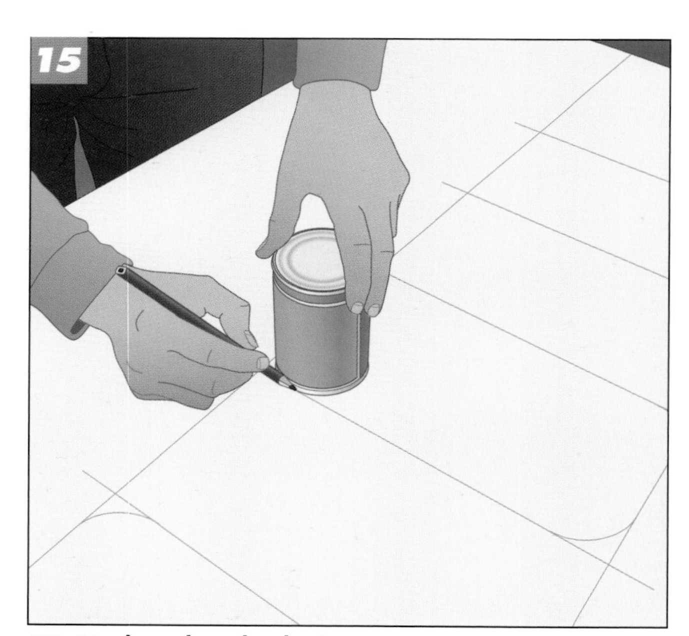

15. Mark and cut back piece.
Cut a piece of sheet goods to 36×55 inches. Mark vertical lines every 12 inches; mark for the ladder cutouts so that the first step is 11 inches from the floor (see page 63). Each step opening is 6 inches high, with 6 inches separating the steps. Use a soup can to mark the radius at each corner of the cutouts. Bore an entrance hole and use a saber saw.

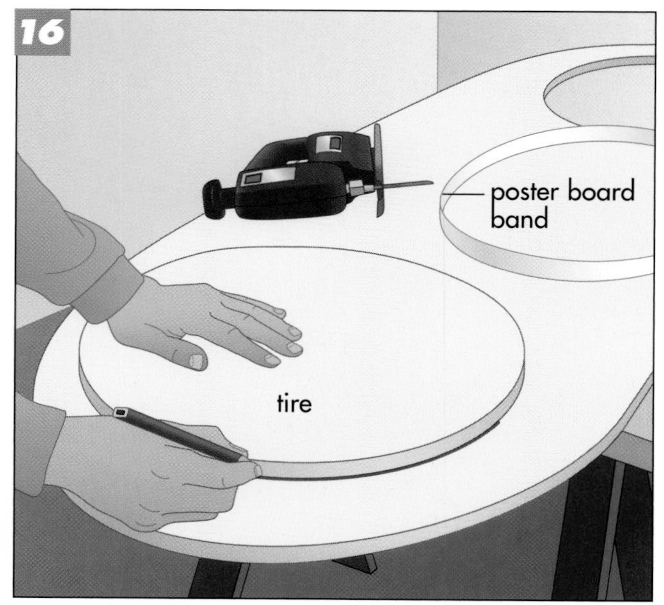

16. Mark and cut tires.
Cut 2-inch strips of poster board or a similar material and glue them together to make 4-foot-long strips. Bend the strip to make an oval 18 inches tall and about 12 inches wide. Use this as a guide for marking the tire on a scrap piece from a window cutout. Cut one and use it as a template for marking the others.

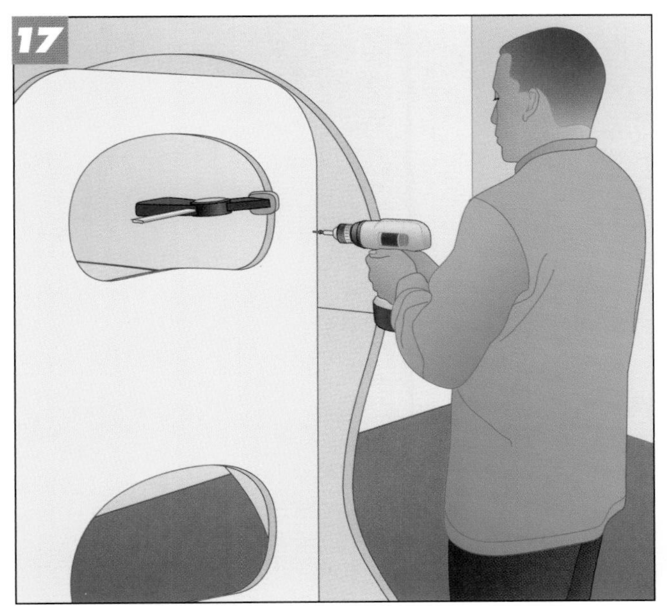

17. Assemble the bunk bed.
This is a large, heavy project, so consider moving it into the bedroom before final assembly and painting. Drill pilot holes and join the four sides with 2-inch all-purpose screws. (You'll need a helper to hold the pieces in place.) Cut, notch, and temporarily install a ¾-inch plywood mattress foundation, using it to square up the project.

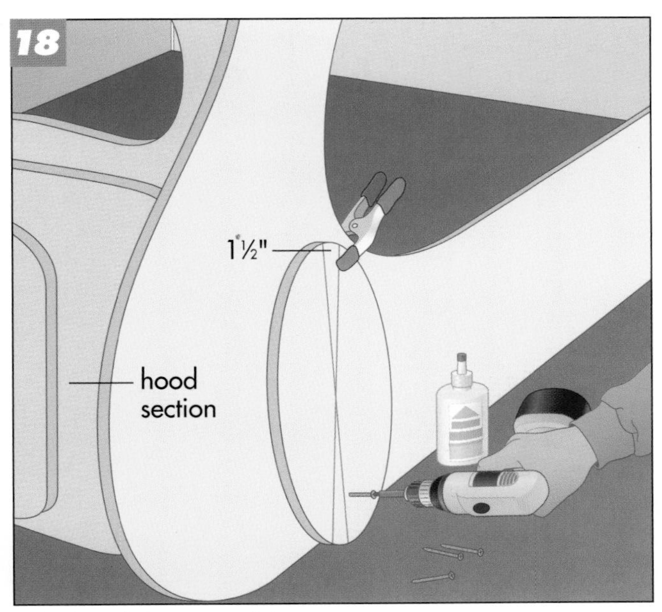

18. Attach hood and tires.
Attach the hood section, drilling pilot holes and fastening with trimhead screws. Note that the tires lean forward slightly. Draw a bisecting line down the length of each tire, then another line 1½ inches clockwise from it as shown. That line should be perpendicular to the floor as you mount the tire. Attach the wheels using 1¼-inch all-purpose screws.

SAFETY

Make sure the mattress you use in the bunk bed leaves at least 5 inches of guard rail. If necessary, lower the supports for the upper bunk foundation. Be sure each mattress foundation is firmly fastened to its support and that the support is fastened and glued as the steps instruct. In addition, follow these precautions from the Consumer Product Safety Commission (CPSC):

- Do not allow children under six to use the upper bunk.
- Prohibit roughhousing on or under the beds.
- Prohibit more than one person in the upper bunk.
- Use a ladder for entering or exiting the upper bunk.

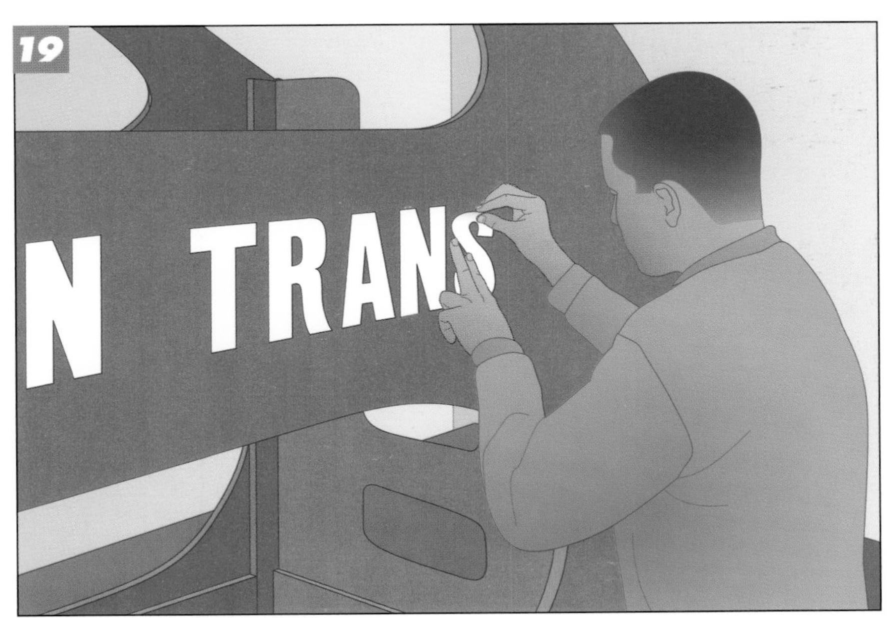

19. Paint and add lettering.
Remove the plywood mattress foundations and detach the hood and tires. Detail the grill, headlights, and tires with black and white paint. Finish painting the bus. When it is completely dry, make a light pencil line 6 inches below the upper window. Apply adhesive lettering. Reattach the hood section and tires, and fasten the mattress foundations with 2-inch screws placed every 12 inches into the 1×4 support.

SITTING WITTY

Designed for any aspiring bookworm, this fanciful chair provides an ideal spot for reading, listening to music, or just lounging. The solid frame is made of doubled ¾-inch plywood joined with three angle brackets. For a book-cover effect, fabric wraps the frame. Sleeping bag pads made of high-density foam serve as the pages. They can be easily sponged off with soap and water. Cut to size and bound together with cord, the pages adhere with built-in "spring" to complete the bookish illusion and also make it a truly comfortable chair. The finished book sits on colorful legs made of wooden deck-post finials.

BELOW: *This comfy chair becomes an ideal centerpiece for the study area of a bedroom. Its simple, stylish form is easily downsized for use by smaller children.*

YOU'LL NEED

TIME: About a day, not including painting the finial legs.
SKILLS: Moderate carpentry skills.
TOOLS: Tape measure, pencil and felt-tip marker, circular saw, variable-speed drill, ¾-inch Forstner or spade bit, ¼-inch and ⅛-inch bits, utility knife, hammer, socket wrench, stapler, straightedge, clamps, coarse file, belt sander, and sandpaper.

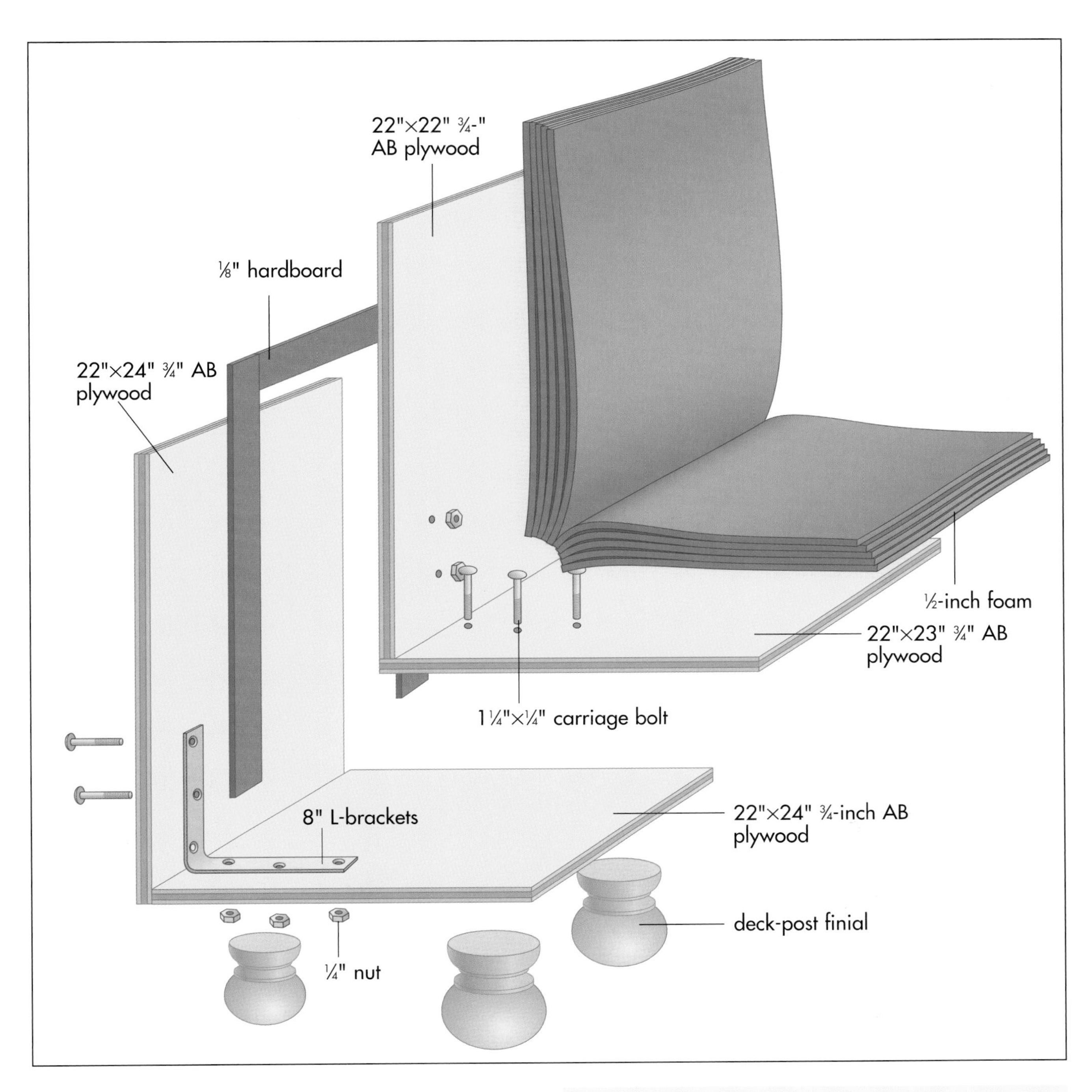

Three 8-inch L-brackets combine to give plenty of strength to this chair, while preserving its book-cover look. The brackets are sandwiched between pieces of ¾-inch plywood, held in place by carriage bolts that pierce both layers. (The ⅛-inch hardboard fills out the gap made by the thickness of the brackets.) Making the base and back of the chair is the most difficult stage of the project, but worth the trouble for a solid, durable frame. Wrap the frame in fabric before adding the pages and legs. Cut the high-density foam pages to size, drill holes, and lace the leaves together before attaching to the chair and to each other with spray-mount adhesive.

Materials

4×4 sheet of ¾-inch AB plywood
2×4 sheet of ⅛-inch hardboard
Three 8" L-brackets
15 1¼"×¼" carriage bolts, washers, nuts
Three 2×6 ½-inch foam
One sleeping bag pad
3 feet ⅛-inch nylon cord
Six ¼" washers
4 yards fabric
Four deck-post finials
12 1½" trim-head screws
Spray-mount adhesive
Wood glue
Paint

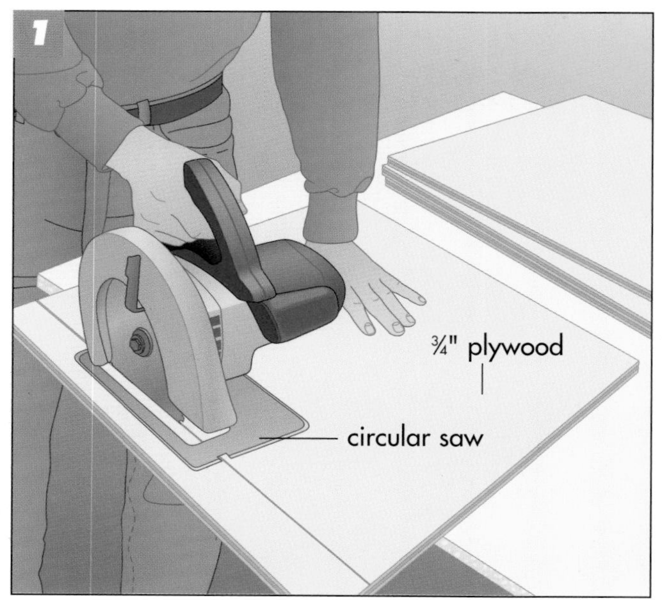

1. Mark and cut ¾-inch plywood.
With a tape measure and straightedge, mark a 4×4-foot piece of ¾-inch pine AB plywood for cutting. Mark 22×24- and 22×22-inch pieces for the back and 22×24- and 22×23-inch pieces for the seat of the chair. Cut with a fine-tooth handsaw or use a circular saw equipped with a combination blade. Set the blade ¼ inch lower than the thickness of the plywood. Sand away any roughness.

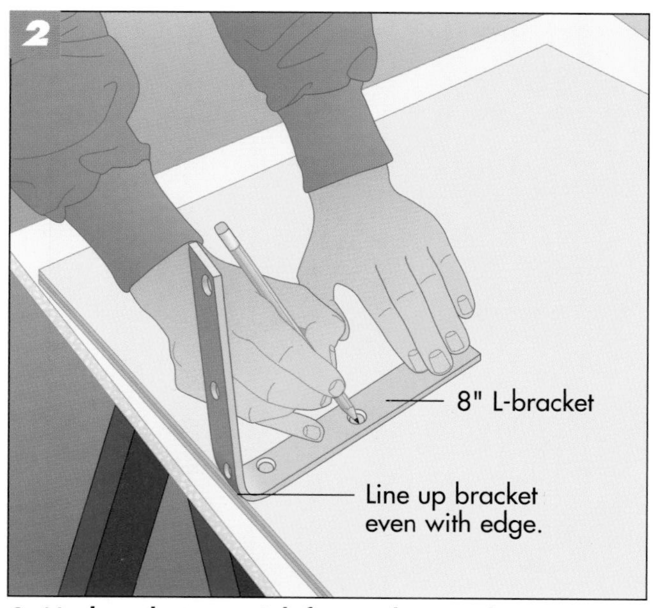

2. Mark and countersink for washers and nuts.
Set the brackets in place as shown and mark for drilling. Begin with an ⅛-inch pilot hole. Then use a ¾-inch spade or Forstner bit to countersink on the seat side for the nut and washer of each carriage bolt.

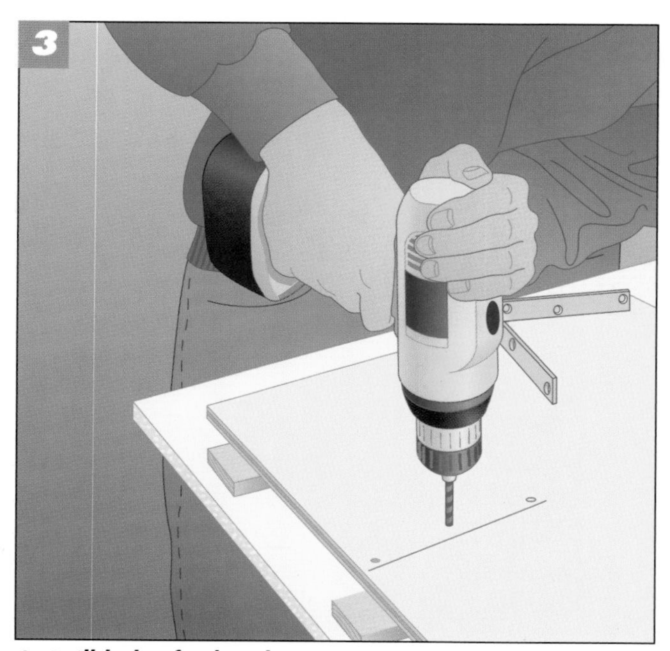

3. Drill holes for brackets.
Drill ⅛-inch pilot holes for each of the bracket bolts. Next, use a ¾-inch bit to drill a ½-inch-deep countersink hole for the nut and washer. Countersink the side of the plywood piece that will be away from the foam pages.

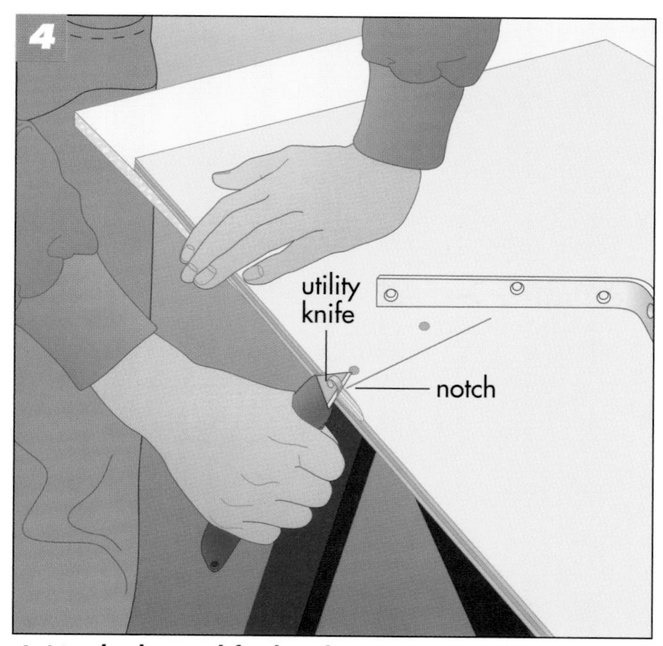

4. Notch plywood for brackets.
Cutting away from yourself, use a utility knife to notch the plywood so each bracket sits fully onto the surface. Don't worry about overdoing this—the notch will be covered.

COVER FABRIC

Choose a plain-colored fabric to stretch over the plywood seat of this chair. Thermal fleece (shown on page 70) works well, as does duck, canvas, denim, and burlap. Upholstery fabrics are excellent for this project. Remnants often are easy to find at inexpensive prices in a fabric store that carries upholstery fabric. Consider covering the plywood first with a layer of batting (see page 60) to pad the chair and give the cover a smoother look.

If you can't find the ideal fabric color, use a plain fabric and paint it with fabric paints or dye, following the manufacturer's directions.

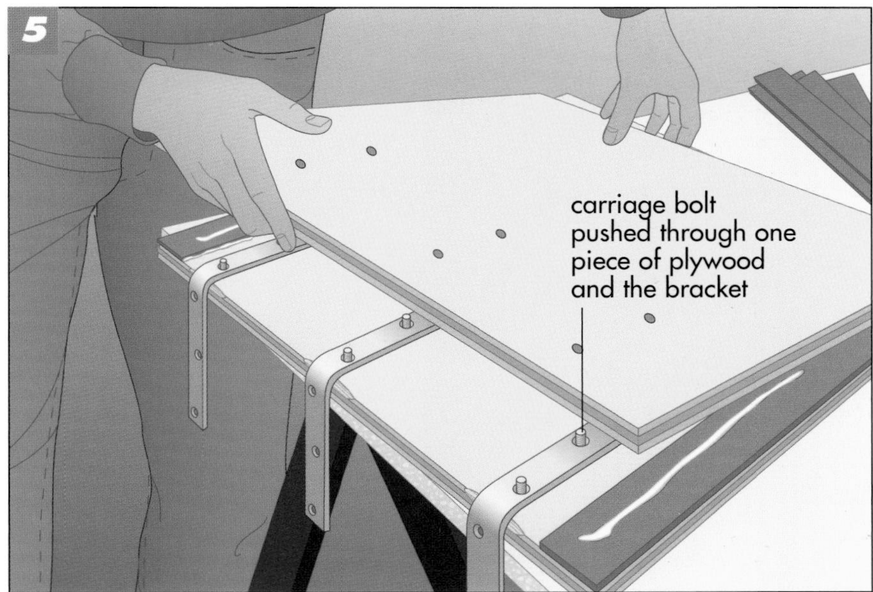

5. Fit pieces together; tighten nuts. Cut six 2×24-inch strips of ⅛-inch hardboard as spacers to compensate for the thickness of the brackets. Glue them to the plywood. Set the brackets in place. Push a 1¼×¼-inch carriage bolt through the plywood and the bracket. Apply glue to the spacers, and set the second plywood piece over the brackets. Use two clamps to hold the pieces of plywood together like a sandwich, and tap the brackets until you can push all the bolts through. You may have to redrill some of the holes.

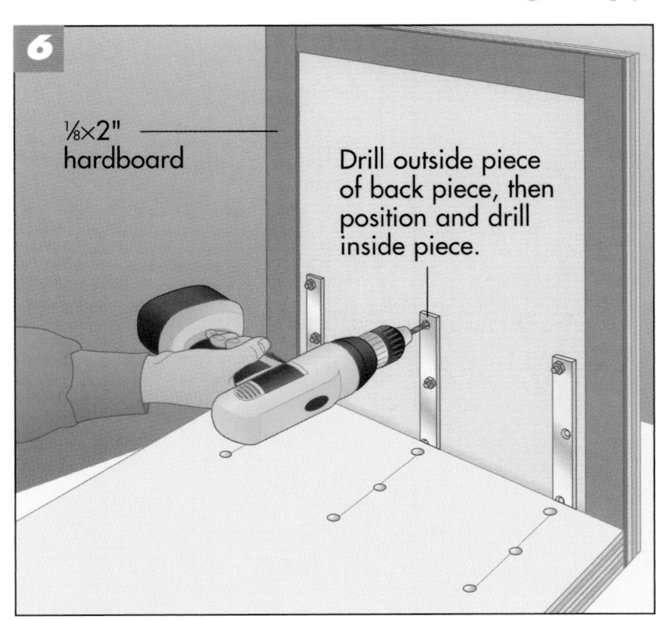

6. Drill for seat back.
Once the chair seat is glued and fastened, set the outside half of the back into place as shown. Drill through the brackets (you'll be able to use only two of the three holes in each bracket). Push in two carriage bolts from behind. Clamp the inside back piece in place and drill holes from behind, using the holes in the outside piece as a guide. Countersink and add the bolts, washers, and nuts.

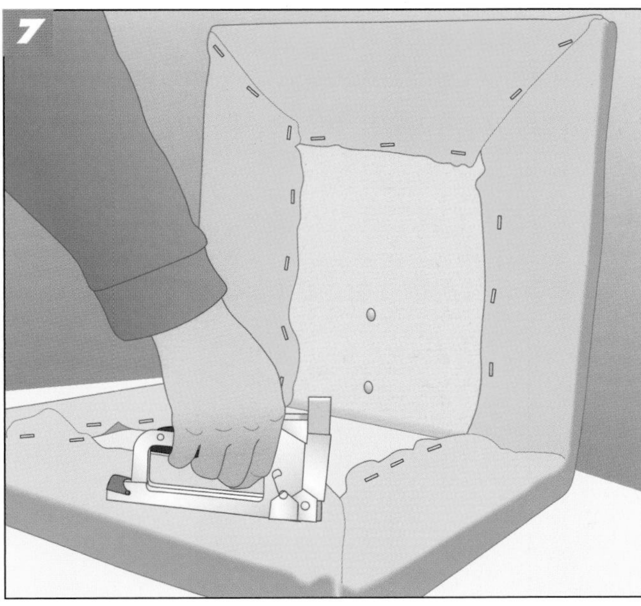

7. Staple cover.
Round the "spine" of the book cover with a coarse file or belt sander. Wrap the chair with burlap, thermal fleece, or other fabric. For a smooth fit, notch each corner of the fabric before stapling. Staple 4 inches in from the edge, with a staple every 1 to 2 inches. Check your work to be sure the fabric is uniformly stretched over the chair frame.

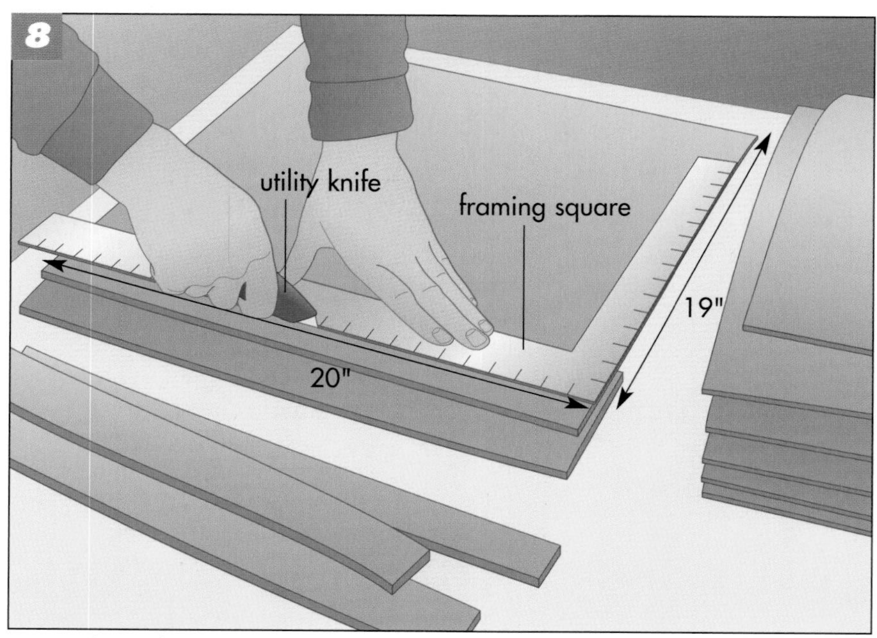

8. Cut foam for pages.
Load a utility knife with a new blade. Using a straightedge (a carpenter's framing square like the one shown is ideal), cut pages so each edge will be about 1 inch in from the edge of chair—20 inches wide by 19 inches deep if you are using the frame dimensions shown on page 71. See box, right, for how to make a neat-looking cut.

EXPERTS' INSIGHT

CUTTING FOAM

You'll have some excess foam, so take the opportunity to practice your cutting technique so that you'll end up with smooth, straight cuts. Keep these hints in mind:

- Use a metal straightedge held firmly in place.
- Hold the knife perpendicular to the foam and tight against the straightedge.
- Cut with one smooth, even motion, end to end.
- Utilize the factory edge (an edge that's been cut by the manufacturer) whenever possible. Usually—though not always—it is straight and smooth.

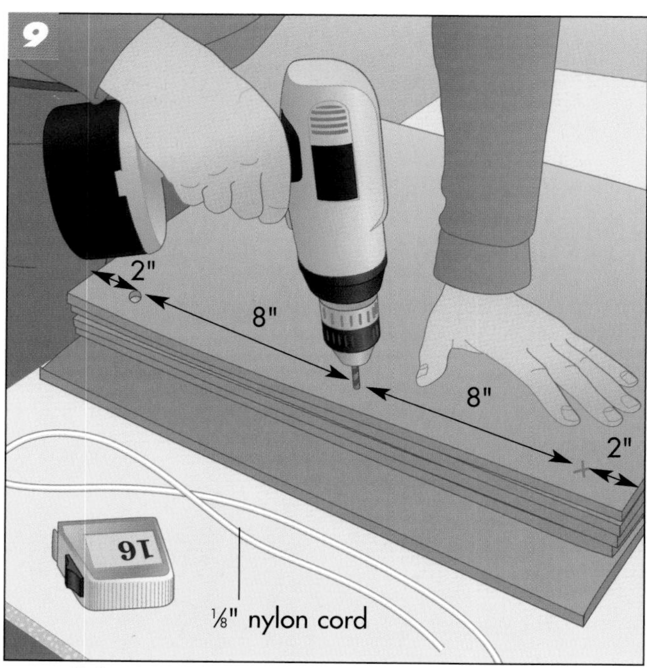

9. Drill foam.
Purchase about 3 feet of ⅛-inch nylon cord. Mark as shown a stack of 4 to 6 pages for drilling. Using a ¼-inch bit, drill through the foam, keeping the bit as perpendicular as possible. Use one of the pages as a template for drilling the others.

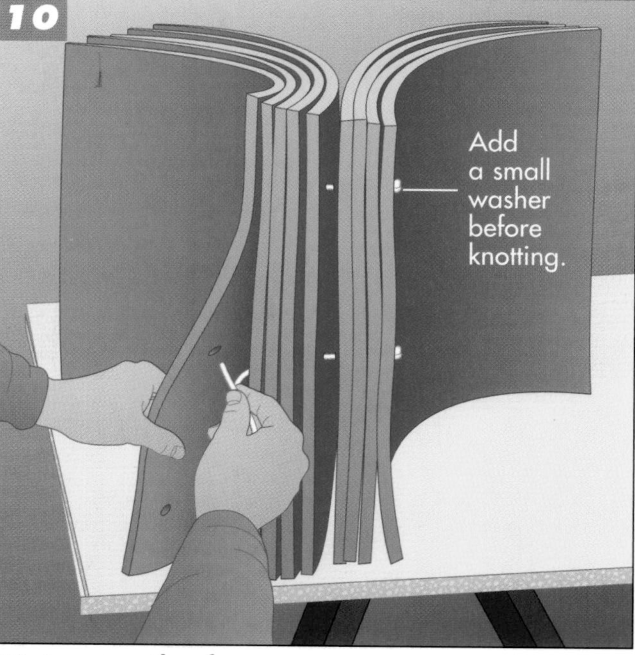

10. Lace together foam pages.
Heat one end of the cord with a match or lighter until it is a hardened nubbin. Knot the other end and string a ¼-inch washer on it. Stack the pages together. For each set of holes, stitch through the pages, then add a washer, snip the cord, melt the end slightly, and tie a knot.

11. Glue bundle of pages in place. Use spray-mount adhesive in a well-ventilated area. Following the manufacturer's directions, spray the back of the foam and the chair base from the recommended distance. Let the adhesive dry as directed before pressing the foam into place. Position it carefully—you'll get only one chance.

STENCILING

Customize your chair by using ready-made letter stencils to spell out a child's name, a literary quotation, or the alphabet. Use masking tape to carefully affix the stencils. Color over, using permanent markers or paint. (Test the paint first on a scrap of foam. Some paints eat into foam; others may bead up.)

Make your own stencils by photocopying special typography or images. Outline the photocopy with a soft pencil. Place the outlined image face down on a piece of poster board. Transfer the pencil image to poster board by firmly running a spoon over the back of the photocopy. Cut out the image using a hobby knife, and stencil it on the foam with markers or paint.

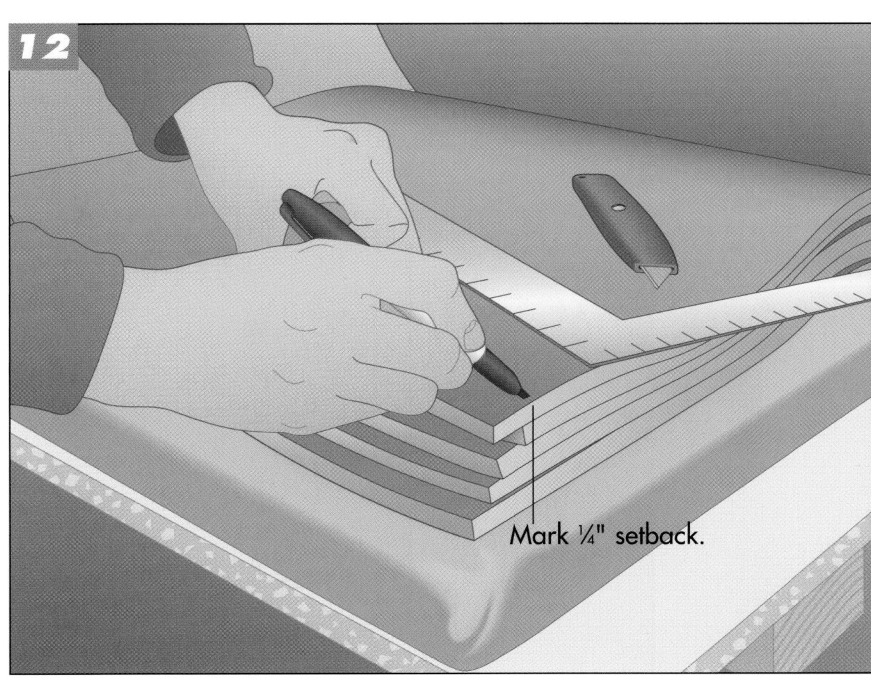

12. Stagger, trim, and glue pages. To truly mimic the look of an open book, trim each page so it sets back from the one beneath by about ¼ inch. Use a scrap of foam as a cutting surface. Masking surfaces you don't want adhered, spray adhesive and press each page in position.

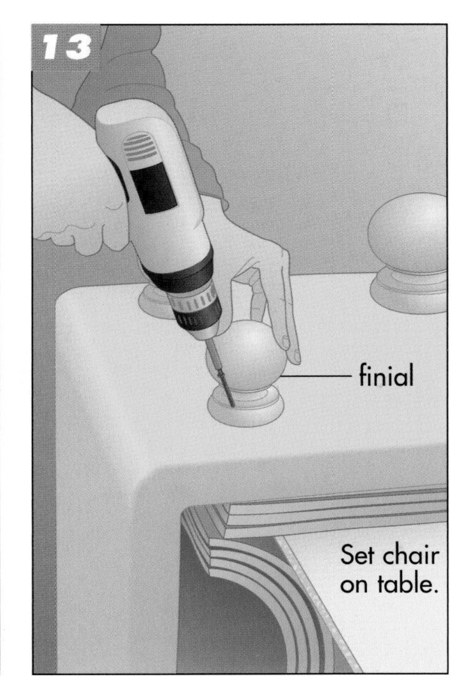

13. Attach legs.
Position the finials in each corner, about 4 inches from each edge. Predrill three holes in the base of each finial at a slight inward angle. Fasten each with 3 1½-inch trim-head screws.

DELIGHTFUL DIVIDERS

What pre-teen wouldn't want to transform his or her bedroom into a multiroom "apartment" with these colorful dividers? With plastic-coated cable and readily available curtain rings, just stretch the cable and adapt floor-length curtains to let your child carve out personal space in almost any size room. By sliding the curtains, entryways can be closed off or opened for a flexible floor plan.

Plan the location of the dividers by first determining what areas lend themselves to special activities, such as studying, sleeping, listening to music, or just hanging around. Several panels per cable give more flexibility than one or two wide panels. Combine them with a clothing rack to designate a closet area. Even shared rooms can be divided with this project.

BELOW: *Decorative and utilitarian, these dreamy curtains turn a room into a mini-apartment.*

YOU'LL NEED

TIME: About 3 hours, including hemming curtains.
SKILLS: Beginner carpentry and sewing skills.
TOOLS: Drill, screwdriver, sewing machine, scissors, cutting pliers, long-nosed pliers, tape measure.
MATERIALS: Sheer fabric, curtain rings with clips, 6-strand plastic-coated wire, cable anchors, 3⁄16-inch-diameter eye hooks and turnbuckles, 1⁄8-inch cable clamps.

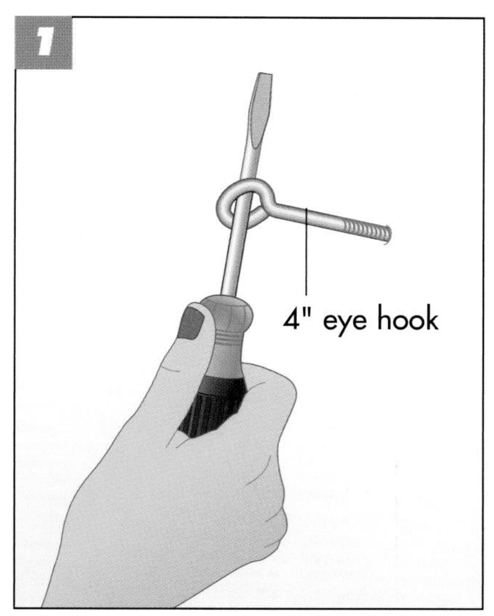

1. Install eye hooks.
Decide where curtain dividers will hang. Measure and mark on opposing walls the approximate location for each eye hook. Find a nearby stud (see page 34) and drill a 3/16-inch hole. Use a screwdriver to twist the eye hook into the wall.

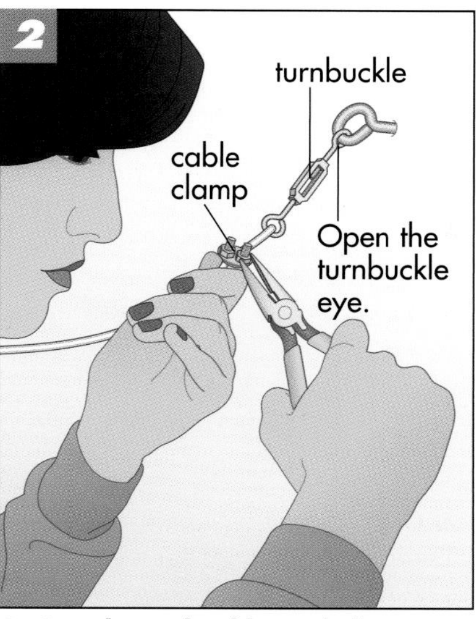

2. Attach turnbuckle and clamp.
Measure from wall to wall, add a foot or so, and cut a length of cable with cutting pliers. Attach the turnbuckle to the anchor—you may have to use pliers to open the turnbuckle eye. Thread the cable through a turnbuckle and attach a clamp, using long-nosed pliers to tighten each nut in turn.

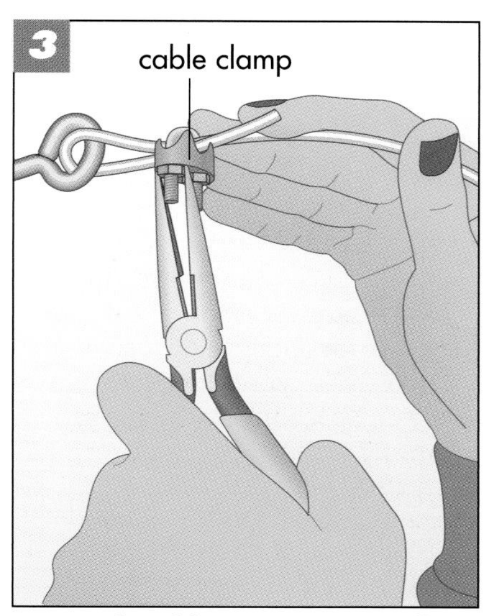

3. Attach cable to opposite wall.
At the opposite wall, install an eye hook. Thread curtain rings onto the cable. Thread a clamp onto the cable, and feed the end through the eye. Pull the cable as taut as possible and tighten the clamp. Return to the opposite wall and tighten the turnbuckle until the cable "twangs" when plucked.

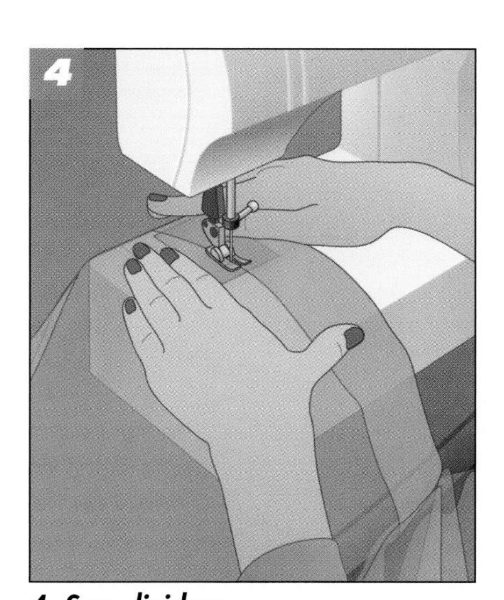

4. Sew dividers.
Measure from the cable to the floor. Add 8 inches to this measurement for curtain length. Determine number of fabric widths needed for each curtain, with fullness twice the width needed. Cut fabric for curtains. Hem each side with double ½-inch seams and the top and bottom edges with double 2-inch seams.

5. Hang dividers.
Pinch the curtain rings to open them and attach the curtain. Place a ring every 8 to 12 inches. If you find you need to add rings, simply loosen the turnbuckle, unhook it, and add rings. If you install a second cable that runs perpendicular to the first, position it about ½-inch down the wall so the rings will slide past each other.

Mood Rings

The simple clip curtain rings shown allow for all sorts of creative fabric possibilities. If a divider is to separate sibling roommates, a double-sided fabric, such as thermal fleece, can lend privacy and give each a unique color scheme. Designate a hangout area with a funky shower curtain in a sheer pattern, glitter design, or an opaque metallic finish. Use sheer fabrics, from netting to bridal lace, to set apart a sleeping haven. Sew stylish touches, such as strings of beads or feather boas, to any of these options. Best of all, dividers can be changed as a child's tastes change. Simply clip new ones into place.

GUM BALL FOOTSTOOL

Often the most enjoyable projects are those that can't be purchased. This unique gum ball footstool cover certainly fits into that category. Made of hundreds of colorful pom-poms glued to a simple slipcover, this project transforms a plain wooden footstool into a real conversation piece. With a little help on the slipcover, a middle schooler can more than handle gluing on the pom-poms.

Multicolored pom-poms give the footstool a light-hearted gumball look. A simpler color scheme of white and blue creates a fanciful cloudlike feel. The sizes of the pom-poms provide variation as well—different sizes of pom-poms lend a variegated effect, while identically sized pom-poms would produce a cloudlike smoothness. Either approach feels great on the feet.

The footstool makes a comforting addition to a bedroom or a fun kid's-only addition to a family room. And it's more than just a footstool: Kids can lean over the top while watching TV or use it with a low table to complete their homework.

YOU'LL NEED

TIME: About 2 hours for a 10"×10"×14" footstool.
SKILLS: Moderate sewing skills.
TOOLS: Bread knife, measuring tape, scissors, straight pins, sewing machine.
MATERIALS: 1 yard cotton muslin, 1¼ yards denim (or other heavy-weight fabric), thread, foam to cover footstool about 10"×10"×14", about 1,500 pom-poms in a variety of sizes and colors, fabric glue.

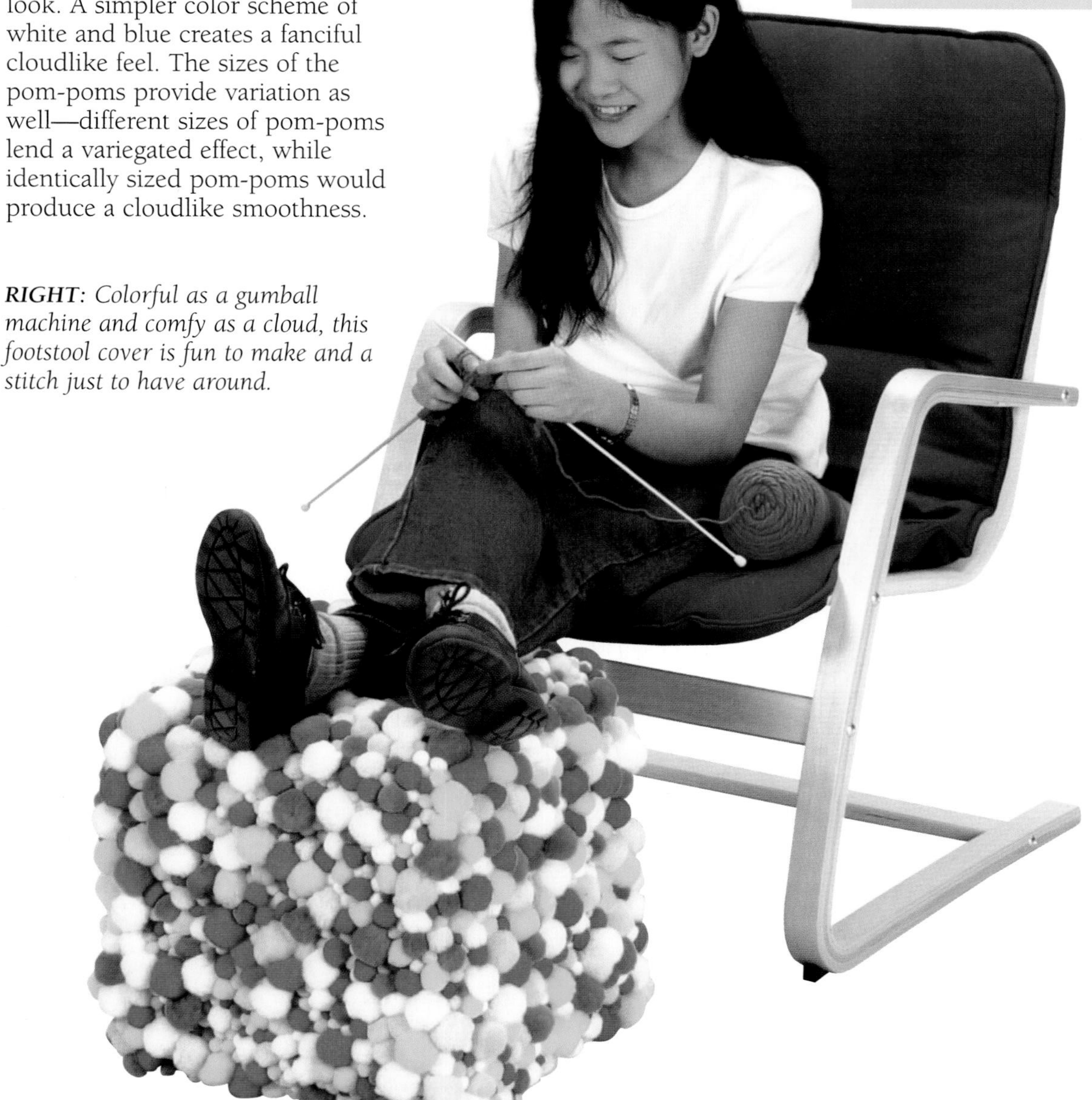

RIGHT: *Colorful as a gumball machine and comfy as a cloud, this footstool cover is fun to make and a stitch just to have around.*

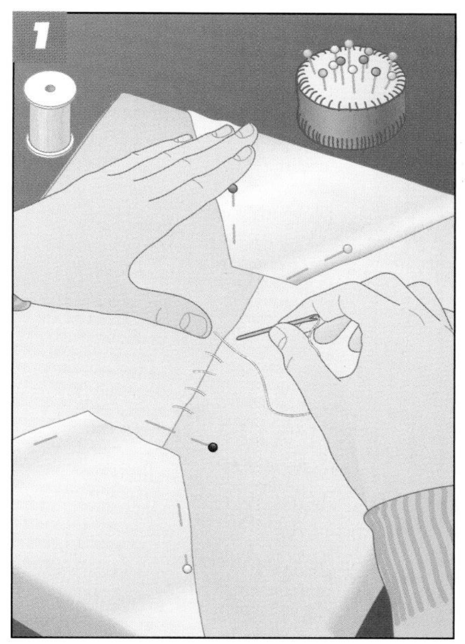

1. Cover the pad.
Using a bread knife (see page 11), cut a square of 2- or 3-inch-thick foam rubber to fit the top of your wooden footstool. Wrap the foam in muslin as though you were wrapping a package. Pin and then tack the ends with large stitches.

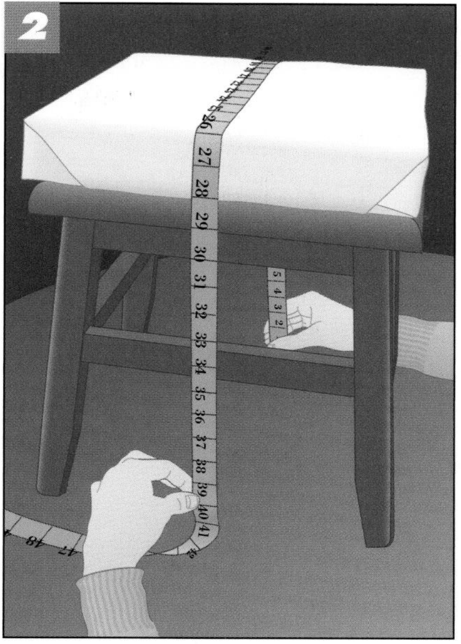

2. Measure for the cover.
Measure the footstool with the foam pad in place. From the floor and go over the top down to the floor again. Add 4 inches for the hems. Using that measurement cut a square of heavyweight fabric.

3. Pin the side seams.
Drape the cover fabric inside out over the top of the footstool, making certain that it is even. Fold the corners of each side together; pin as shown. Remove the cover; using your pins as a guide, sew each side, taking out the pins as you come to them.

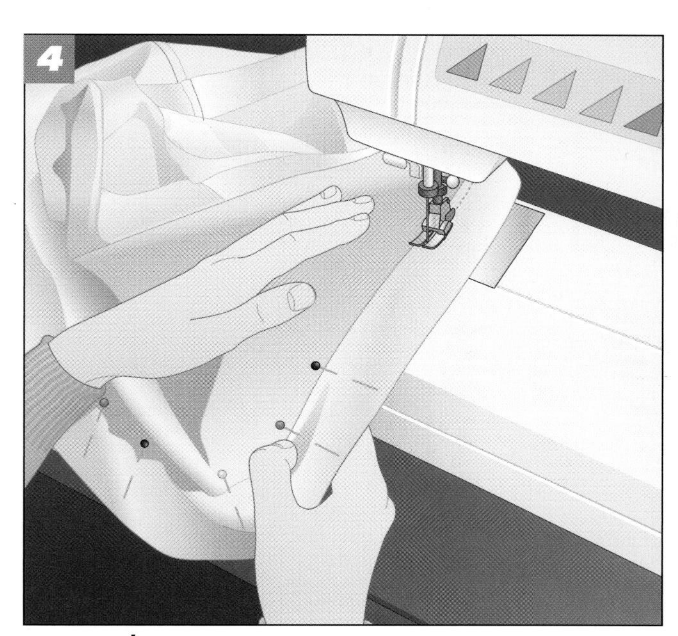

4. Hem the cover.
Cut off the excess fabric at each corner, leaving a ½-inch seam allowance. Iron a 2-inch hem, turning under the raw edge ¼ inch. Pin the hem and sew with matching thread. Tip: When sewing a heavyweight fabric, such as denim, use a needle in your sewing machine made for heavyweight fabric and stitch slowly over the seams.

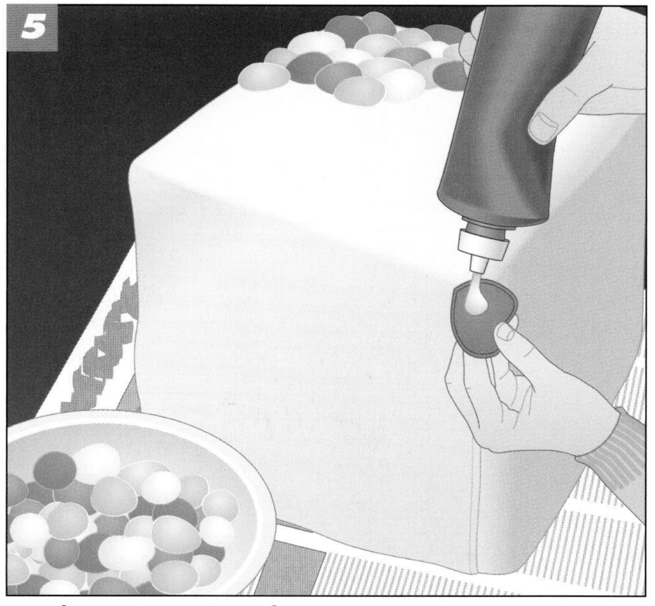

5. Glue pom-poms to the cover.
Place a dollop of fabric glue on a pom-pom and press it on the cover. (Or pour glue into a disposable lid and dip each pom-pom into the glue.) Add more pom-poms, gluing them close to each other until all the fabric is covered. Vary the size and colors of the pom-poms. Let it dry before you put your feet up.

MADE IN THE SHADE

Romantic as a soft spring night, the moon and stars on this lampshade softly glow through a deep blue sky. Adaptable to any size smooth-surfaced, white or off-white lampshade, it can add a truly personal touch to a child's bedroom. Glass beads set over the star cutouts are an added dimension. Otherworldly minded children might want to decorate planets, a spaceship, or even a flying saucer.

YOU'LL NEED

TIME: About 2 hours.
SKILLS: Moderate drawing skills.
TOOLS: Hobby knife, cutting mat, scissors, clothespins, small cutting pliers, pencil, straight pin, paintbrush.
MATERIALS: Lampshade, rickrack trim, tracing paper, a piece of heavy blue paper, spray adhesive, white glue, 20 glass or plastic beads, jewelry wire, spray glitter.

ABOVE: Delicate beaded curlicues dangle starlike beads near a waxing moon. ***RIGHT:*** *Bedecked with a storybook nighttime sky, this lampshade transforms a plain bedside lamp into a keepsake.*

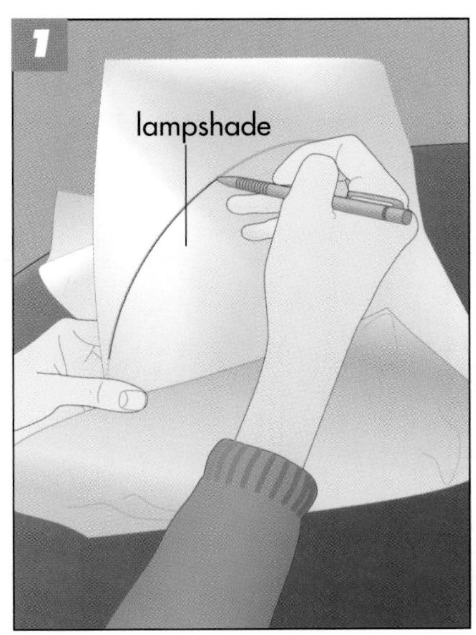

1. Make a template.
Wrap a lampshade with a large piece of white tracing paper. Trace the outline of the lampshade, and cut out along the top and bottom lines. Wrap the template around the shade again, and fold the overlap to make a straight seam. Add a ½-inch overlap and cut out.

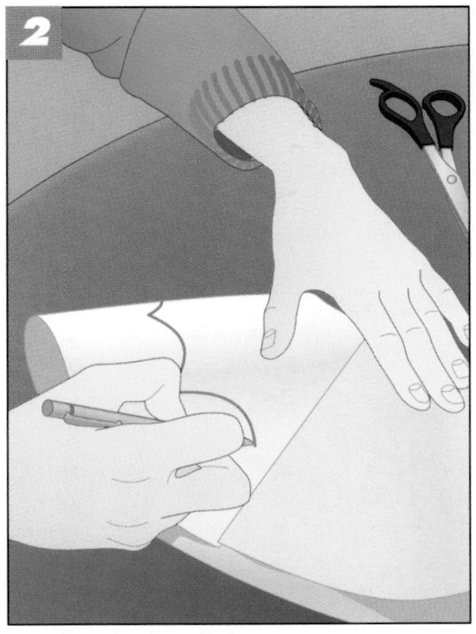

2. Sketch cloud shapes.
Lay the template flat and sketch cloud shapes so the tops of the clouds will be 2 to 4 inches above the bottom edge of the shade. Turn the template over, align the seam (shown), and continue sketching the cloud motif. Cut out the template with scissors.

3. Transfer pattern to blue paper.
Lay the shade template on top of a large sheet of heavyweight blue paper, and trace the cloud outline. Sketch a crescent moon and stars in the sky. Cut out the cloud forms with scissors.

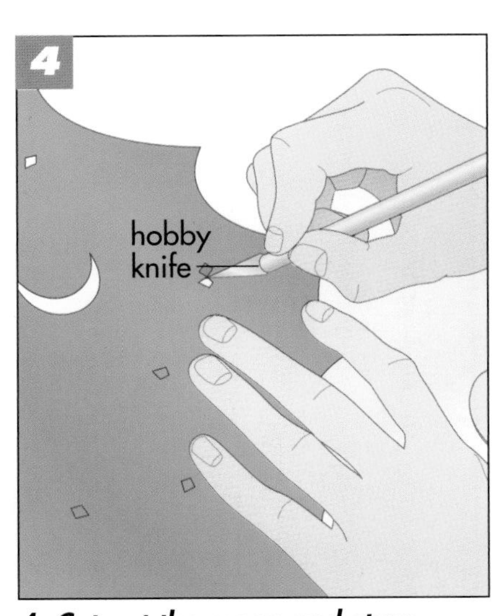

4. Cut out the moon and stars.
Using a hobby knife on a cutting mat, cut out the crescent moon and star shapes. In a well-ventilated area, spray the back side of the blue paper with spray-mount adhesive. Check the label on the can for how long to let the adhesive dry. Wrap the paper around the shade, overlapping the straight edge.

5. Glue rickrack to the edges.
Dust the shade with spray glitter. Glue rickrack along the top and bottom edges. Hold the rickrack with clothespins while it dries. Use a straight pin to poke two holes in each star for beading.

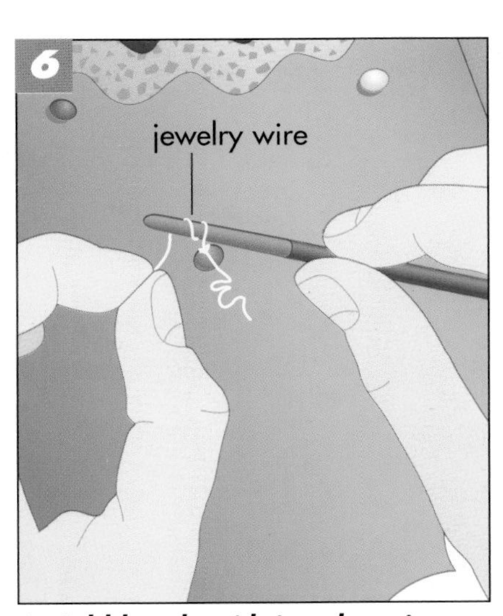

6. Add beads with jewelry wire.
Push jewelry wire in one hole and back out the other. Trim wires so two 3-inch lengths are left. Place a bead on one end of the wire, then thread the other length of wire back through the bead in the opposite direction. Pull snugly. Coil the leftover wire around a paintbrush and carefully remove the brush.

WORK SPACE STATION

If you have a computer-savvy youngster in your house, this colorful, mod workstation provides a welcome control central. Made of medium-density fiberboard (MDF) and readily available plumbing parts, this workstation goes together quickly.

This is a flexible and forgiving project. You can follow the pattern on page 102 to draw out the desk and the monitor shelf, or expand the desk to suit your child's needs, using the pattern as a guide only.

***BELOW:** The dimensions of this free-form workstation reflect a standard desk height of 30 inches.*

YOU'LL NEED

TIME: About 6 hours, not including painting.

SKILLS: Moderate carpentry skills.

TOOLS: Drywaller's T square, framing square, or other straightedge; pencil; felt-tip marker; saber saw; coarse file, router, or belt sander; drill; 2-inch hole-cutting saw; ¼-inch drill bit; screwdriver; adjustable wrench or socket wrench; sandpaper; painting tools.

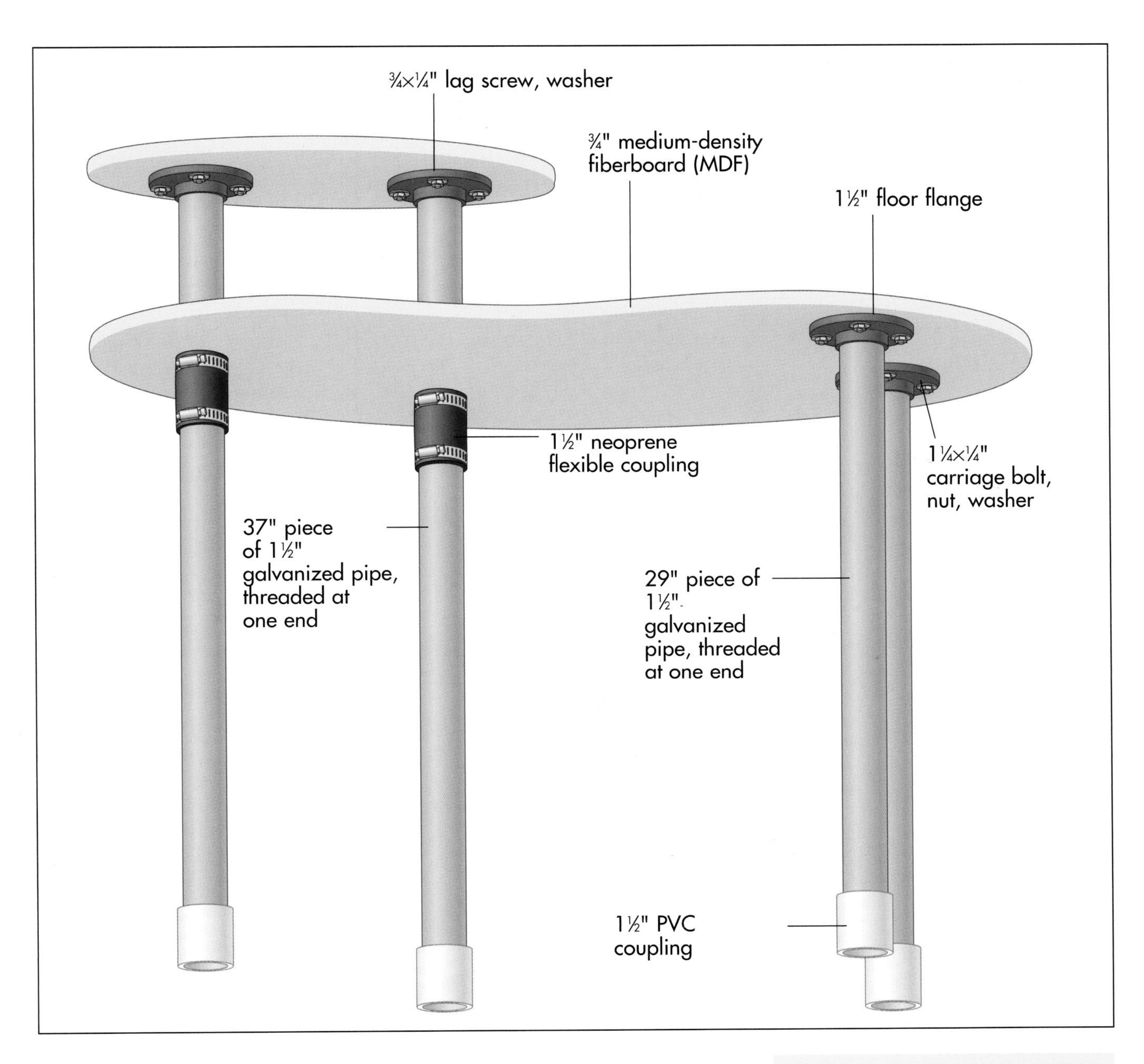

This workstation has a desk surface and monitor shelf made of medium-density fiberboard (MDF) to which flanges attach to hold the 1½-inch galvanized pipe legs. Neoprene flexible couplings support the desk surface beneath the monitor shelf. PVC couplings fasten on the legs to keep the pipes from marring the floor.

Your local home center or lumberyard may have 4×4 pieces of ¾-inch MDF available. If not, have them cut a 4×8 sheet into two 4×4s for easy transport. Full sheets are heavy and, because MDF sheets are actually 49×97 inches, are big enough to tax the cargo bay of any minivan.

Most home centers and hardware stores will cut and thread pipe for you. Let them know you are using the pipe for desk legs and ask for clean, smoothly galvanized pieces. Once the pieces are cut and threaded, be wary of the oil that these pipes will shed—a byproduct of threading. Stand the pipes upright over a rag overnight; the next day, clean the pipes with mineral spirits.

Use tinted primer on the MDF if you are using dark colors (see page 87). Apply several coats of paint for a durable finish.

MATERIALS

4×4-foot, ¾" medium-density fiberboard (MDF)
Two 29" pieces of 1½" galvanized pipe, threaded at one end
Two 37" pieces of 1½" galvanized pipe, threaded at one end
Eight ¼" ×1¼" carriage bolts, washers, and nuts
Eight ¼"×¾" lag screws, washers
Four 1½" floor flanges
Two 1½" flexible couplings
Four 1½" PVC couplings
Primer and paint

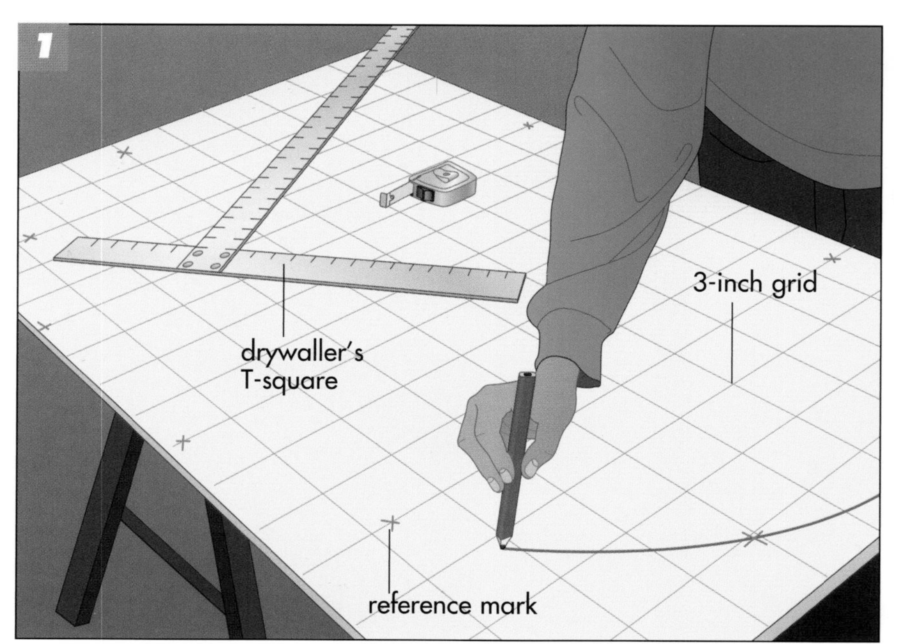

1. Mark the top.
Lay two 2×4s across sawhorses so the sheet of MDF is solidly supported. Using a drywaller's T square (shown) or a framing square or other straightedge, mark a grid of 3-inch squares. Transfer the pattern shown on page 102. Begin by making reference marks where the outline of the project crosses an intersection of grid lines. Then lightly sketch the desktop. Use broad, sweeping strokes so the curves of the shape are smooth.

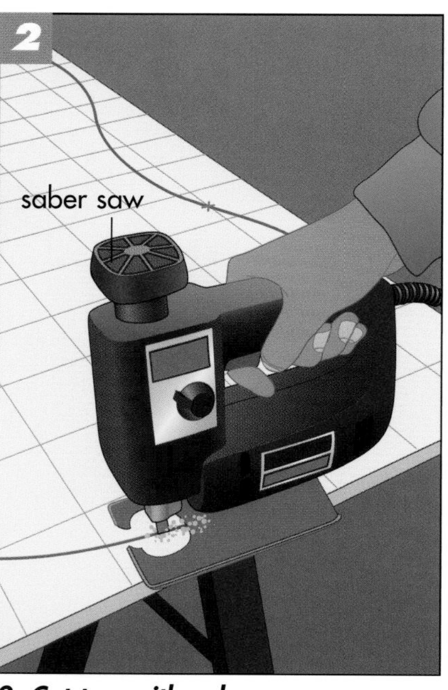

2. Cut top with saber saw.
With a felt-tip marker, draw a single cutline. Cut the shape using a saber saw with a 00 blade.(See page 106 for how to use a saber saw.) Cut smooth curves even if you deviate from the cut line slightly.

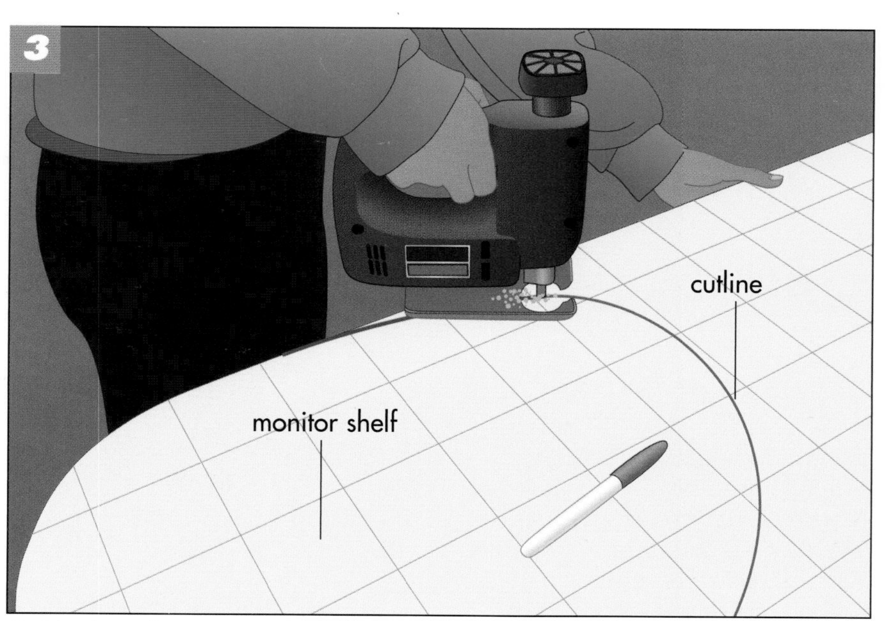

3. Mark and cut monitor shelf.
On the remaining scrap, sketch the shape of the desk shelf and mark a cutline. Position the scrap on 2×4s on the sawhorses, and cut out the shelf using the saber saw. As with the desktop, the exact size of the piece is not critical. If the saw blade wanders slightly from the cutline, don't make an abrupt adjustment; instead, go for a smooth shape.

MEASUREMENTS

Desk and Monitor Shelf Height

To determine the ideal height for the desk and monitor shelf, have your child sit in the desk chair that will be used with the work space station. Adjust the chair so the user's feet are flat on the floor. The desk height should allow the forearms to be level or tilted up slightly when using the keyboard. The monitor shelf should be high enough that the top of the monitor screen is at or just below eye level. When positioning the monitor, tip the screen upward slightly to avoid glare.

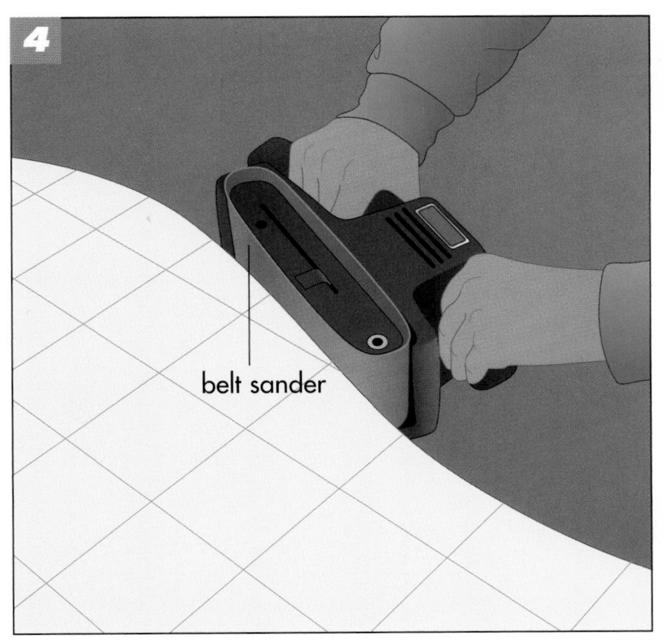

4. Round, smooth edges.
Use a coarse file (see page 66), a router (see page 107), or a belt sander (shown) to smooth and round out the edges of the desktop and the monitor shelf. As with the cutting, aim for smooth, flowing curves, even if they vary somewhat from the pattern shape.

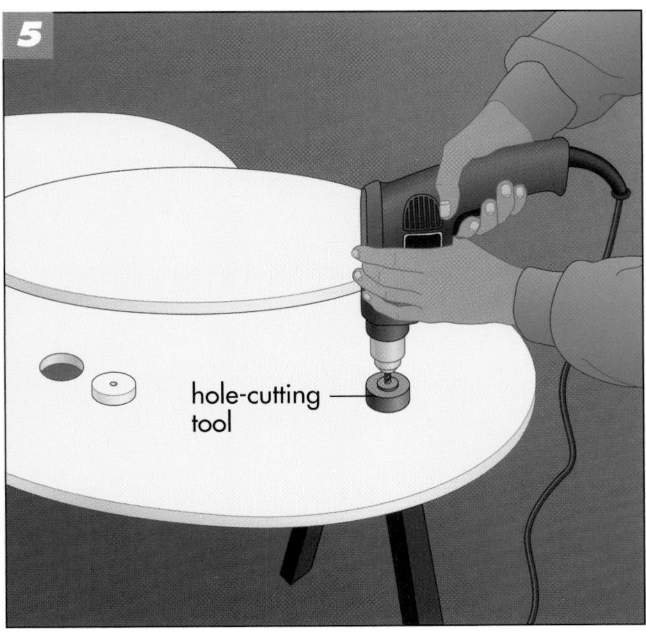

5. Bore leg holes.
Check the pattern and mark the centers of the holes for the shelf supports. Use a power drill with a hole-cutting tool to bore 2-inch holes (1½-inch pipe has an outside diameter of just under 2 inches). Lightly sand the edges of the holes.

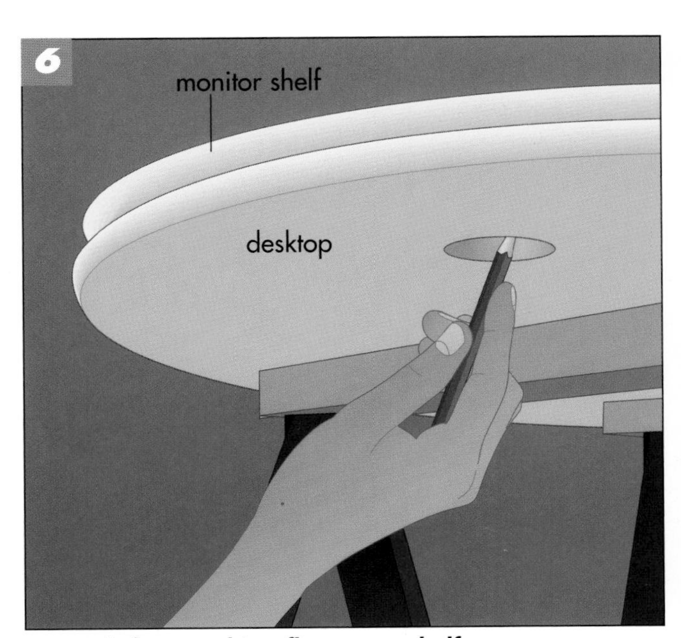

6. Mark for attaching flanges to shelf.
Set the monitor shelf on top of the desktop, positioning its edge so it matches that of the desktop. With a standard pencil, carefully mark the location of each floor flange. Flip the shelf over and set a flange in place to mark each of the bolt holes. Drill 3/16-inch holes ½ inch deep. Fasten each flange with ¾×¼-inch lag screws and washers.

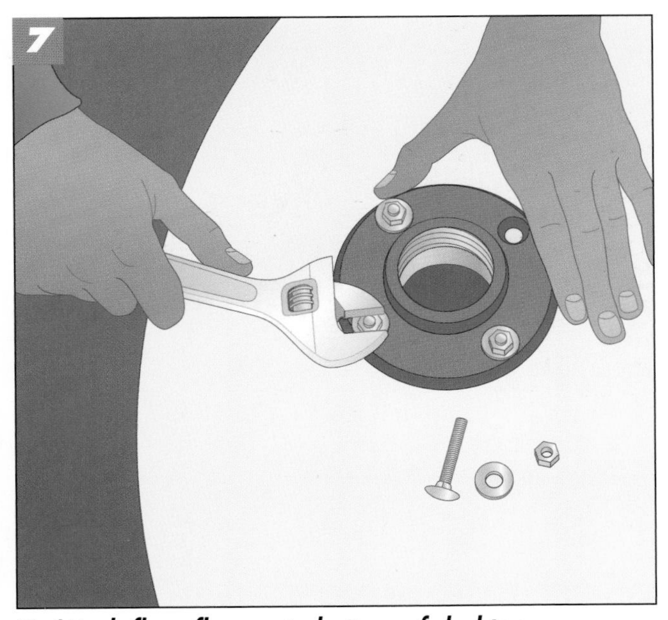

7. Attach floor flanges to bottom of desktop.
Flip the desktop so it is bottom up. Set a floor flange over a hole in the desktop and mark for drilling the bolt holes. Drill ¼-inch holes for each flange. Push in ¾×¼-inch lag screws from underneath, tapping them with a hammer to set the head into the board. Add washers and nuts, and tighten.

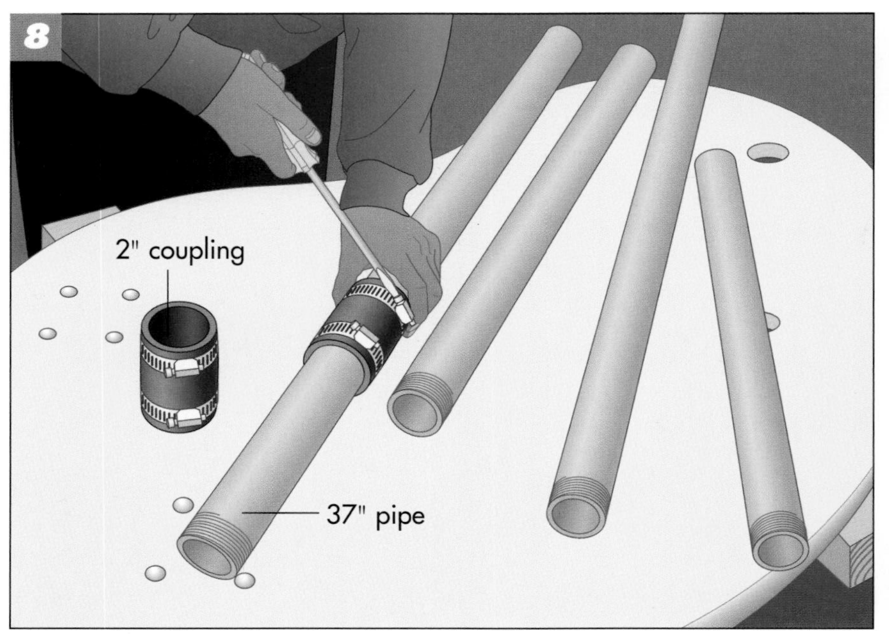

8. Get pipe cut; add clamps.
Have four sections of galvanized 1½-inch pipe cut to size. For a standard-height desk, ask for two cut 37 inches long, and two cut 29 inches long. Have one end of each pipe threaded. Slip a 1½-inch flexible coupling loosely onto each of the long legs. (You may have to loosen the screws to slide it into place.) Position the top of the coupling so it's even with the top of one of the short legs. Tighten both adjustable rings.

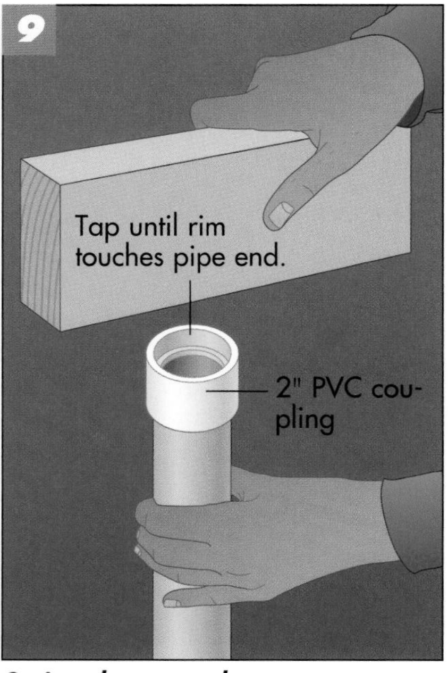

9. Attach caps to legs.
On the unthreaded end of each leg, set a 2-inch PVC pipe connector. Tap it in place with a piece of 2×4 until the rim inside the connector touches the threads. (Don't use a hammer—you'll crack the plastic.)

EXPERTS' INSIGHT

GETTING PIPE CUT

Most hardware stores or home centers will have 1½-inch galvanized pipe in stock. For a small fee, they will cut and thread the pipe to the dimensions you specify. Mention that you are using the pipe for a desk project and ask for clean and unmarred sections of pipe. No allowance for the threads is necessary—the total length of the pipe, threads included, will be the final length of each leg. Expect a wait while the pipe is cut and threaded—you might want to call in your order in advance.

10. Screw pipe into the flanges.
Flip the desk top upside down. Set a pipe leg in the flange, checking that it is perpendicular to the surface before you twist it. Turn the pipe clockwise. Start again if you sense resistance—forcing it may cross-thread the pipe and ruin the joint. Screw the pipe all the way into the flange.

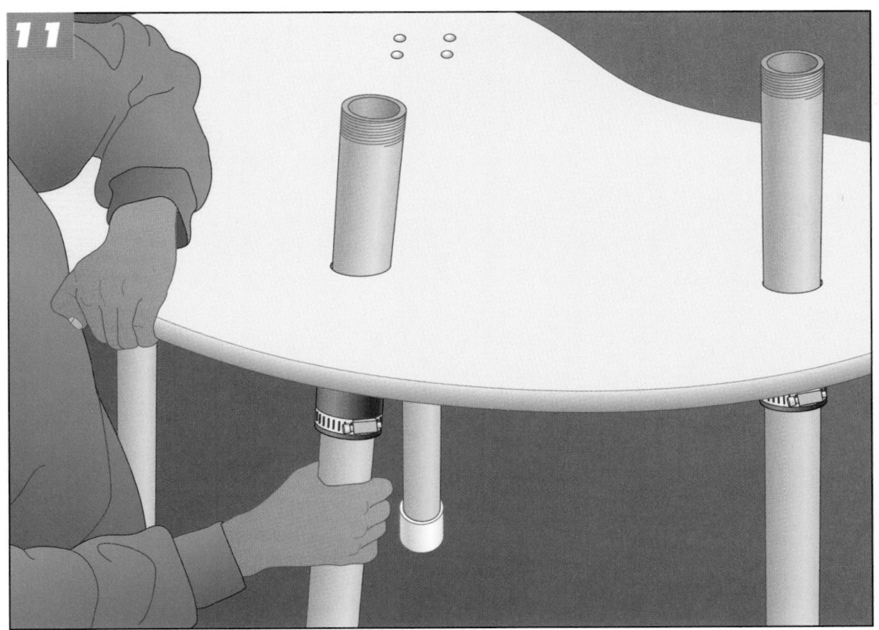

11. Insert the monitor stand legs. With the desk legs attached to their flanges, flip the desk upright. Have the monitor legs handy so you can slip them into their holes. Be careful not to chip the holes as you do so. Slip both monitor legs in place. Check that the desk surface is level; adjust the flexible couplers as needed.

12. Twist legs into shelf. Set the monitor shelf in place, setting both flanges atop their respective legs. Twist the threaded end into each flange, starting slowly to make sure the threads engage. Twist tight.

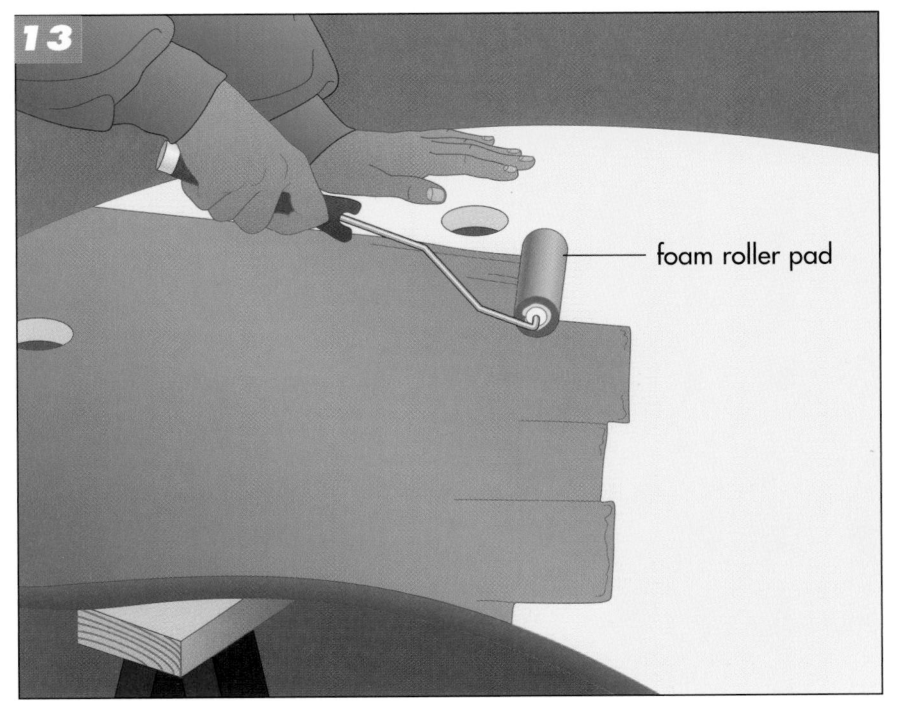

13. Disassemble, prime, paint. Once the desk is complete, disassemble it for painting. For a smooth finish, use a foam roller pad. For intense color, use a tinted primer and several coats of paint, particularly on the absorbent edge of the fiberboard.

PRIMER FOR DARK COLORS

If you intend to use an intense color on your work space station, keep in mind that primers come in colors other than white. A gray primer is a preferable base for a dark color. Or, have your paint supplier provide a tinted primer. While the tinted primer will not be as intense in value as the finish paint, it will save an extra coat or two. For a durable finish, choose an alkyd gloss enamel instead of water-base paint.

CITYSCAPE SCREEN

Two children to a room? This cityscape screen is a kid-friendly (and parent-friendly) alternative to running masking tape down the center of the room. The simple spraypaint technique leaves room for individuality. Each child can paint a separate side of the screen in his or her own color scheme, or use the stenciling method shown here to devise a personalized design.

Purchase a ready-made folding screen, or make one from mahogany-veneer bifold doors available in a variety of widths at home centers. Use the doors full length or cut them down with a circular saw (see page 105). Bifold doors come with three hinges to a pair. Use the middle hinge from each to join the pairs. Lightly sand and prime your screen before stenciling.

BELOW: *Keep peace in a shared room; create a room within a room with this colorful divider.*

YOU'LL NEED

TIME: About 3 hours.
SKILLS: Basic carpentry.
TOOLS: Phillips head screwdriver, hobby knife, ruler, drop cloth.
SUPPLIES: Masking tape, folding screen, three colors of spray paint, 8 pieces of poster board.

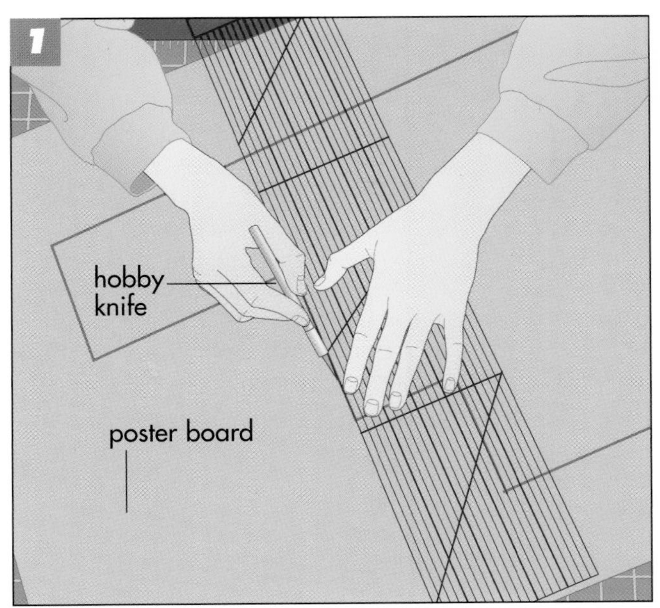

1. Make the stencils.
Using the pattern and measurements shown on page 103. transfer the building forms onto poster board. (Expand the width of each building if your screen panel is larger than 18 inches.) Use a hobby knife and a straightedge to cut the positive image from the background. Create two building stencils for the background, two for the foreground, and one window stencil.

2. Paint the first layer.
Remove the hinges from the screen and prime the panels. Place the sections of the screen next to each other on a drop cloth. Tape the background stencils onto the screen, being sure to secure the openings. Cover all areas that you do not wish to be painted. Use the lightest paint color first, spraying the openings using a circular motion.

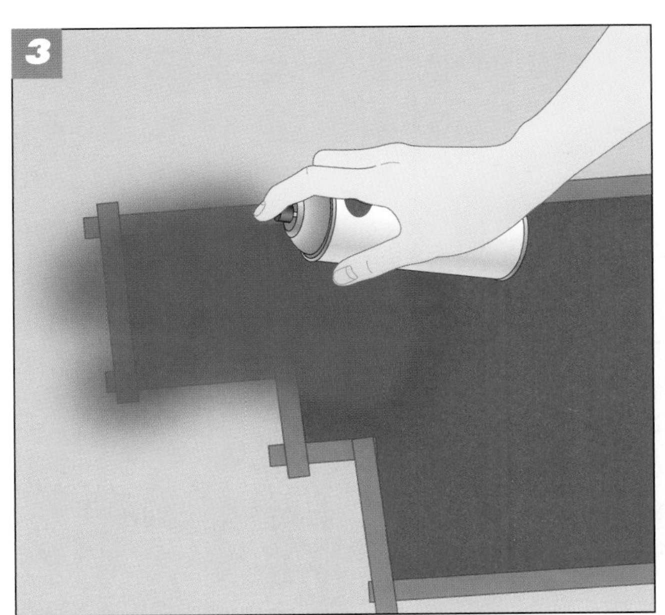

3. Paint the second layer.
When the first coat is completely dry, tape the foreground stencils onto the dry background images. Cover all areas outside the stencil. Spray with the darker color paint.

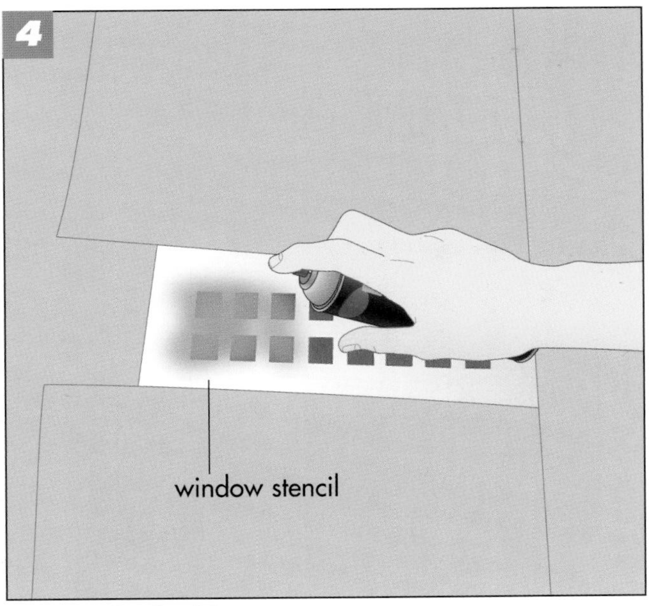

4. Paint the final layer.
Remove all building stencils. Tape the window stencil onto a building. Cover all areas outside the stencil with poster board or newspaper. Spray with silver paint. Let dry, then repeat as desired. Reattach the screen hinges.

HOMEGROWN LOFT

This dorm-room classic can be adapted for the student under your roof. It combines college glamour with space-saving efficiency, putting to dual use about 24 square feet of floor space. The desk is large—about 14 square feet of work area, with 7 feet of shelf above for books or collectibles. The flat surfaces in this example are painted a popular bright blue but any color that suits your child will work. The sturdy PVC can remain white (acetone cleans off the manufacturer's lettering), or painted silver or black for an industrial look.

PVC appears simpler to assemble than it actually is. Work methodically and be prepared to redo some of your work.

This is a sturdy project, but no bed stands up to unlimited roughhousing. Note the warnings about bunk bed safety on page 69—they apply to lofts, too.

YOU'LL NEED

TIME: About 2 days.
SKILLS: Advanced carpentry or PVC plumbing skills.
TOOLS: Tape measure, backsaw or PVC saw, miter box, PVC reamer, felt-tip marker, circular saw, saber saw, variable-speed drill, wooden or rubber mallet; channel-lock pliers; square, coarse file or belt sander or router and corner round bit; sandpaper, clamps.

ABOVE: *With a twin mattress on top and plenty of desk and shelf area below, this loft maximizes floor space.*

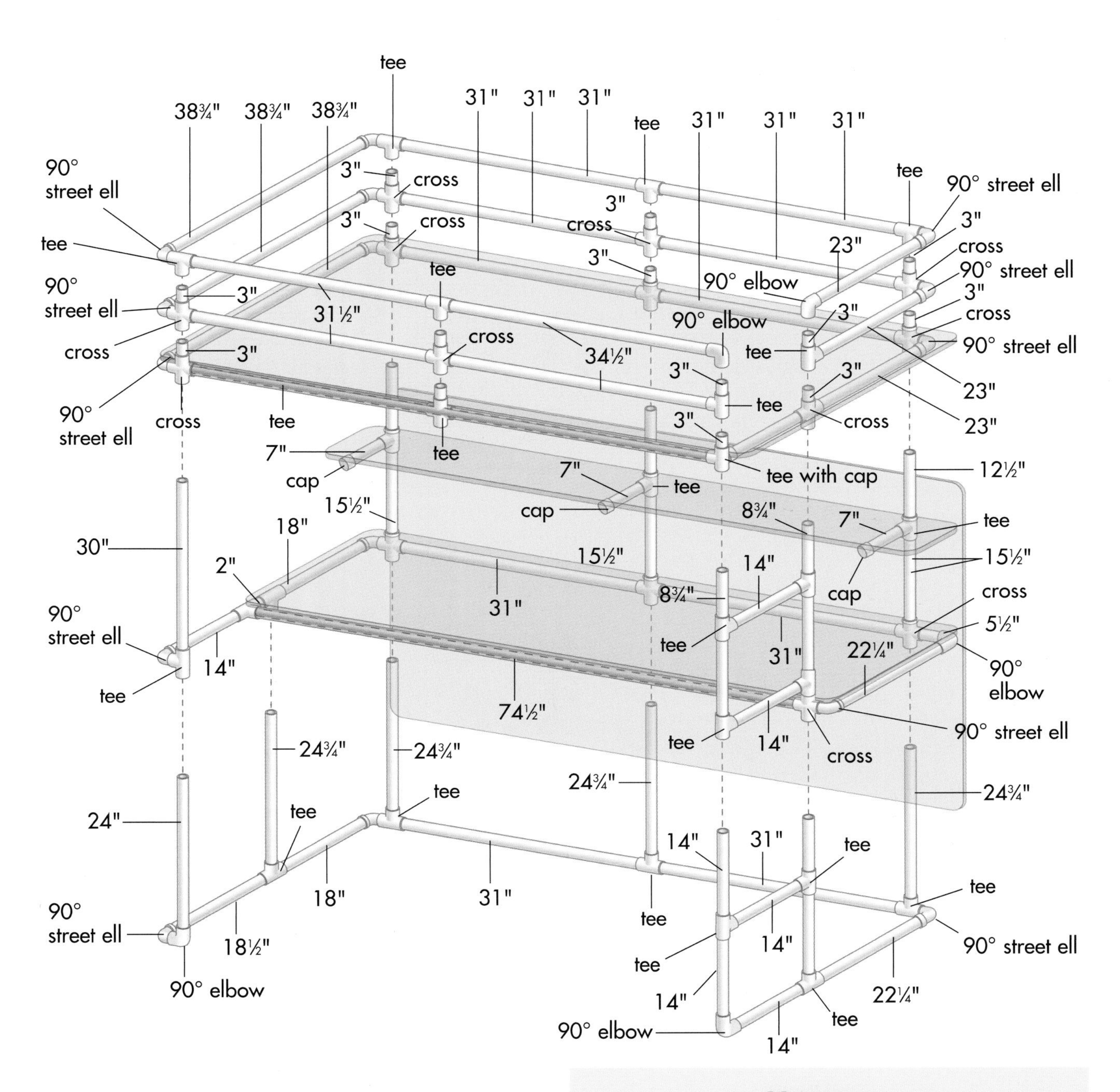

The frame of the loft is made of 1½-inch PVC pipe with a ½-inch plywood base for the bed. The desk surface and shelf are made of ¾-inch medium-density fiberboard (MDF), with a bulletin board of ½-inch plywood. The first stage of assembly—cutting and dry-fitting sections of the frame—is essential to make sure everything joins together, dimensions are consistent, and the project squares up correctly. Work methodically, double-checking measurements. Expect to make mistakes. Fortunately, PVC pipe is inexpensive, and miscut pieces can be replaced. Use the measurements above as a cutting list as you tackle each section.

MATERIALS

- 12 10-foot, 1½" PVC pipes
- 27 1½" PVC tees
- 14 1½" PVC crosses
- 16 1½" PVC 90° street elbows (ells)
- Four 1½" PVC 90° elbows (ells)
- Four 1½" PVC caps
- Two 1¼"×10' metal conduit
- Two 4×8 sheets of ½" AB plywood
- One 49"×97" sheet of ¾" MDF
- 1" and 2½" screws
- Adhesive, primer, paint

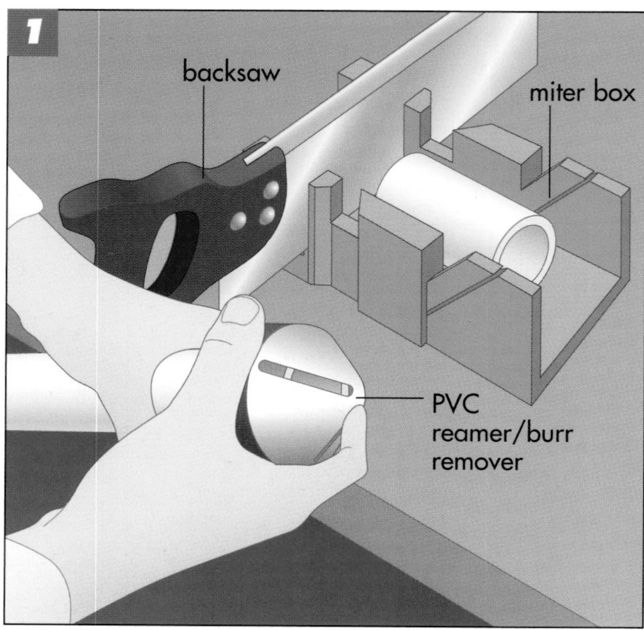

1. Cut and ream edges of PVC.
Because you will assemble the loft frame, mark it, take it apart, and reassemble it as you glue it. Having even cuts and smooth edges is important. Use a sharp backsaw (or a saw designed especially for cutting PVC also works well) and a miter box. Or, use a chop saw (box, *opposite page*) with a combination blade. A reamer/burr-removal tool easily smoothes pipe ends.

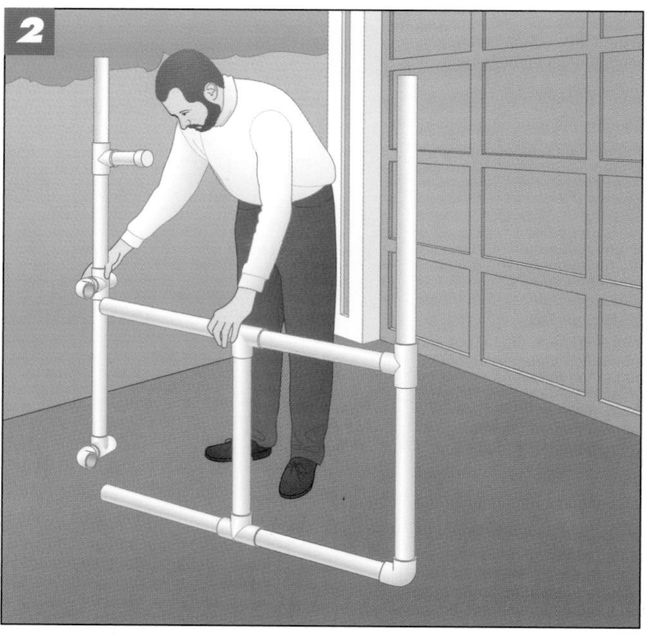

2. Assemble the first side.
Precut the pieces of 1½-inch PVC pipe to the dimensions for this side as shown in the illustration on page 91. As you do so, use a felt-tip marker to mark each piece with its length. Assemble the side without gluing it. Use a wooden or rubber mallet to completely seat each piece into its respective fitting.

3. Assemble the ladder side.
Cut and assemble the pieces of the ladder side of the loft. As you work, some pieces may come apart—this is a sometimes frustrating side effect of dry-fitting. Confirm that the uprights are a consistent length, the same as those of the first side (see Step 2). Inconsistencies might be the result of poorly seated pipe sections or mismeasurement.

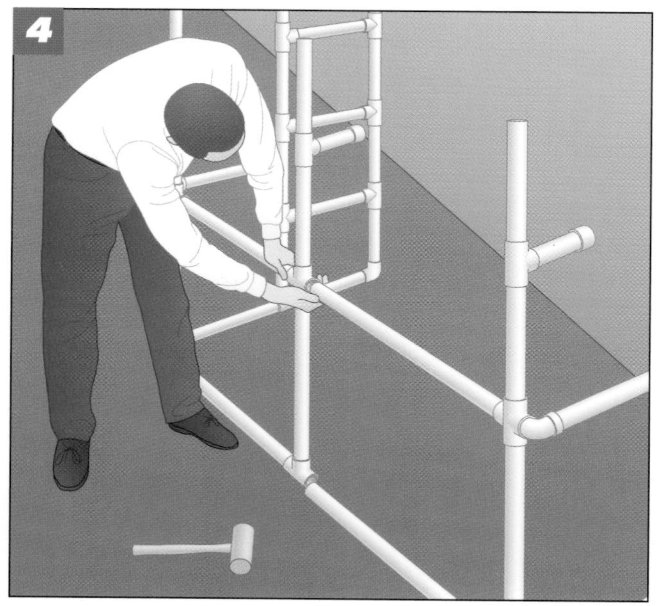

4. Assemble back to ends.
With the two sides assembled, complete the back section. Once the back is pieced together, attach the side sections. (The job will go easier if you have a helper or two holding the sides in place.) Check over the whole project, retapping any joints that may have loosened during assembly.

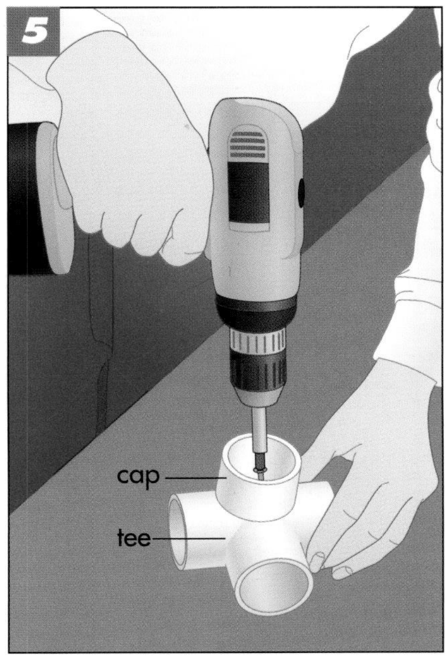

5. Make a custom fitting.
To assemble the bed base, you need to fabricate a custom fitting. With PVC adhesive, glue a 1½-inch PVC cap to a 1½-inch tee as shown. Let it dry for five minutes, and fasten it with a 1-inch all-purpose screw.

6. Assemble bed base.
Cut to size and assemble the base of the bed, using the dimensions shown on page 91. For added support, slip a 10-foot piece of 1¼-inch metal conduit into the section of railing shown. Trim the conduit so it runs from tee to tee fitting. Confirm that the heights of all of the six uprights of the bed are equal. With a helper, lift the base in place and push the fittings onto the uprights. Seat each of the joints.

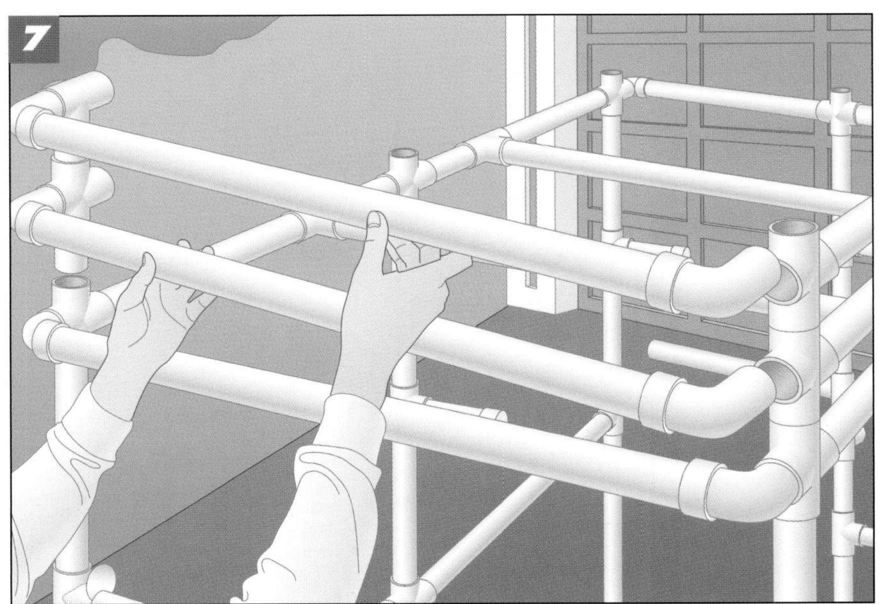

7. Assemble the side railing.
Assemble the side railing in sections before joining it to the overall structure. You can gang-cut the 3-inch pieces (14 pieces are needed in all for the loft) that join the tees and crosses on the uprights of the bed. Note that this design assumes a mattress about 4 inches thick. Your railing should extend 5 inches above the top of the mattress. If you choose to extend your railing, be sure that the opening between the rails is not more than 3½ inches.

EXPERTS' INSIGHT

USING A CHOP SAW

This project requires that you cut more than 60 pieces of PVC. Renting a chop saw can make the job go easier and faster. When you're cutting long pieces, support the full length of the pipe to avoid binding.

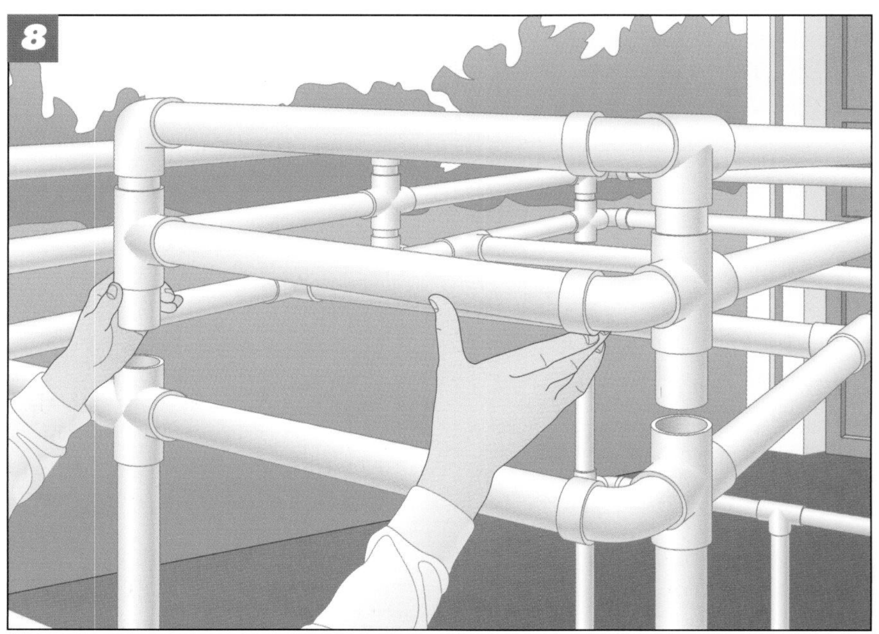

8. Assemble the back rail.
Measure and cut the pieces for the back section of the railing, using the dimensions shown on page 91. When it is complete and in place, review the overall dimensions of the loft. Check that the distance between the side railing posts is 40 inches and that the height of the loft bed is consistent at all four corners. Measure the height of the desk area—is it the same at all four corners? Is the overall length of the bed 77 inches?

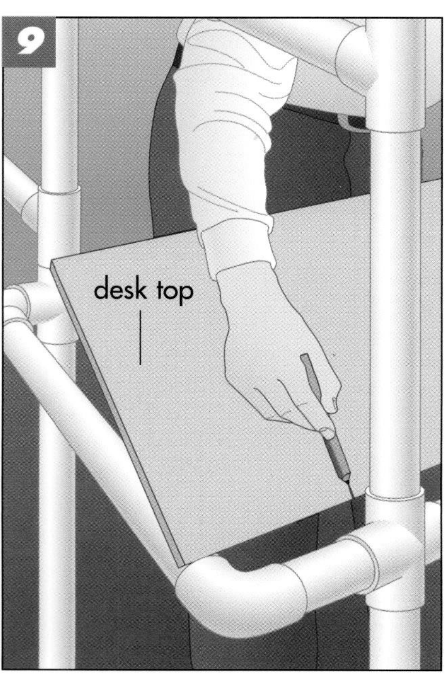

9. Mark desk surface.
Confirm the length and width of the desk surface by measuring the frame. Cut the MDF sheet to size (the scrap will be used for the shelf). Set the piece in place and mark the location of the posts.

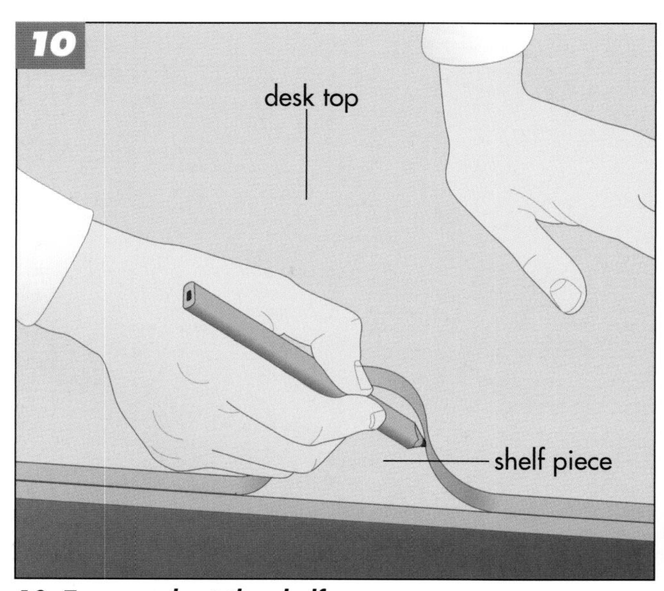

10. Trace and cut the shelf.
Use a soup can to mark each radius on this project. Complete the cutouts using a saber saw (see page 106) and confirm the fit on the frame. Redo any cutouts, leaving enough play so that the desk fits in place easily. Cut a 10-inch-wide strip of MDF for the shelf. Lay the desk top on the shelf piece and transfer the cutouts. Trim the shelf to length and make the cutouts in the shelf.

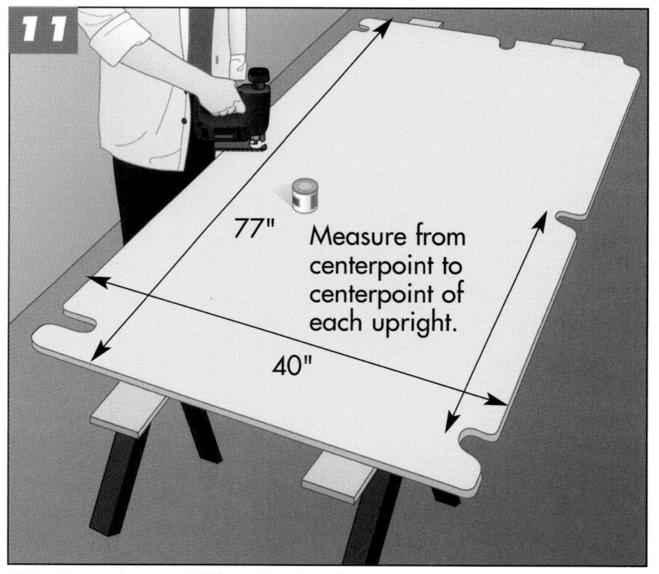

11. Cut plywood for the bed.
Confirm the length and width of plywood for the bed base. The plywood should extend to the outside edge of the bed base frame. Carefully measure the cutouts for the uprights along the sides of the bed base. Make the cutouts with a saber saw, and sand the edges with 100-grit sandpaper.

12. Pound joints.
Remove the desk top, shelf, and plywood bed base. Make a final review of the entire frame, tapping each member fully in place. Measure the height, width, and length of all sides of the complete project, and adjust so that opposite sides are the same dimensions.

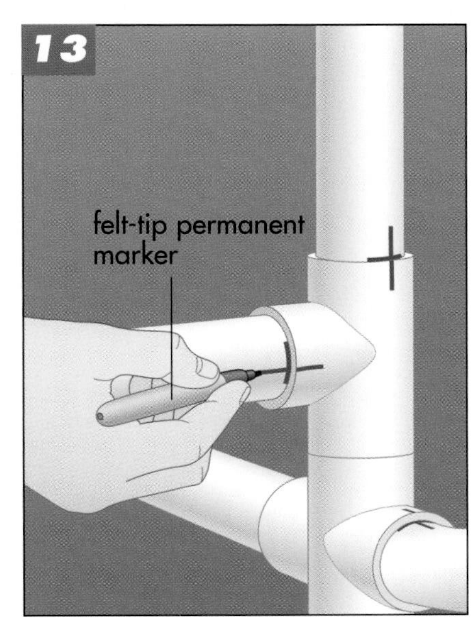

13. Mark all joints.
Make alignment and depth marks on all the pipes and fittings (see box at right). Dismantle one section at a time, laying out the pieces in "exploded" fashion so it will be easy to remember which fittings attach to which pipes.

EXPERTS' INSIGHT

GLUING PVC

It's challanging to glue PVC. The PVC adhesive sets very quickly, leaving you little time to align pieces. Follow these pointers:

- Wipe every joint clean.
- Mark each joint with felt-tip marker to indicate how far each piece of pipe goes into a fitting.
- Make a mark to show how a pipe lines up with the fitting.
- Mark an arrow to indicate which end of the fitting is up.
- Use a carpenter's square to quickly check that you've lined up pieces correctly.
- Have a wooden or rubber mallet handy; you will need to coerce some pipe pieces into their fittings.

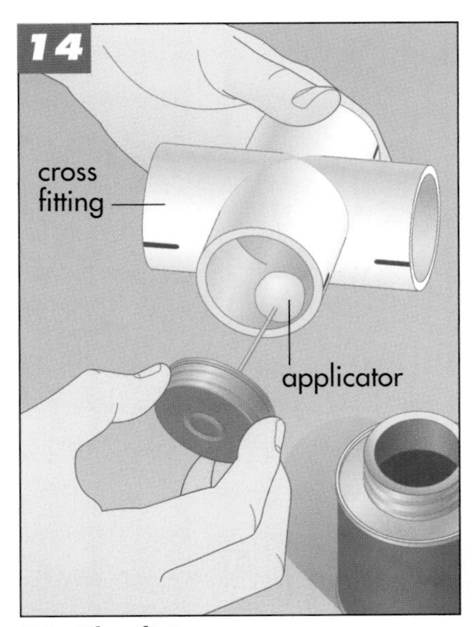

14. Glue fittings.
Using the applicator provided with the container, apply PVC cement inside the socket of each fitting. Insert the pipe and twist it until the marks line up. Work from the bottom of the section up. Glue each section shown in Steps 2, 3, 4, 6, 7, and 8.

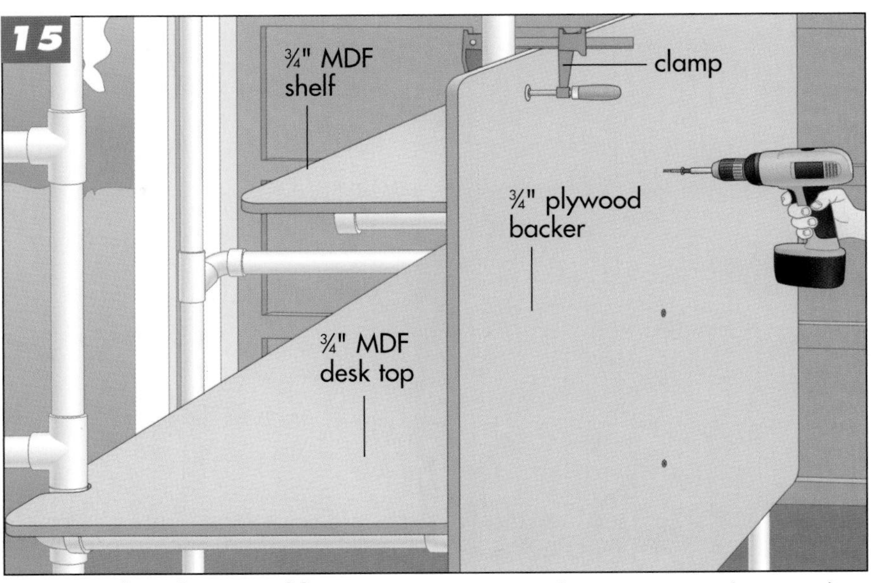

15. Complete the assembly.
Assemble the sections. Drill pilot holes and attach the desk and the shelf from underneath and the backer from behind, using 2½-inch all-purpose screws. When satisfied with their fit, remove the pieces and paint them with alkyd paint. In the bedroom, glue the loft sections (except one rail section) together. Install the bed base, and fasten from above every 2 feet. Glue the final section of railing in place. Use acetone to clean the frame. Push the bed against a wall and fasten the backer board to the framing members at four points with ¼-×3½-inch lag screws.

PROJECT PATTERNS

One square equals 1 inch

A BEDSPREAD THAT GROWS UP (Project on page 18)

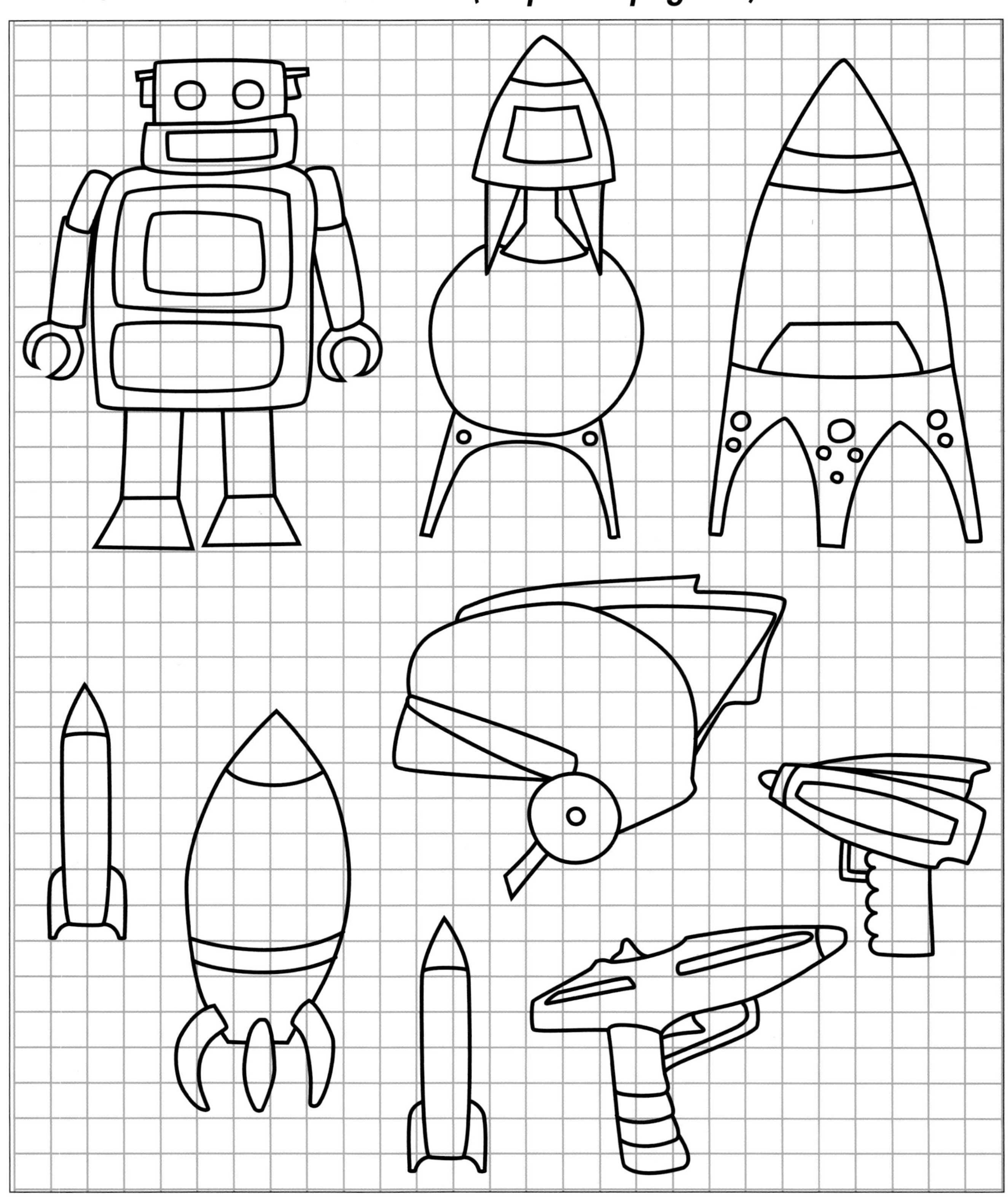

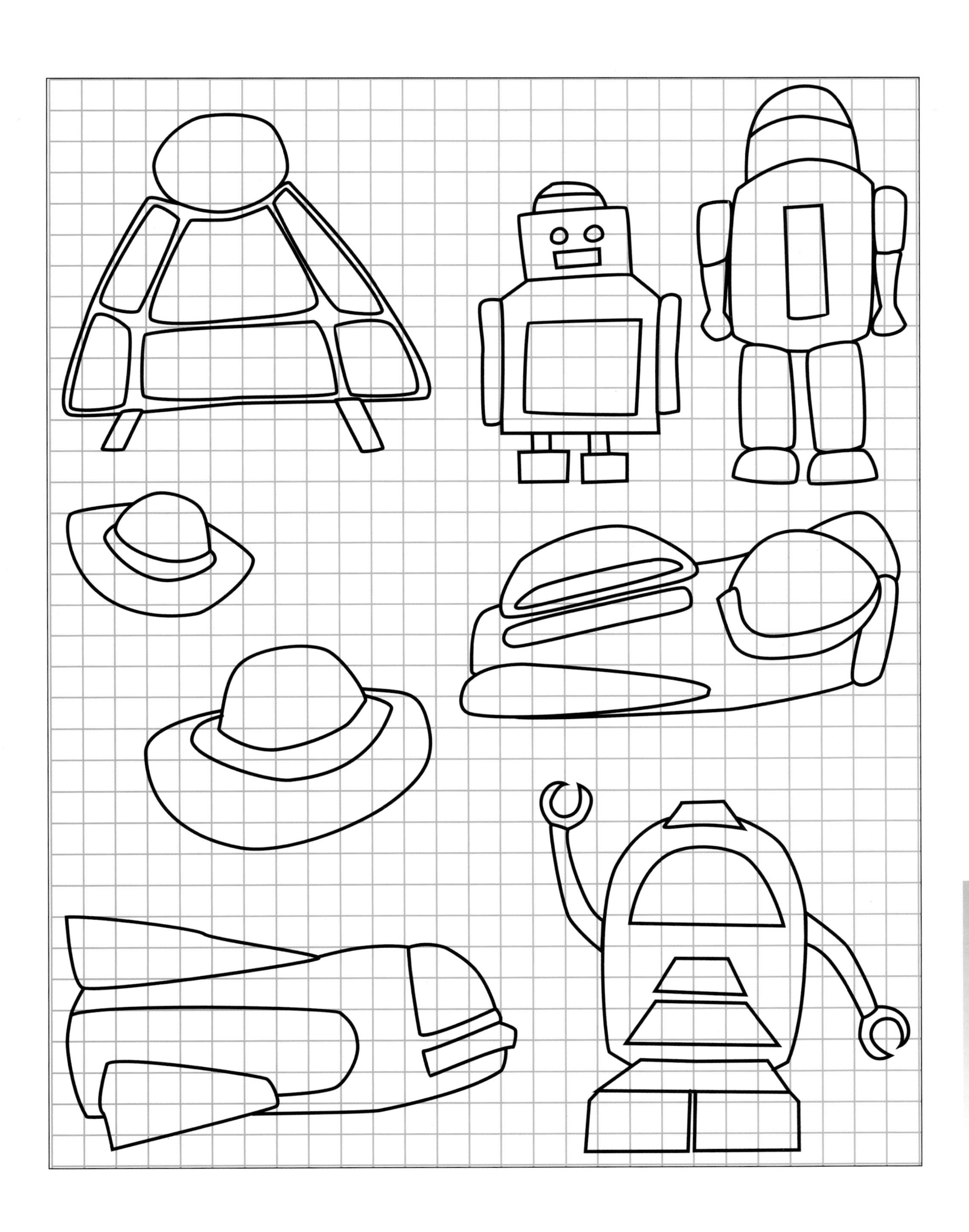

BIG TOP TENT (Project on page 22)

One square equals 2 inches

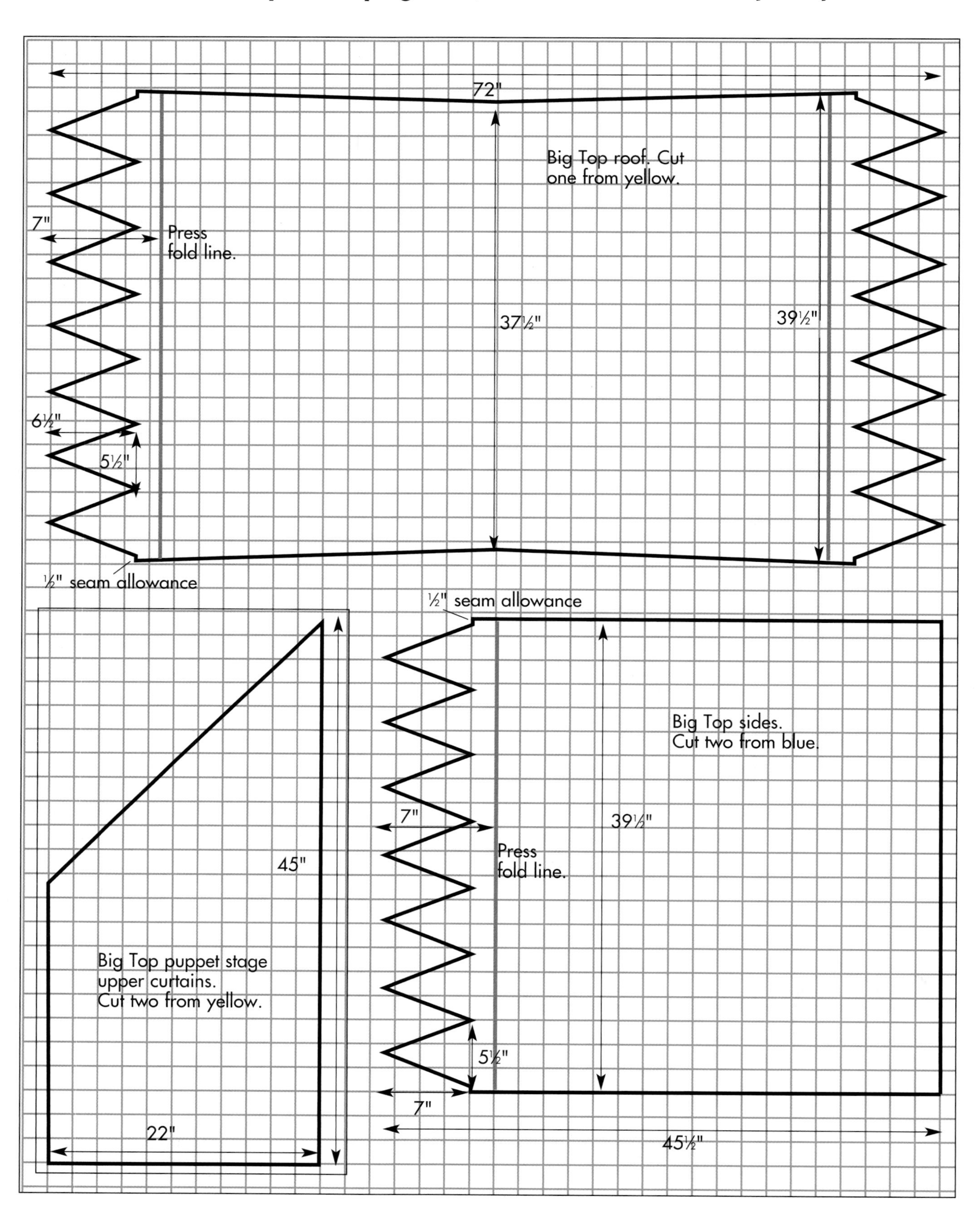

One square equals 2 inches

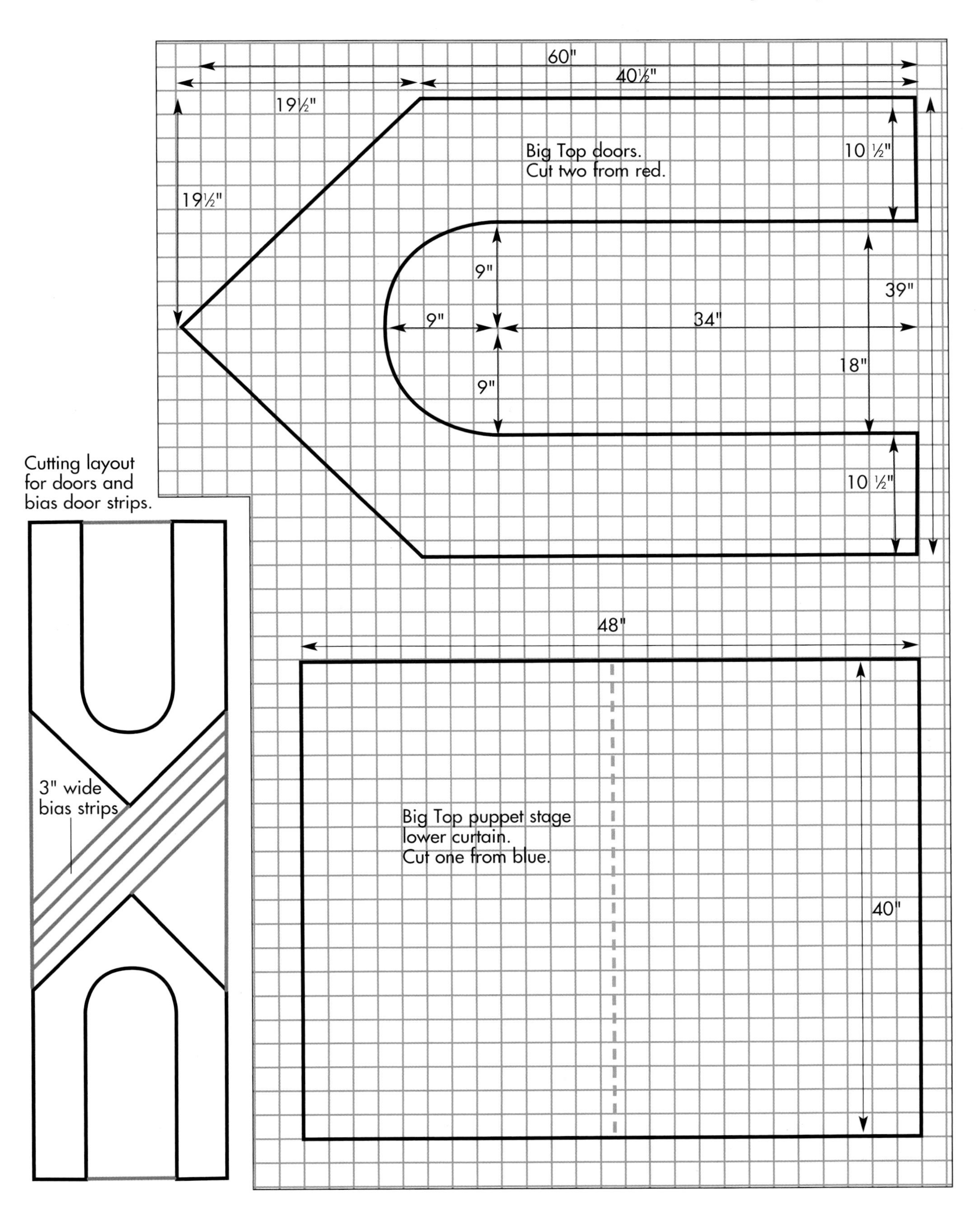

LAUNDRY MONSTER (Project on page 26)

One square equals 1 inch

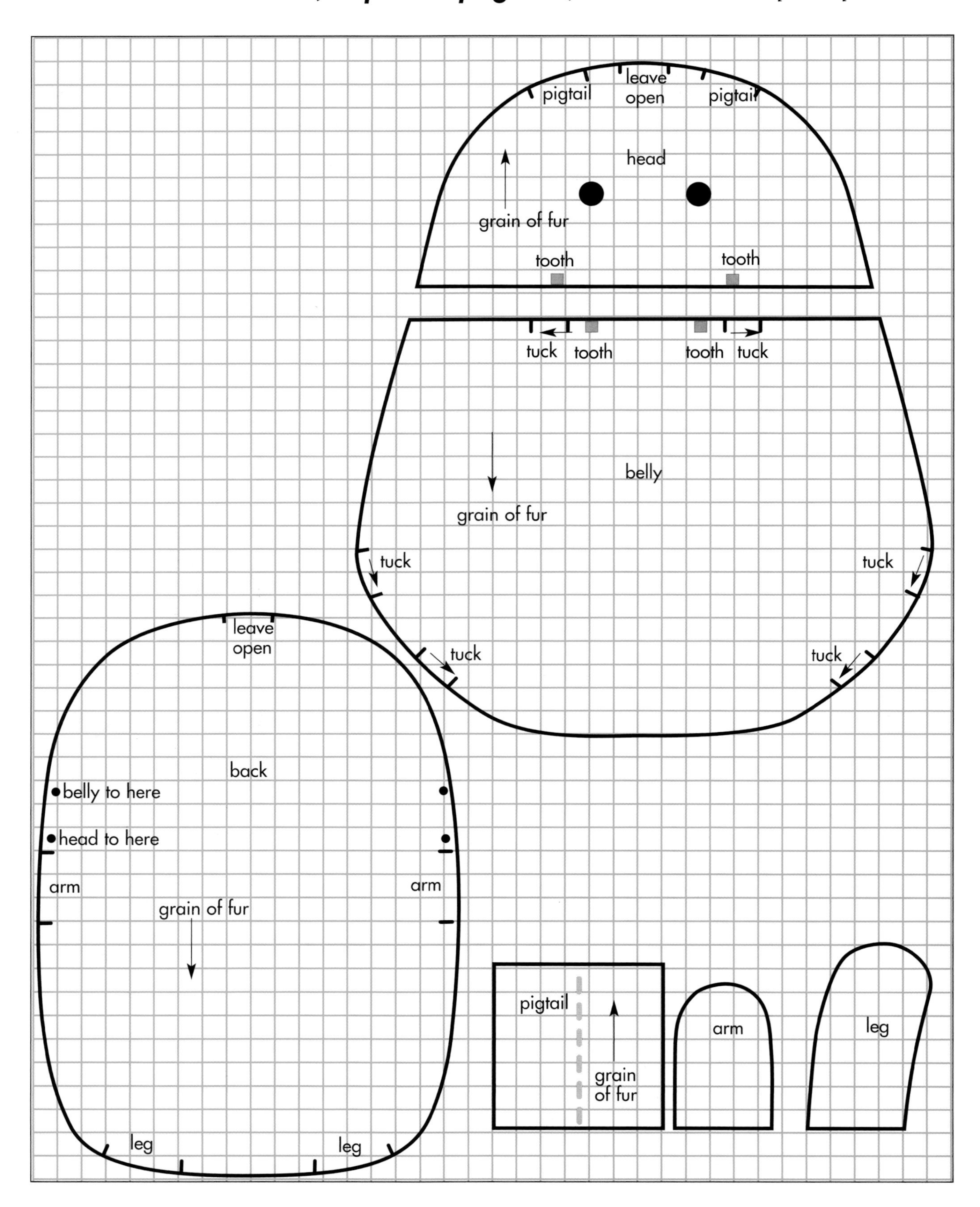

IT'S A JUNGLE IN THE CLOSET (Project on page 58) One square equals 6 inches

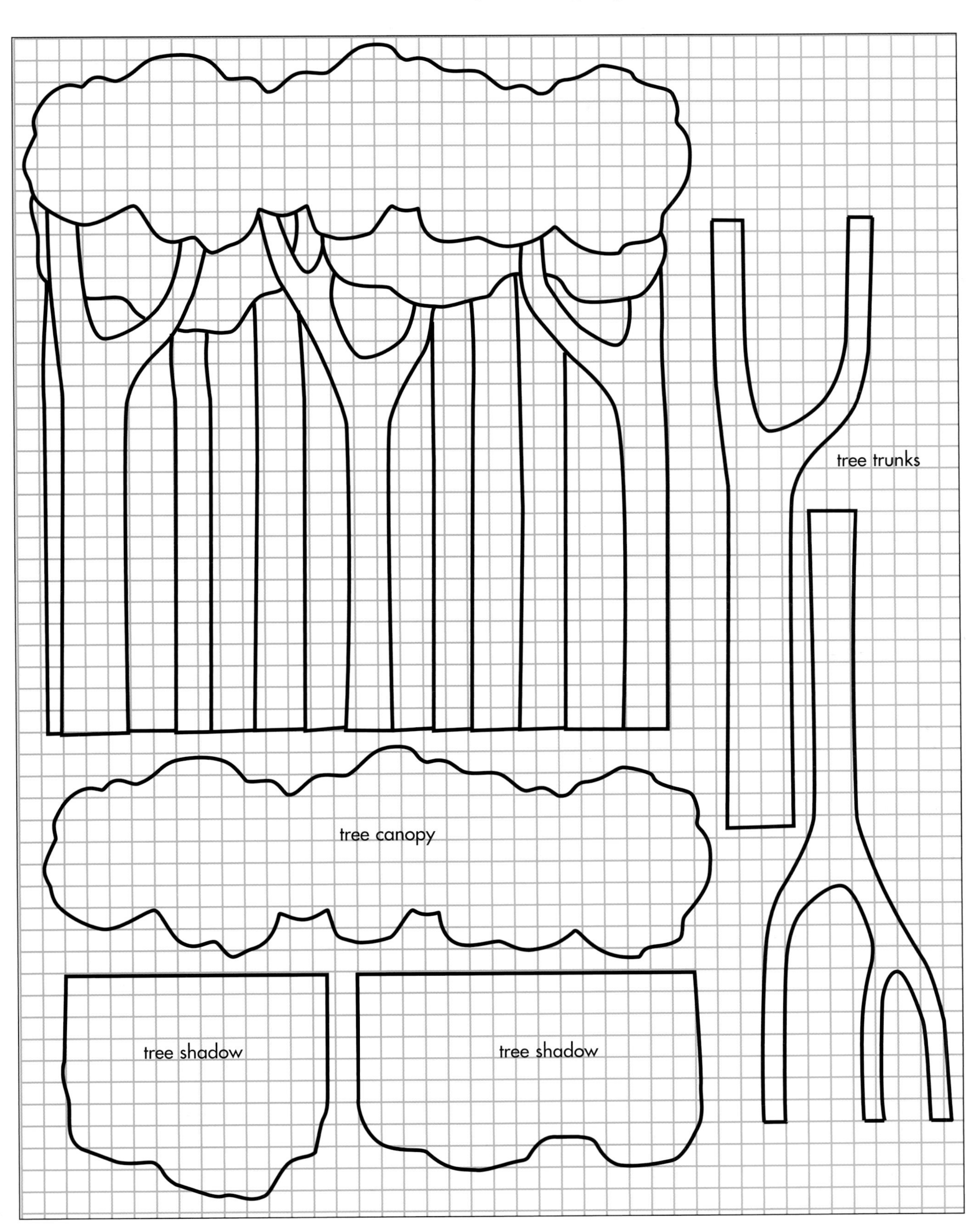

DREAMY DOUBLE-DECKER (Project on page 62)

One square equals 3 inches

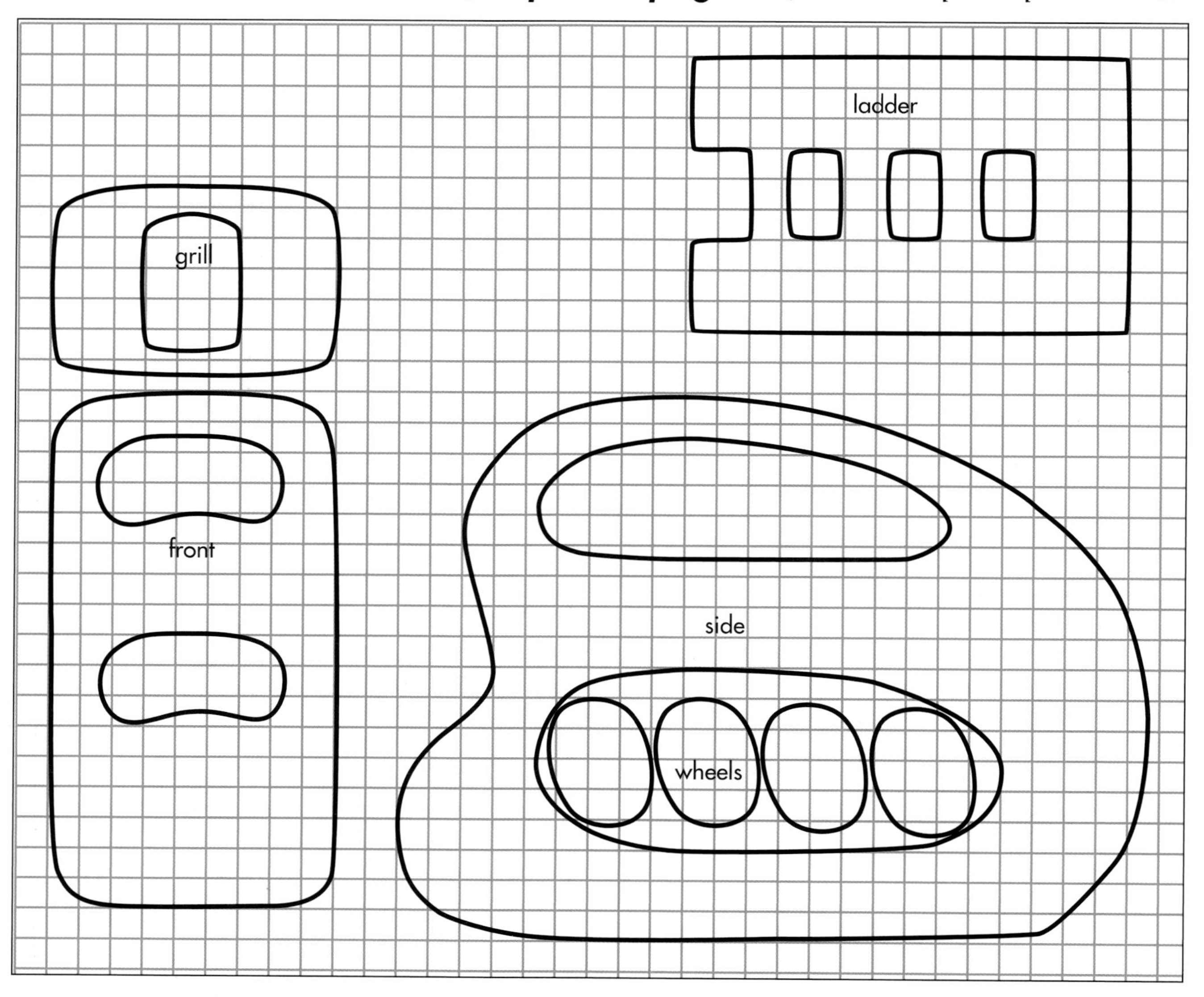

WORK SPACE STATION (Project on page 82)

One square equals 3 inches

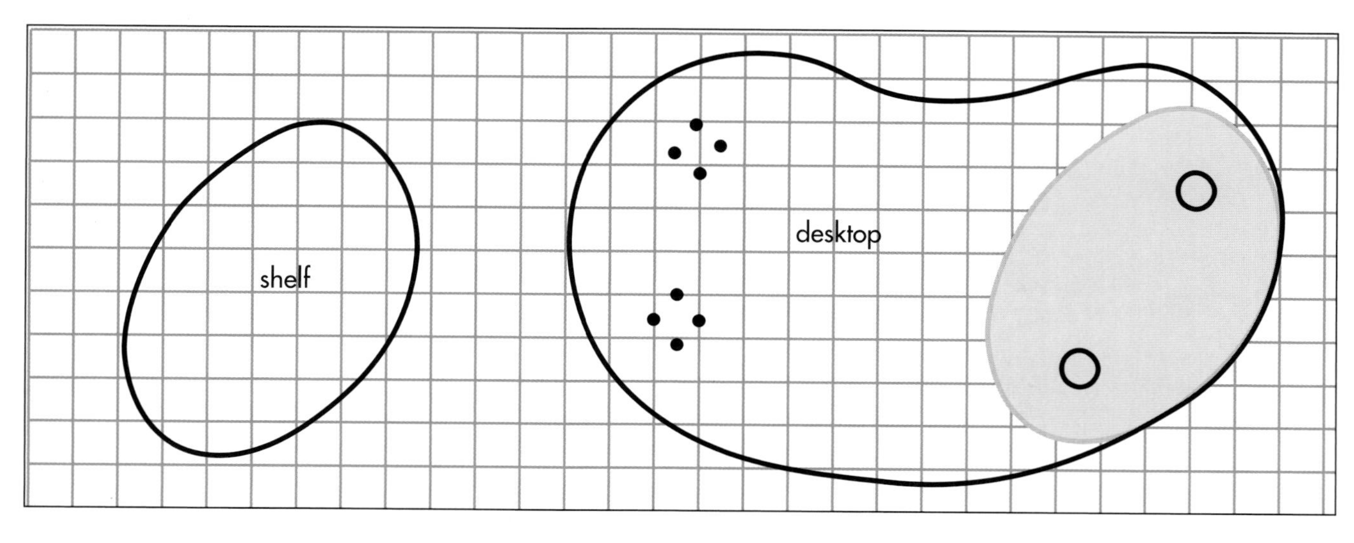

CITYSCAPE SCREEN (Project on page 88)

One square equals 3 inches

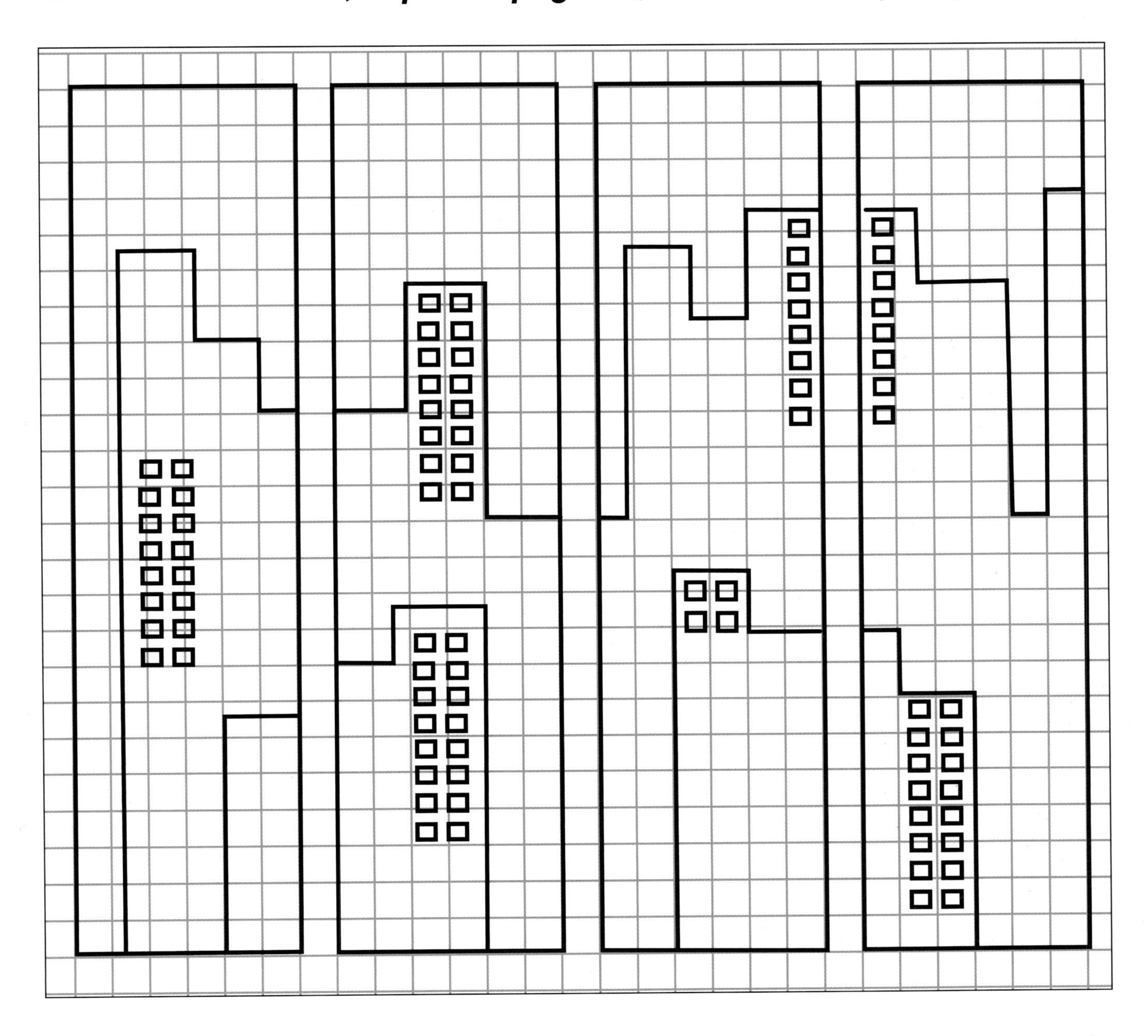

CUTTING AND SHAPING

For a wood project to look good and hold up for years, the parts must be cut with precision. Keep these basic guidelines in mind:

- Assemble a few reliable cutting tools, and keep them sharp. If a handsaw is so dull that cutting is a struggle, replace it or have it sharpened.
- Replace circular saw and saber saw blades when they no longer slide easily through the wood.
- To gain proficiency and to avoid wasting valuable lumber, measure and cut scrap pieces for practice. Once you are sure you can make cuts that are straight and crisp, you're ready to cut the real thing.

These pages give tips for the most basic cutting tools—handsaw, circular saw, and saber saw. If it's in good shape, a shop tool, such as a radial arm saw or a table saw, can produce clean cuts with ease. Read the manufacturer's instructions to make sure that you are working safely.

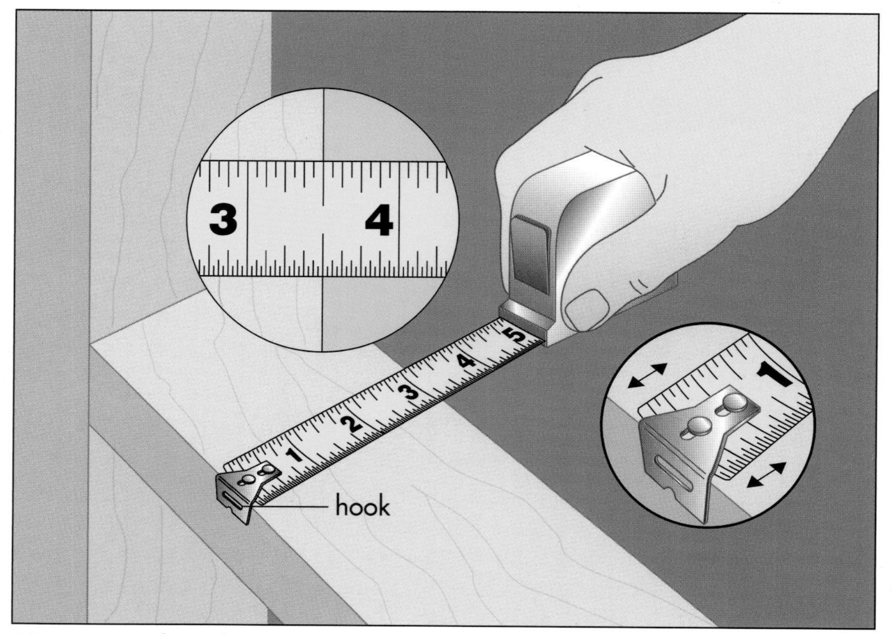

Measure and mark. A 1-inch-wide steel tape measure handles a variety of measuring jobs. Its hook slides back and forth slightly to compensate for its own thickness, so you get the same result for both an inside measurement and an outside measurement. Even the length of the body is marked, just in case you have to take an inside measurement. Mark the spot with a sharp pencil, and draw a straight cutoff line using a square.

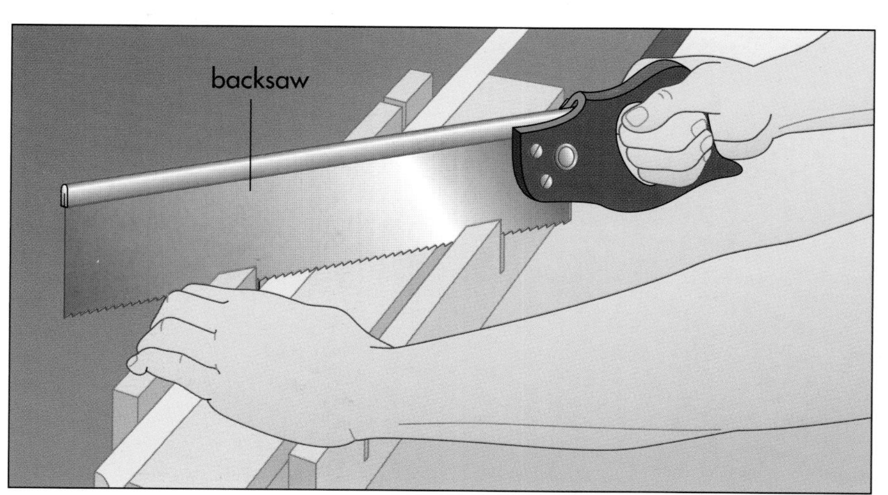

Use a miter box. Use a miter box to make an accurate 90-degree cut, or to cut two pieces (usually at 45 degrees) for a miter joint. An inexpensive plastic or wood miter box, like the one shown, can make precise cuts if you take care; a more expensive model can make the work even easier. When using a miter box, cut with a backsaw, which has a rigid blade.

When making a miter joint, cut two scraps of wood and hold them in place together to see whether you need to adjust the angle slightly. Whenever possible, make the miter cut first (and recut it if needed), then hold the piece in place to mark for cutting to length.

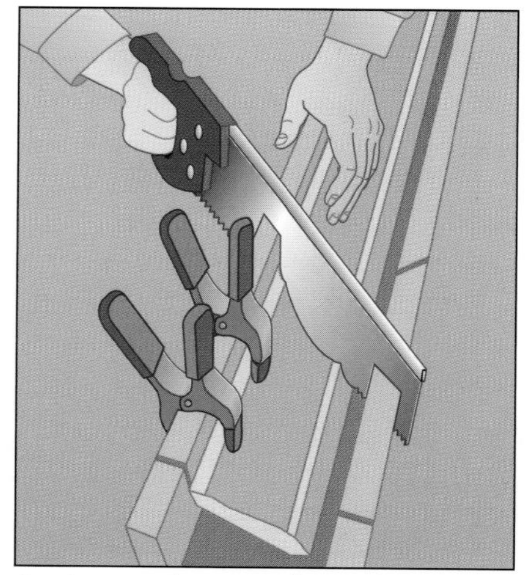

Setting up for complicated cuts. Two common mistakes when making miter cuts are cutting at the wrong angle and cutting upside down. Hold the piece near the place where it will go, and eyeball it to make sure you're cutting in the right direction. Hold the work firmly as you cut. Use clamps to prevent slipping.

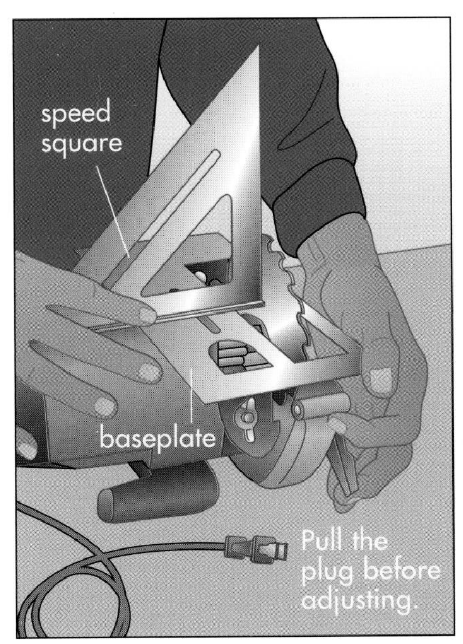

Adjust a circular saw.
Set the blade depth about ¼ inch deeper than the thickness of the work. Check that the blade is square to the baseplate, and make a test: Cut through a board, and flip one piece over. If the cut edges meet perfectly, the blade is square.

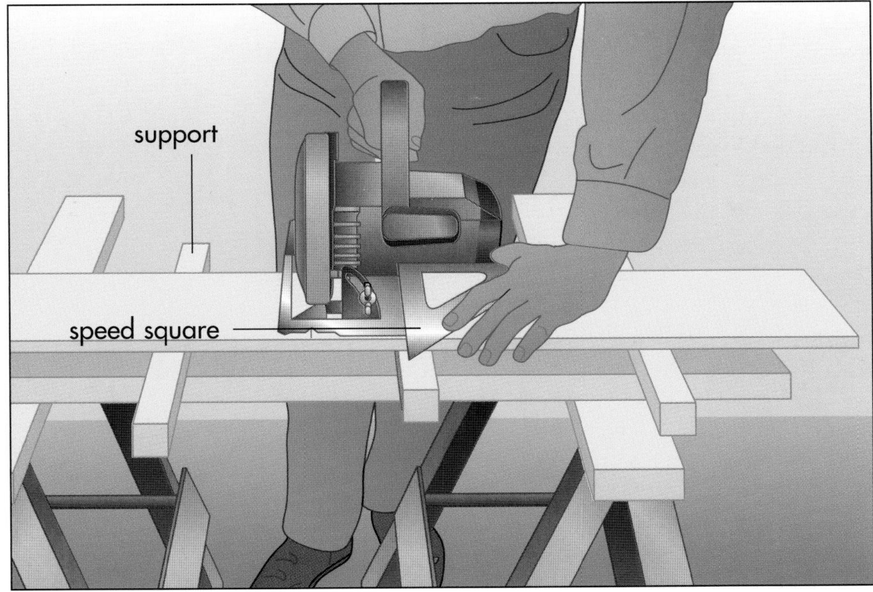

Support the material.
If the board to be cut is not supported correctly, it may cause kickback (see box *below*). Never hold a board up on the waste side or the blade will bind. If the waste piece will be short, simply support the board on the good side of the cut, and let the waste piece fall. If the waste side is long, its weight could crack the board as it falls, so support the board in four places, as shown. Or cut the piece a few inches too long, then cut it precisely with the waste end unsupported.

SAW SAFETY

A circular saw usually slices through wood with ease. But if the blade is squeezed by the board, the saw may kick back dangerously. To avoid kickback, take precautions:

- *Support the work correctly (see above right).*
- *When making a long cut (as through plywood), don't try to change direction mid-cut if you stray from your cut line. To make a correction, shut off the saw, back up, and start again.*
- *When a blade becomes dull, change it.*
- *Don't wear overly loose clothing that could get caught in the blade.*
- *Keep the extension cord well away from the cut line.*

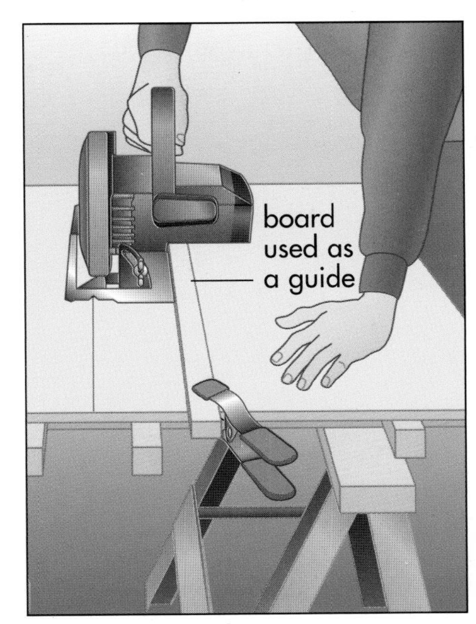

Cutting plywood.
Support plywood in four places, as shown *above*. Use a straight board as a guide. To position the guide correctly, take into account the distance from the outside of the baseplate to the inside or outside edge of the blade, depending on which side of the line you will cut.

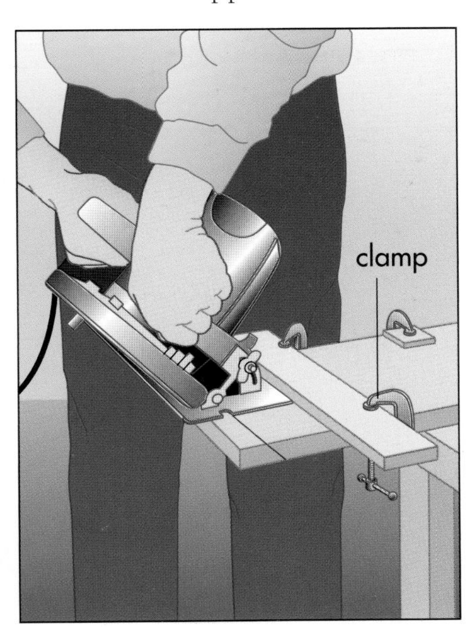

Use a circular saw for bevel cuts.
If you need to cut a board at a bevel, practice on scrap pieces to make sure the blade is set at the correct angle; circular-saw bevel guides are usually not accurate. Rest the large portion of the baseplate on the board. You may need to pull back the blade guard before cutting.

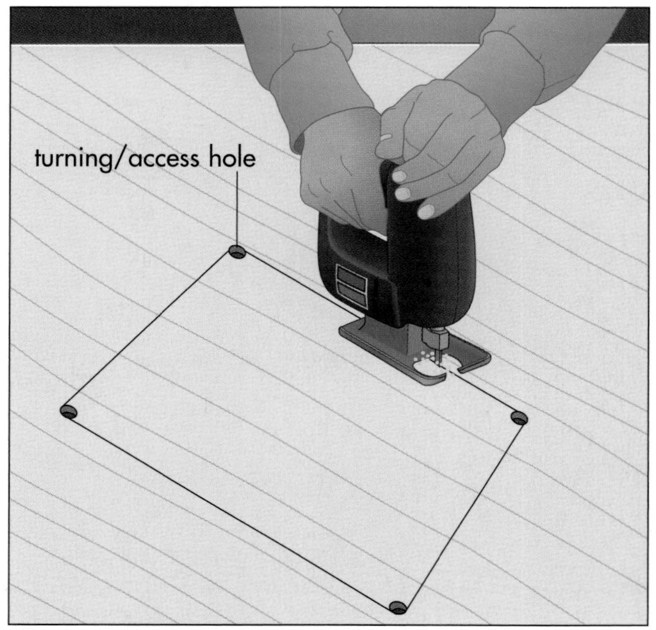

Cutting with a saber saw.
Saber saw blades break easily, so keep plenty on hand. Baseplates tend to go out of alignment and blades tend to bend, so practice on scrap pieces to make sure that your cut will be at 90 degrees to the face of the board. The narrower the blade, the more easily you can make tight turns. Often it helps to drill holes—large enough for the saw blade—at one or more corners first.

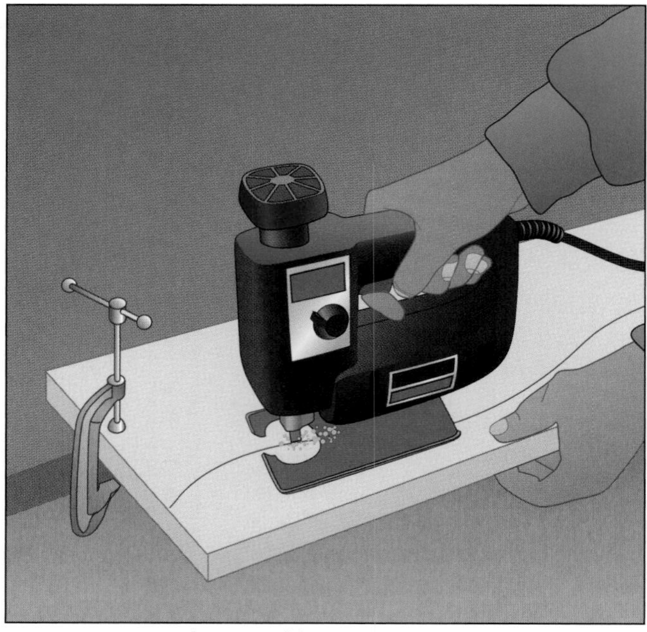

Cutting a smooth curved line.
When possible, clamp the board firmly and position it so you can make the entire cut without moving the board. Press the baseplate firmly onto the board as you cut. Push with steady pressure and a consistent speed. You may have to continually blow the sawdust away so that you can see the cut line. If the blade heats up—sometimes you can smell smoke—slow down and perhaps change the blade.

Sand with a power sander.
A belt sander (shown) removes a lot of material quickly, so use one with great care; one false move can gouge the wood. Always hold it so it sands with the grain, never across the grain, and apply very light pressure. Vibrating or "random-orbit" sanders work much more slowly but are safer.

Hand-sanding.
A sanding block produces a much smoother surface than a handheld sheet of sandpaper. To produce a silky-smooth surface, sand three times, using sandpapers of decreasing roughness: first 80-grit, then 120-grit, then 180- or 240-grit. Always sand with the grain. Press lightly, and blow away dust every so often.

ROUTING AND DRILLING

Woodworkers use routers with elaborate guides to carve designs in wood and to custom-make moldings. The projects in this book, however, use piloted bits, which cannot go awry as long as the router is adjusted correctly.

Choose the right drill and drill bits for your project:

- A reversible, variable-speed drill with a ⅜-inch chuck will capably handle most projects.
- A cordless drill is a joy to use, but unless it pulls at least 12 volts, it can't handle wide holes or hardwoods.
- In addition to a selection of bits (see below), buy a magnetic sleeve with a variety of screwdriver bits so you'll be equipped to drive screws quickly and easily.

To avoid splitting wood, drill pilot holes before driving screws. The drill bit should be slightly thinner than the screw shaft.

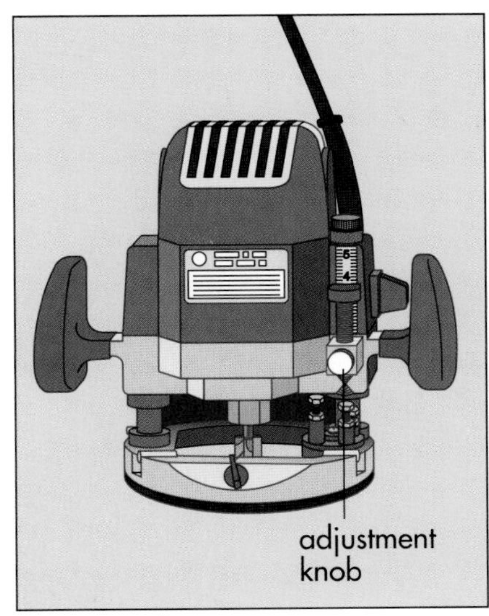

Adjusting the router. Follow manufacturer's directions for inserting and tightening a router bit. Adjust the depth of the bit, experiment on a scrap board, and readjust if necessary. Before using the router for real, make sure the hold-down clamp is very tight so the bit cannot slip down.

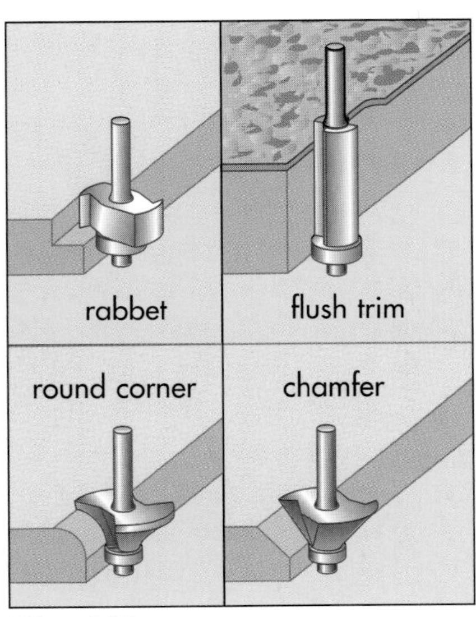

Piloted bits. Better piloted bits have guide wheels that run on ball bearings so that you won't burn the edge of the board. Use a piloted bit to produce a rounded, angled, or rabbeted edge.

Drilling holes. If you need to drill to a certain depth, wrap a piece of tape on the bit as a guide. As you drill, exert gentle pressure. If the drilling gets tough, pull out the bit and remove sawdust and chips from its grooves with a nail.

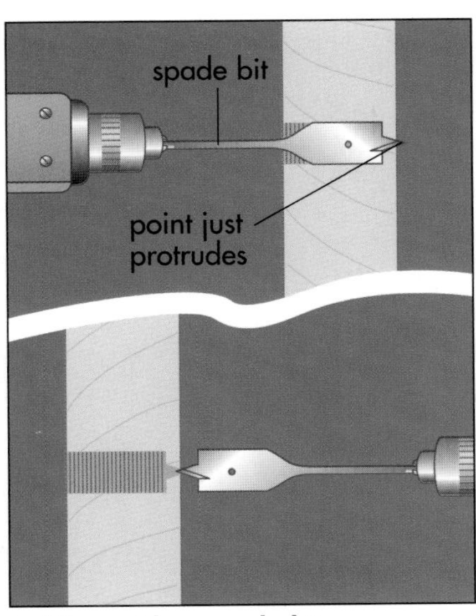

Drilling with a spade bit. A spade bit will splinter the back side of the board if you drill all the way through. Instead, drill until the point sticks out the back side, then drill from the other direction.

TOOLS TO USE

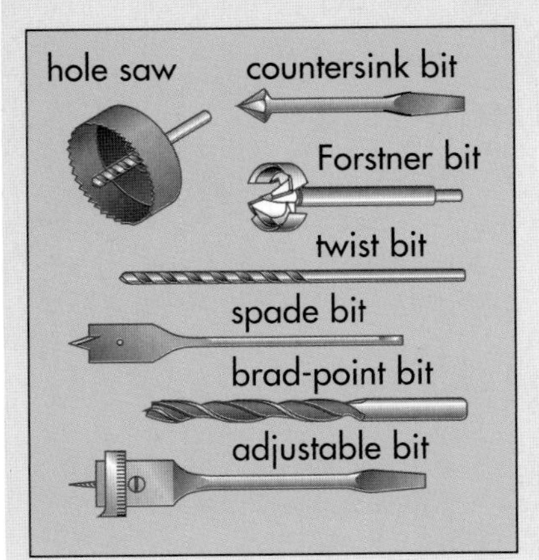

Standard twist bits bore holes up to ¼ inch in diameter. A brad-point bit costs more but makes a cleaner hole. For larger holes, use an inexpensive spade bit, or spend more and get cleaner results with a Forstner bit or a hole saw.

FASTENING

To join pieces of wood, screws are generally stronger than nails, but a joint that is both nailed and glued is plenty strong. Use woodworking glue. When fastening, try to keep these guidelines in mind:

- For a finished look, drive a nail or trimhead screw just below the surface, and fill it with wood putty. Or, use trim washers and let the screw heads show (see page 40).
- Practice driving nails until you achieve a smooth, fluid motion and rarely miss. Keep your elbow loose rather than rigid, so the hammer head snaps at the end of the stroke.
- Use screws or nails that are as long as at least twice the thickness of the board being attached.

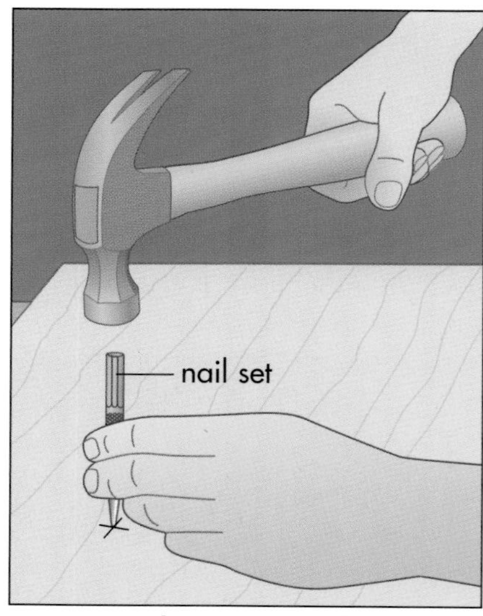

Driving and setting a nail.
Drive a nail until its head is close to flush with the wood surface. Then, to avoid marring the board, use a nail set to drive the head slightly below the surface.

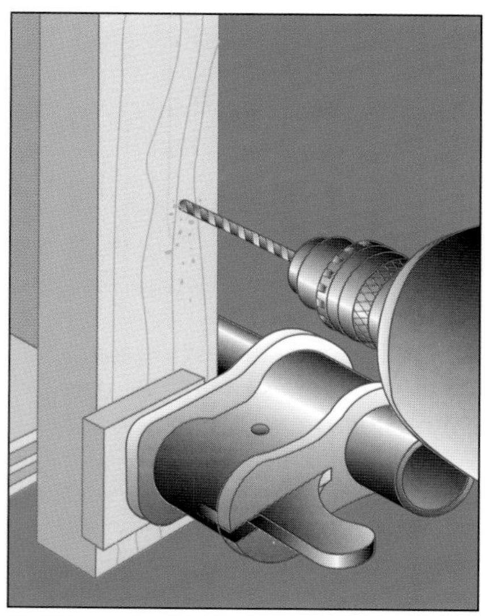

Drilling pilot holes.
Avoid splitting wood—especially when driving a screw or nail near the edge of a board—by drilling a pilot hole first. Clamp the board firmly, drill a series of pilot holes, and then drive the screws or nails.

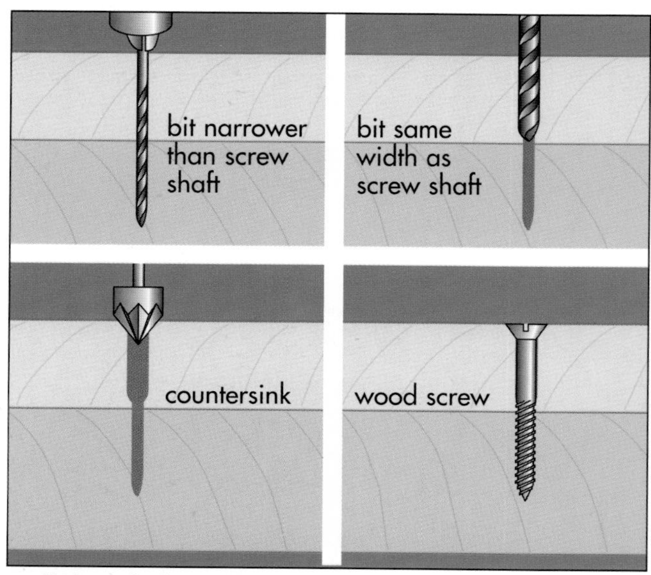

Drill three holes.
For the cleanest appearance and the strongest joint, drill three holes before driving a screw. First, drill the pilot hole, using a bit slightly narrower than the screw shaft. Next, enlarge the hole in the piece to be fastened using a bit the same thickness as the screw shaft. Then use a countersink bit to make a shallow, wide hole for the screw head. A combination bit bores all three holes at once.

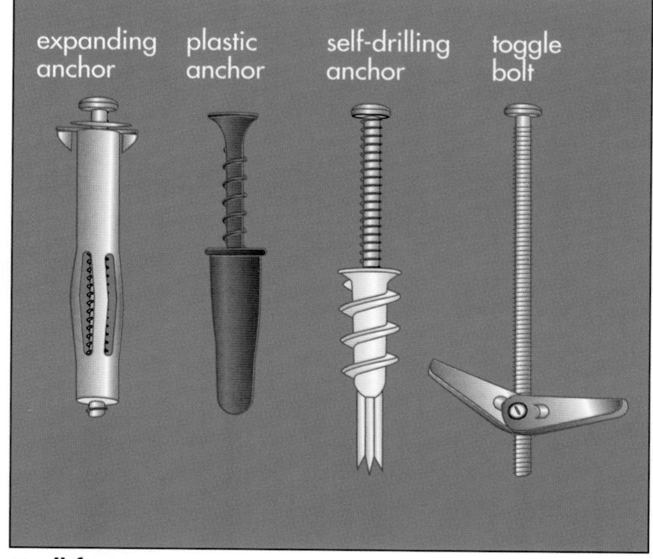

Wall fasteners.
Driving a screw into framing is the strongest way to attach it to a wall or ceiling. Use a stud finder to locate the framing member. If that isn't possible, or if the fastener doesn't have to be very strong, a fastener designed to attach to drywall or plaster will suffice. For an expanding or plastic anchor, drill a hole and tap the anchor into the wall, then drive the screw. For a toggle bolt, drill a hole, push the bolt through, and tighten. A self-drilling anchor just drives right in.

SEWING

For successful machine sewing, follow these tips:

- Iron your fabrics before cutting so the cuts will be straight.
- Use a needle that is appropriate for the weight of fabric you are using. Replace your needle at the start of each new project—needles get dull with use.
- Stitch slowly and accurately, pulling out the straight pins just before coming to them—don't sew over pins.
- Place a self-stick note or a piece of masking tape on the sewing machine plate to mark the correct seam allowance.
- Iron the seam open or to one side (as directed) before joining another piece to the first.
- Keep your sewing machine in good repair.

Machine-sewing isn't necessary for all projects. Hand-sewing is an inexpensive alternative for many projects.

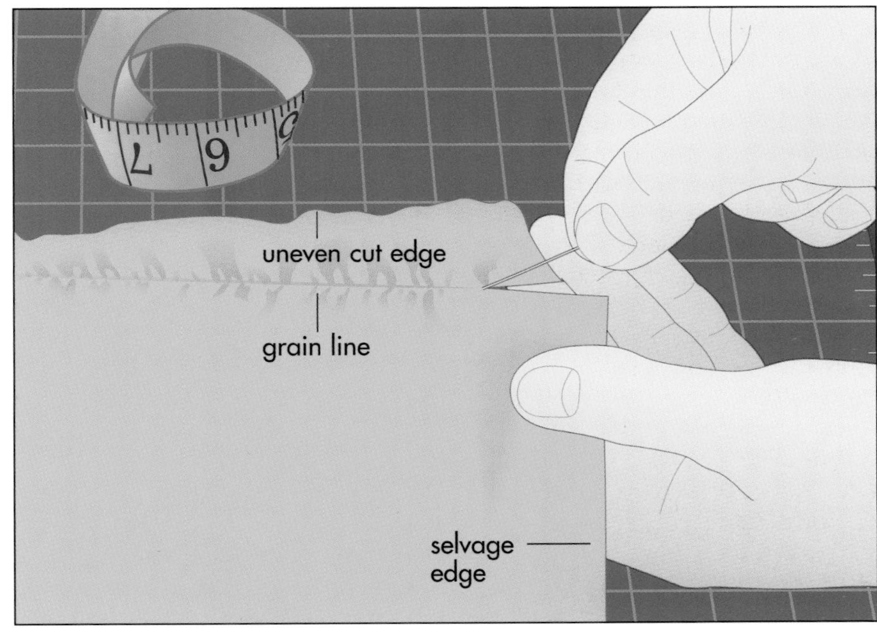

Find the grain of the fabric.
If you measure from the straight grain of your fabric, your curtains or panels will hang evenly. To find the grain, clip the selvage with scissors. Pick out a thread from the weave, and gently pull it to find the cross grain of the fabric. Cut along the resulting line. If the thread breaks, just pull another from the cut edge and continue.

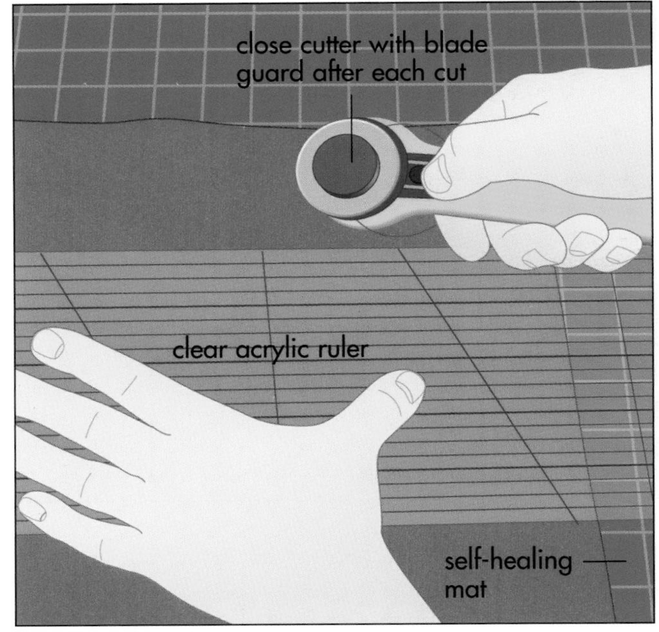

Rotary cutter safety.
Rotary cutters, rulers, and mats are useful for quick, accurate fabric cutting. But the blade of the cutter is razor-sharp. Train yourself to shut the safety guard of the blade after each and every cut. Keep the rotary cutter out of the reach of children.

No-sew hemming.
To make hems without sewing, consider washable glues or fusible webbing. Fusible webbing comes in 20-inch-wide sheets sold by the yard, or ½-inch-wide strips. Follow the manufacturer's directions for use. Be careful not to touch the fusible web with the iron.

WORKING WITH KIDS

When planning your kid's room, don't overlook the most obvious source of expertise: your child. Kids possess a natural talent for creativity and invention. And while an adult may pursue daily activities throughout many rooms of the house, a child's room is a sanctuary—a nucleus of countless hours of playing, learning, daydreaming, entertaining friends, and unleashing of imagination.

Balancing Restraint with Imagination

Of course, you'll want to strike a balance between your child's needs for self-expression and your budget, time constraints, and good judgment. If your 6-year-old insists on orange-and-black bedroom walls, carpet, and furniture, complete with a soda machine and climbing wall, it's time for a little parental intervention.

In setting limits, you need not squelch your child's imagination. After all, the more involved your child is in creating the room, the more apt he or she will be to assume responsibility for its care and upkeep. Children are masters of improvisation—with a little coaching, they will delight you with their versatility. Instead of painting your child's walls orange, for example, compromise by accenting the room with orange lamp shades, sheets, or storage containers. Keep in mind that in the long run it will be easier to alter a trendy wall color than to paint over desks and dressers, or replace carpet and window treatments.

The Allure of Color

A room decorated with the right colors can improve a child's sense of aesthetics and sensory stimulation while promoting learning, discovery, and imagination. If a child under the age of 5 is too young to express preferences verbally, pay attention to the colors of the crayons and toys that he or she chooses. Children five and older will typically not hesitate to point out the colors that complement their personality and tastes.

Children under the age of 10 usually gravitate toward bright primary colors (yellow, blue, and red) and secondary colors (green, orange, and purple). Children 10 and above opt for a slightly more subdued palette. In such cases, aim for intermediate colors—produced by mixing primary colors with secondary colors—or add a little white, black, or gray to your preteen's favorite hue to create a more sophisticated look.

When working with a limited amount of space, remember that light colors open up a room, while dark colors tend to diminish it. Choosing walls, carpets, and window treatments in the same color family will help convey a sense of spaciousness.

And keep in mind that strategic use of color can help you organize the contents of a room or delineate space when a room is shared by more than one occupant.

MEASUREMENTS

IDEAL FURNITURE DIMENSIONS

Age	Height	Eye Level	High Reach	Table	Chair
3	37"	33"	41"	15"	8"
5	39"–47"	35"–43"	43"–52"	18"	10"
7	44"–52"	40"–48"	49"–59"	19"	11"
9	47"–57"	43"–53"	53"–65"	21"	12"
12	53"–64"	49"–60"	61"–73"	23"	13"
15	61"–71"	57"–66"	70"–82"	26"	15"
Adult woman	61"–70"	57"–66"	70"–81"	29"	18"
Adult man	65"–75"	61"–70"	74"–86"	29"	18"